MONITORING GLOBAL POVERTY

MONITORING GLOBAL POVERTY

Report of the Commission on Global Poverty

WORLD BANK GROUP

ISBN (paper): 978-1-4648-0961-3
ISBN (electronic): 978-1-4648-0962-0
DOI: 10.1596/978-1-4648-0961-3

Cover design: Critical Stages.

Library of Congress Cataloging-in-Publication Data has been requested.

Contents

Figures

Tables

Foreword

In 2013, the World Bank Group announced two overarching goals: the end of chronic extreme poverty by 2030; and the promotion of shared prosperity, defined in terms of economic growth of the poorest segments of society. The United Nations has also now declared the eradication of poverty by 2030 as a primary development goal.

Poverty is, at the same time, stark and conceptually elusive, especially when we try to track it statistically across nations and over time. The World Bank Group has been at the vanguard of developing measures of living standards. It has played a major role in providing and collating data on poverty and inequality, and thereby providing a framework for discourse and policy making.

To build on this work and carry out this responsibility more effectively, in 2015 I convened a high-level Commission led by Sir Anthony Atkinson, distinguished economist with seminal research on poverty and inequality, along with an Advisory Board of 23 renowned economists from around the world. I am delighted that we are able to present to you the *Report of the Commission on Global Poverty*.

The Commission was asked to advise the World Bank on the methodology currently used for tracking poverty in terms of people's consumption, given that prices change over time and purchasing power parities across nations shift. It was also asked to give advice on other dimensions and relativities of poverty and deprivation that ought to be measured.

Tony Atkinson and the Commission have listed and elaborated upon a comprehensive agenda of recommendations for the World Bank Group which would make poverty measurement more comprehensive, collaborative, and reliable. The recommendations range from the need to invest in better data and have better national-level poverty statistics, with elaboration of the possible sources and magnitudes of statistical errors, to recommendations for handling price movements and developing a range of complementary indicators and nonmonetary measures of poverty. It also calls for greater external scrutiny of the Bank's work.

I am confident that this report will go down as a major work of scholarship in an area of urgent global concern. The World Bank Group staff and I thank Tony and the Commission for their thoughtful analyses and recommendations. I would like to hope that they will be instrumental in improving our understanding of the extent of poverty and in making progress toward the goals of ending extreme poverty and promoting shared prosperity.

Kaushik Basu
Chief Economist and Senior Vice President
The World Bank Group

Preface

The *Report of the Commission on Global Poverty* is solely my responsibility as the Chair of the Commission. None of those whom I am about to thank should be held accountable for the contents and recommendations. But I have benefited greatly from their contributions. First of all, members of the Advisory Board, whose names are listed on the next pages, have played two roles. Without exception, they responded to my initial request for submissions dealing with the key issues. These submissions, and their earlier writing on the subject, have been invaluable. Members of the Advisory Board were sent the draft Report, and the comments received from them led to significant revisions. Circumstances have meant that I have not in all cases been able to respond as fully as I would like to their thoughtful suggestions, and I hope that they will understand that these limitations were outside my control. Second, a subgroup of the Board (the "Core Group") provided active support throughout the process. The Core Group had two meetings, and members read the Report twice. The writing of the Report would not have been possible without their guidance regarding the overall structure and the detailed contents.

The second meeting of the Core Group was attended by Martine Durand, Director of Statistics and Chief Statistician at OECD and Chair of the Executive Board of the International Comparison Program. I am most grateful to her for assisting our work, while making it clear that she is in no way responsible for the conclusions reached.

In preparing the work of the Commission, and in drawing up the Report, I have been keen to consult widely. In September 2015, I wrote to 71 organizations and individuals with research interests in the area. The World Bank, in a conversation launched on September 28, 2015, asked people to "share your thoughts with us" on the measurement of global poverty. There were a series of eight questions, and responses were requested by November 30, 2015. All together, 122 submissions were received. My warm thanks go to all who responded. The responses provided valuable material, which has been taken into account in writing the Report. They suggested issues that had not been on the original work plan, which have been followed up where possible. The main omission in this respect is that the Report does not examine policies to achieve reduction in global poverty. This naturally engaged many of our respondents, and involves members of the Advisory Board in other roles, but lay outside the remit of the Commission, which is concerned only with the *monitoring* of the extent of global poverty.

The preparation of this Report would not have been possible without the support and encouragement of World Bank staff. I would like to take this opportunity to thank them most warmly, while making clear that they too are in no way responsible for the views expressed in the Report. I have also been greatly helped in Oxford by (Chloe) Qianzi Zeng, who has recently completed her doctorate at Nuffield College and worked on the underlying research, and by Maarit Kivilo, Publications Officer of OPHI, who provided most valuable assistance in the preparation of the Index—an essential element in a Report where issues appear at several different points in the analysis.

The final version of the Report has been prepared after its launch at the World Bank on July 13, 2016. I am most grateful to those who participated in the panels at the launch: Kaushik Basu, François Bourguignon, Shaohua Chen, Andrew Dabalen, Himanshu, Germano Mwabu, Martin Ravallion, Sabina Alkire, Laurence Chandy, Francisco Ferreira, James Foster, and Ravi Kanbur. They are absolved from any responsibility for the Report, but their comments have led to significant improvements in this final version.

Tony Atkinson
Oxford
July 28, 2016

Members of the Advisory Board

Sabina Alkire is Director of the Oxford Poverty and Human Development Initiative (OPHI), University of Oxford, and Oliver T. Carr Professor and Professor of Economics and International Affairs at George Washington University.

Robert Allen is Global Distinguished Professor of Economic History at New York University, Abu Dhabi, and a Senior Research Fellow, Nuffield College, Oxford.

*Sir Tony Atkinson (Chair) is Centennial Professor at the London School of Economics and Fellow of Nuffield College, Oxford. He was previously Warden of Nuffield College.

Haroon Bhorat is Professor of Economics and Director of the Development Policy Research Unit (DPRU) at the University of Cape Town, South Africa. Prof. Bhorat's research interests cover labor economics, poverty, and income distribution.

*François Bourguignon is Emeritus Professor of Economics at the Paris School of Economics. He has been the Director of the Paris School from 2007 to 2013. Before that he was the Chief Economist and Senior Vice President of the World Bank.

*Andrea Brandolini is Head of the Statistical Analysis Directorate in the Directorate General for Economics, Statistics and Research at the Bank of Italy. He represented the Bank of Italy in the Poverty Commissions established by Italian governments (1994–2007).

---

* indicates member of the Core Group.

Laurence Chandy is a Fellow in the Global Economy and Development Program and the Development Assistance and Governance Initiative at the Brookings Institution.

Shaohua Chen is a Lead Statistician in the Development Economics Research Group of the World Bank, where she has managed the Global Poverty monitoring and online computational system, PovcalNet, at the World Bank since 1991.

Angus Deaton is the Dwight D. Eisenhower Professor of Economics and International Affairs at the Woodrow Wilson School of Public and International Affairs and the Economics Department at Princeton University. He received the Nobel Prize in Economic Sciences in 2015.

Stefan Dercon is Professor of Economic Policy at the Blavatnik School of Government and the Economics Department, University of Oxford, and Director of the Centre for the Study of African Economies. He has been Chief Economist of the Department of International Development (DFID) since 2011.

*Francisco H. G. Ferreira is a Senior Adviser in the World Bank's Development Research Group, where he oversees the Bank's research programs on poverty, inequality, and agriculture. He was formerly the Bank's Chief Economist for the Africa Region, and has also served as Deputy Chief Economist for Latin America and the Caribbean, and as co-Director of the *World Development Report 2006: Equity and Development*.

James Foster is Professor of Economics and International Affairs at the George Washington University.

Ana María Ibáñez is Professor of Economics at Universidad de los Andes.

*Ravi Kanbur is T. H. Lee Professor of World Affairs, International Professor of Applied Economics and Management, and Professor of Economics at Cornell University. He is President-elect of the Human Development and Capability Association (HDCA).

*Peter Lanjouw is Professor of Development Economics at VU University, Amsterdam, since January 2015. Prior to his appointment to the VU, he was Research Manager of the Poverty Team in the Development Economics Research Group of the World Bank.

*Nora Lustig is Samuel Z. Stone Professor of Latin American Economics and Director of the Commitment to Equity Institute (CEQI) at Tulane University.

She is also a Nonresident Fellow at the Center for Global Development and the Inter-American Dialogue.

*Eric Marlier is the International Scientific Coordinator of the Luxembourg Institute of Socio-Economic Research (LISER). He has been managing the European "Network for the analysis of EU-SILC [Net-SILC]" since 2008.

Germano Mwabu is Professor of Economics at the University of Nairobi.

Martin Ravallion holds the Edmond D. Villani Chair of Economics at Georgetown University. Prior to joining Georgetown in December 2012, he was Director of the World Bank's research department, the Development Research Group.

Ana Revenga is the Senior Director of the Poverty Global Practice at the World Bank Group. Until July 1, 2014, she was Director of Human Development in the Europe and Central Asia Region and Acting Vice President for the Poverty Reduction and Economic Management Network at the World Bank.

Peter Saunders was Director of the Social Policy Research Centre at Australia's University of New South Wales (UNSW) from February 1987 until July 2007, and now holds a Research Chair in Social Policy within the Centre.

Amartya Sen is Thomas W. Lamont University Professor, and Professor of Economics and Philosophy, at Harvard University and was, until 2004, the Master of Trinity College, Cambridge. He received the Nobel Prize in Economic Sciences in 1998.

S. Subramanian is a former Indian Council of Social Science Research (ICSSR) National Fellow and a former Professor of the Madras Institute of Development Studies.

Zhu Ling is a Member of the Academy and Professorial Research Fellow, Institute of Economics, Chinese Academy of Social Sciences.

Key Features of the Report

A Middle Way

The subject of this Report—measuring global poverty—is highly contro-versial. There are those who believe that the current exercise is futile. The obstacles to making such a calculation are so great, it is argued, that it makes no sense to even attempt an estimate of the number of people living in extreme poverty. This view is not one that I share and it is not one that underlies this Report. The aim of the Report is to explore—within a context glossed in two key respects—what can be said.

The first gloss is that, as the title of the Report indicates, the principal aim is to determine the extent to which global poverty is *changing over time*. Put simply, the World Bank figure of 900 million (in round numbers) living in extreme poverty may be criticized as too low or too high, but the focus here is on whether a reduction is being achieved over time. Many of the same issues arise in such monitoring over time as in the determina-tion of the level of poverty, but there are certain points in the argument where it is the focus on *change* that drives the Recommendations. To give a concrete example that will no doubt generate discussion, the position taken in the Report is that purchasing power parity comparisons play an essential role in establishing the *baseline* poverty estimates (those based on the 2011 International Comparison Program), but that in order to evalu-ate the subsequent *changes over time* up to 2030 the local currency pov-erty line should be adjusted in line with domestic consumer price inflation.

The second gloss is that the Report stresses that any estimate—of level or of change—is surrounded by a margin of error. This is often lost from sight in public pronouncements, and it is important to convey to policy makers and other users that they are operating with numbers about which there is considerable uncertainty. Indeed, this could take us back to the position that nothing concrete can be said. However, the more positive response adopted here is the "total error" approach, which seeks to identify different potential sources of error and to attach an indication of their possible size. Pursuing the example of the previous paragraph, it can be asked how large would the error in the measurement of domestic inflation have to be to reverse the conclusion reached regarding the direction of the change in recorded poverty? The identification of such possible sources of error should be the first step in the process of creating new poverty estimates. Making sense of uncertain magnitudes is one of the main challenges of social science research, and the Report seeks to contribute to that end.

With these two important glosses, the Report attempts to follow an intermediate path. The estimates of global poverty are flawed but not useless. By focusing on changes over time, we can learn—taking account of the potential margins of error—about the evolution of global poverty. The confidence to be placed in these conclusions can be increased by improvements in the methods of analysis and in the underlying data. These are the subject of chapter 1, where the Recommendations—if adopted— can significantly improve the quality of the global poverty estimates.

The Report goes further. There is a second line of criticism that accepts that the exercise of measuring global poverty is worth pursuing but believes that the World Bank estimates have chosen the wrong point of departure. The aim of chapter 2 of the Report is to explore alternative approaches and their implications, with Recommendations for new developments, including the proposal for the World Bank to produce a set of Complementary Indicators that extend the scope of monetary poverty measures and introduce nonmonetary measures. The Report recognizes that there is a wide range of views as to how poverty should be gauged, whether about the details of poverty indicators or about the broad dimensions to be recorded. By making this plurality of judgments explicit, and by seeking common ground, the Report hopes to offer a richer analysis of global poverty.

Building Bridges with National Poverty Estimates

In the preparation of the Report, a major consideration has been the relation between the measurement of global poverty—both the extreme poverty target and the Complementary Indicators—and the measurement of poverty at the level of the individual country. The implementation of the recommendations made in the Report will depend on the engagement of statistical agencies and other actors at the country level. This is where, as one commentator said, "the rubber hits the road." The issues that arise at the country level may well differ in different parts of the world and, indeed, be specific to a particular context. While the Report focuses, as requested, on global poverty measurement, one important recommendation is that the two levels of analysis—global and national—should be viewed in conjunction. This does not mean any unwarranted imposition of uniformity of approach, but rather that there should be a better understanding of the relationship between global estimates for a country and the estimates of poverty made at the national level. The proposal of brief (two-page) National Poverty Statistics Reports for each country is intended to produce greater coherence between the two activities, with, it is hoped, benefits on both sides.

The World Bank as Producer and as User of Statistics

The Report has been prepared at the request of the World Bank, but the implementation of many of the recommendations depends on collaboration with other international agencies. Indeed, some of the proposals, such as those concerned with population statistics or with nonmonetary poverty indicators, involve areas where other UN institutions have lead responsibility. This does not, however, mean that the World Bank should not engage. It is already actively participating in collaboration, but this should be given greater prominence. The Report stresses that it is incumbent on the users of data supplied by other bodies to ensure that the data are fit for the purposes for which they are employed. The World Bank should not be a purely passive user of these key data. Just as macroeconomists should have an appreciation of how national accounts are constructed, so those responsible for the poverty estimates in the World Bank should have an understanding of the potential strengths and weaknesses of inputs into their calculations that may affect the reliability of the resulting estimates. Outside the World Bank, it is hoped that the Report will be of value to all those engaged in poverty measurement across the world and be a positive force in encouraging partnerships. There is already valuable cooperation between different bodies and individuals, but—given the scarcity of statistical resources—as much use as possible should be made of joint working.

Realism

The monitoring of global poverty is important but it is necessary to be realistic about what can be achieved. Limited statistical resources, the need for collaboration, the diversity of circumstances in different countries, and differing priorities at national level, all mean that the estimate of changes in global poverty—improved in the light of the Report's Recommendations—will still be approximate and in need of careful interpretation. This should be to the fore in the presentation of the findings. The measures proposed here may in economists' terms be seen as moving from a current "third-best" to the "second-best," where the second-best recognizes the limits to what is feasible. Or, for those who prefer a more homely analogy, there is the example of the English writer P. G. Wodehouse, who used to revise a novel by pinning each page of a chapter round the wall of his study, with the height reflecting his degree of satisfaction with the contents. The aim of the Report is to move the pages upward where there is most scope for improvement of the World Bank's monitoring of poverty.

Going Forward

If the World Bank is minded to accept the broad thrust of the Report's recommendations, then it involves:

- Recommendations for the future monitoring of SDG Goal 1.1
- Preparation of (two-page) National Poverty Statistics reports for each country
- Establishing a portfolio of World Bank Complementary Indicators
- Progress in terms of external engagement and joint statistical working parties

List of Recommendations (in order of appearance):

Chapter 1: Monitoring Extreme Poverty

Recommendation 1: The global extreme poverty standard should be cited in general terms as "the International Poverty Line," and expressed in each country in terms of the currency of that country.

Recommendation 2: There should be National Poverty Statistics Reports (NPSR) for each country, giving the Global Poverty estimates, explaining the local currency value of the International Poverty Line and the relation to the official poverty line(s) in that country (where they exist), considering how the trends in poverty measured according to the International Poverty Line relate to those shown by national statistics, and incorporating a set of World Bank Complementary Indicators, as proposed in chapter 2 of this Report.

Recommendation 3: There should be an investigation of the extent to which people are "missing" from the global poverty count, and proposals made for adjustments where appropriate at the national level for survey underrepresentation and noncoverage by surveys; more generally, the World Bank should carry out a review, in conjunction with other members of the UN statistical system, of the fitness for purpose of the baseline population data for each country, and the methods used to update from the baseline to the years covered by the global poverty estimates.

Recommendation 4: The World Bank should take the lead in a standing Joint Statistical Working Group for household consumption statistics, with a remit to set guidelines for the measurement of household consumption, to examine the relation between consumption and income, and to investigate the relation among household survey, national accounts, and other data sources.

Recommendation 5: The World Bank poverty estimates should be based on a "total error" approach, evaluating the possible sources, and magnitude, of error, particularly nonsampling error and the error introduced by the process of determining the International Poverty Line.

Recommendation 6: The World Bank should make public the principles according to which household survey data are selected for use in the global poverty count; and there should be an assessment at national level of the availability and quality of the required household survey data, and a review of possible alternative sources and methods of ex post harmonization.

Recommendation 7: The World Bank, in conjunction with national statistical agencies and other statistical bodies, should explore the construction of an annual national accounts–based indicator of household living standards, as measured by consumption defined in a way that matches as far as possible household survey practice.

Recommendation 8: There should be an investigation for a small number of countries by the World Bank of alternative methods of providing up-to-date poverty estimates using scaled-down surveys, or the SWIFT or other surveys, plus modeling, where the appropriate methods may vary across countries.

Recommendation 9: The World Bank, as a user of Consumer Price Indexes (CPI), should, in conjunction with the responsible international bodies and with the national statistical agencies, seek to improve the quality of the domestic CPI, with particular references to those aspects most relevant to global poverty measurement; this should include examination of the likely magnitude of any bias, and exploration of special price indexes for the poor.

Recommendation 10: The global poverty estimates should be updated up to 2030 on the basis of the International Poverty Line for each country set in local currency, and updated in line with the change in the national CPI or, where available, national index of prices for the poor; the estimates would not be revised in the light of new rounds of the ICP.

Chapter 2: Beyond Goal 1.1

Recommendation 11: The Bank should publish, alongside the global poverty count, a portfolio of Complementary Indicators, including a multidimensional dashboard of outcome indicators, where the number of such indicators should be sufficiently small that they can receive prominence in public debate and in policy making; the selection of the Complementary Indicators should be based on an explicit set of principles, and the implementation of these principles should follow external consultation, including with the proposed external audit body.

Recommendation 12: The portfolio of Complementary Indicators should include the mean poverty gap, relative to the International Poverty Line measured over the whole population and expressed as a percentage of the poverty line.

Recommendation 13: The global poverty figure, and the counterpart national figures, should be accompanied by estimates of the numbers of women, children, and young adults living in households with consumption below the International Poverty Line, as well as the number of female-headed households below the International Poverty Line.

Recommendation 14: The World Bank should explore the use of subjective assessments of personal poverty status (in "quick" surveys of poverty), and of the minimum consumption considered necessary to avoid extreme poverty, as an aid to interpreting the conclusions drawn from the global poverty estimates.

Recommendation 15: The World Bank should develop a program of work, in conjunction with other international agencies, on a basic needs–based estimate of extreme poverty; these estimates would, when developed, form an alternative indicator to be included in the portfolio of Complementary Indicators, and serve to provide an interpretation of what the International Poverty Line would buy.

Recommendation 16: The World Bank should introduce a "societal" head count measure of global consumption poverty that takes account, above an appropriate level, of the standard of living in the country in question, thus combining fixed and relative elements of poverty.

Recommendation 17: The indicator for the shared prosperity goal should be unambiguously stated as raising the living standards of the bottom 40 percent in each country (not confounded with their relative share), and extended to include an indicator identifying the growth of per capita real consumption of the bottom 40 percent of the world distribution of consumption.

Recommendation 18: The World Bank should establish its own requirements with regard to the measurement of nonmonetary poverty, for inclusion in the Complementary Indicators (including the overlapping poverty measure) and in other World Bank uses, and ensure that these are fully represented in the activities of the international statistical system, particularly with regard to the proposed SDG indicators.

Recommendation 19: The Complementary Indicators should include a multidimensioned poverty indicator based on the counting approach.

Chapter 3: Making It Happen

Recommendation 20: There should be a major investment in statistical sources and analysis, with these activities being accorded a high priority in the work of the World Bank.

Recommendation 21: The International Poverty Line estimates and the proposed Complementary Indicators should be audited on a regular basis by a body fully external to the World Bank, and this body should be consulted about major changes in methodology.

Abbreviations

ADB	Asian Development Bank
ATD	All Together in Dignity (Fourth World)
BMI	body mass index
BNPI	Basic Needs Price Index
CONEVAL	National Council for the Evaluation of Social Development Policy
CONPES	National Council on Economic and Social Policy
CEDLAS	Center for Distributive, Labor and Social Studies
CEPALSTAT	Statistical Department of the Economic Commission for Latin America and the Caribbean
CEQI	Commitment to Equity Institute
CI	Complementary Indicators
CPI	consumer price index
CWIQ	Core Welfare Indicator Questionnaire
DEC	Development Economics Vice Presidency
DECDG	Development Data Group in DEC
DECIG	Development Indicators Group in DEC
DECPG	Development Prospects Group in DEC
DHS	Demographic and Health Surveys
DFID	Department for International Development
DPRU	Development Policy Research Unit
ECLAC	Economic Commission for Latin America and the Caribbean
ENIGH	Household Income and Expenditure Survey (Mexico)
EU	European Union
EU-SILC	European Union Statistics on Income and Living Conditions
FAO	Food and Agriculture Organization
FGT	Foster-Greer-Thorbecke measures of poverty
GDI	gross domestic income

GDP	gross domestic product
GLSS	Ghana Living Standards Survey
GNI	gross national income
GNP	gross national product
GPWG	Global Poverty Technical Working Group
HDCA	Human Development and Capability Association
HDI	Human Development Index
HDR	Human Development Report
HFCE	Household Final Consumption Expenditure
HIC	high-income country (definition varies over time)
ICLS	International Conference of Labour Statisticians
ICP	UN International Comparison Program (purchasing power parities)
ICSSR	Indian Council of Social Science Research
IFAD	International Fund for Agricultural Development
IHSN	International Household Survey Network
ILO	International Labour Organization
IMF	International Monetary Fund
ISO	International Organization for Standardization
KIS	Key Indicator Survey
LAC	Latin America and the Caribbean
LCU	local currency unit
LDC	least-developed country
LIC	low-income country (definition varies over time)
LIS	Luxembourg Income Study (Database)
LMIC	lower-middle-income country
LSMS	Living Standards Measurement Survey
MDGs	Millennium Development Goals
MENA	Middle East and North Africa
MICS	Multiple Indicator Cluster Survey
MPI	Multidimensional Poverty Index
NA	National Accounts
NPSR	National Poverty Statistics Reports
NSS	National Sample Survey (India)
ODI	Overseas Development Institute
OECD	Organisation for Economic Co-operation and Development
OPHI	Oxford Poverty and Human Development Initiative
OPL	Official Poverty Line
PARIS21	Partnership in Statistics for Development in the 21st Century
PPP	purchasing power parity

SDGs	Sustainable Development Goals
SEDLAC	Socioeconomic Database for Latin America and the Caribbean, (a joint venture of the Center for Distributive, Labor and Social Studies (CEDLAS) and the World Bank)
SSA	Sub-Saharan Africa
SWIFT	Survey of Well-being via Instant and Frequent Tracking
UN	United Nations
UNDESA	UN Department of Economic and Social Affairs
UNDP	UN Development Programme
UNICEF	United Nations Children's Fund
USAID	United States Agency for International Development
WDI	World Development Indicators
WDR	World Development Report
WHO	World Health Organization
WPP	World Population Prospects

Introduction

The Scope of the Report

In 2013, the World Bank Group announced two goals that would guide its development work worldwide. The first is the eradication of extreme poverty. More precisely, it was the target by 2030 of reducing below 3 percent of the world population the number of extremely poor people, defined as those living on less per day than 1.25 international dollars in 2005 purchasing power parity (PPP) terms (to allow for differences in purchasing power). (The International Poverty Line has subsequently been revised in 2015 to 1.90 PPP-adjusted dollars a day per person in 2011 PPP terms.) The second is the boosting of shared prosperity, defined as promoting the growth of per capita real income of the poorest 40 percent of the population in each country.

In June 2015, the World Bank established the Commission on Global Poverty to advise it on how to monitor global poverty in light of the Twin Goals, with the remit of advising on two questions:

1. What should be the interpretation going forward of the definition of extreme poverty, set in 2015 at 1.90 PPP-adjusted dollars a day per person in 2015, in real terms?

2. What choices should the World Bank make regarding complementary poverty measures to be tracked and made available to policy makers?

In other words, the Commission is charged with one quite specific technical question—(1) How should the World Bank measure of extreme poverty be monitored between now and 2030? And it is charged with a more general question—(2) What other kinds of poverty indicators should guide policy? It should be noted that the specific technical question takes as given its starting point the World Bank 2015 level of 1.90 PPP-adjusted dollars a day per person. Although the Report begins by summarizing the history of the World Bank measure leading up to this figure, the Commission was not asked to redo this analysis. The Report looks to the future, while seeking to learn from the lessons of the past.

The work of the Commission acquired additional significance with the agreement at the United Nations (UN) meeting in September 2015 on a new set of global Sustainable Development Goals (SDGs—discussed further below), and committed themselves to the achievement of these Goals by 2030. The opening SDG is Goal 1.1: the eradication by 2030 of extreme poverty for all people everywhere. The first question addressed by the Commission may therefore be seen as advising the World Bank as to how it should monitor progress toward achieving this goal, for which it has been identified as possible custodian agency, together with the International Labour Organization (ILO) (UNDESA 2016, 3).

The Report of the Commission comes correspondingly in three parts. Chapter 1 addresses question 1, and chapter 2 addresses question 2. Chapter 3 is concerned with "Making It Happen" and deals with issues common to chapters 1 and 2—investment in statistics, governance structure, and building a coalition of support. Together chapters 1, 2, and 3 contain 21 Recommendations to the World Bank.

Readers may well focus on either chapter 1 or chapter 2, so it may be helpful in this introduction to provide a context within which their differing purposes may be understood. The distinction has been neatly drawn by Commission member S. Subramanian, who contrasts the *Merriam-Webster Dictionary* definition of the "poverty line" as "a level of personal or family income below which one is classified as poor according to governmental standards" with that in the *Oxford English Dictionary*, according to which the poverty line is "the estimated minimum level of income needed to secure the necessities of life." In chapter 1 of the Commission Report, the World Bank extreme poverty definition is taken as a "governmental standard." It reflects a political judgment about the extent of ambition on the part of the Member States of the United Nations: the members of the UN have signed up to this particular poverty target. An alternative poverty line may be more intrinsically defensible, but it does not have the same claim on political leaders. Chapter 1 is therefore concerned with the implementation of the $1.90 standard, taking it as a given.

Chapter 2 of the Report steps back and asks more generally how poverty standards can be rationalized. The underlying justification may be in terms of "basic needs," as in the *Oxford English Dictionary* definition, but this is not the only alternative approach and the Report discusses "capabilities" and "minimum rights." Although unable to be fully encompassing, the aim in chapter 2 is to open the measurement of global poverty to a wide range of different perspectives and to multiple dimensions of deprivation. This means considering how the measurement of poverty relates to the second Twin Goal of the World Bank (the boosting of shared prosperity) and how the monetary poverty goal relates to the SDGs that deal with nonmonetary indicators. In short, the reader of chapter 2 should bear in mind the "governmental" role of chapter 1; and the reader of chapter 1 should bear in mind the wider scope of chapter 2.

The analysis of chapter 2 leads to the proposal of a set of Complementary Indicators that provide the Report's answer to the question: What other kinds of poverty indicators should guide policy? The set is deliberately small in number, and there are other indicators that are strong candidates for inclusion. They are put forward in the spirit of encouraging constructive discussion. In each case, the proposed Complementary Indicators raise issues of implementation. Many of these issues are similar to those that arise in chapter 1. The quality and coverage of household surveys, and the need for better population data, for example, are relevant to the measurement of nonmonetary indicators in analogous ways as to the measurement of monetary poverty. Rather than repeat the discussion, the Report refers the reader of chapter 2 back to the appropriate sections of chapter 1.

In preparing the Report, the Chair has been very conscious that time is of the essence. This is all too evident for those who are living in conditions of extreme poverty. For the SDGs, the clock has been ticking since January 1, 2016. New estimates of the extent of global poverty are already under preparation in the World Bank. From the outset, it was clear that there are issues the Commission could not cover, and, as the work proceeded, the ambitions for the scope of the Report had to be further curtailed. In particular, it has not proved possible within the tight timescale to do justice to the important topic of multidimensional poverty indexes. The way forward is the subject of—the relatively brief—chapter 3 ("Making It Happen"), which focuses on investment in statistics and external accountability. (While there are implications of the analysis for the *internal* organization of statistical activities in the World Bank, these are not the subject of this Report.)

Reference

UNDESA (United Nations Department of Economic and Social Affairs). 2016. *Provisional Proposed Tiers for Global SDG Indicators.* New York: United Nations.

Monitoring Extreme Poverty

Chapter 1 of this Report is concerned with the first of the two remits of the World Bank's Commission on Global Poverty: the monitoring of extreme poverty according to Sustainable Development Goal 1.1. The measurement of extreme poverty has long been a high-profile activity of the World Bank, covering initially developing countries and now extended to the world as a whole. The first section, "From $1 a Day to Sustainable Development Goal 1.1," gives a brief account of the historical background in the World Bank's research.[1] The next section describes the 2015 World Bank estimates that are our point of departure. This sets the scene for the assessment of the future monitoring of global poverty in the sections "Assessment: Household Surveys and Population Data" and "Assessment: Monitoring over Time." These contain recommendations as to how the monitoring up to 2030 should be conducted. The introduction of the recommendations sequentially in the course of the analytical sections means, however, that their internal coherence may be obscured. The concluding section, therefore, brings together the recommendations under the three headings: raw materials (data), analysis, and presentation.

From $1 a Day to Sustainable Development Goal 1.1

The adoption of a global goal for the abolition of extreme poverty has been much contested, but its formulation has served as a focal point. The existence of the $1 a day poverty line, and the associated estimates of the number of people living in extreme poverty, provided a concrete foundation for the first and most closely watched of the Millennium Development Goals (MDGs) adopted in 2000. The MDGs in turn have been succeeded by the Sustainable Development Goals (SDGs) in 2015.

Measuring Extreme Poverty

The adoption of a global goal only makes sense if progress can be monitored, and rendering such monitoring possible has been a major contribution of the World Bank. Over the past 40 years, the calculations made by the World Bank have moved from being a largely academic exercise to playing a prominent role in public policy. With the MDGs, and now the SDGs, they have become the vehicle for monitoring progress toward an objective that is defined in global political terms.

The capacity of the World Bank to make such estimates dates back to the research initiated by Hollis Chenery, chief economist in the 1970s. It was on the basis of the studies of Ahluwalia (1974) and of Ahluwalia, Carter, and Chenery (1979), that Robert McNamara, the president of the World Bank at the time, was able to write in the foreword to the first World Development Report in 1978 that "some 800 million individuals continue to be trapped in what I have termed absolute poverty: a condition of life so characterized by malnutrition, illiteracy, disease, squalid surroundings, high infant mortality, and low life expectancy as to be beneath any reasonable definition of human decency" (World Bank 1978, iii). This definition is clearly broad, covering multiple dimensions of deprivation, but the concrete numbers were based on poverty measured in terms of economic resources. Ahluwalia, Carter, and Chenery made estimates for 36 developing countries of the percentage of people living with incomes below a poverty line set on the basis of Indian experience, and went on to extrapolate to the developing world as a whole.

The approach adopted by Chenery and colleagues to the measurement of global monetary poverty—based on data from household surveys—was the forerunner of that employed by the World Bank today, but there have been major developments, notably as a result of the research carried out in the past 25 years at the World Bank by Martin Ravallion and colleagues, where the output of this research is embodied in the PovcalNet database on which today's estimates are based.[2] The importance of this research, and the decisions taken in the past to support this work, should be underlined. Without the investment by the Research Department in the 1990s, the World Bank would not have been in a position to implement the monitoring of the extreme poverty goal. It cannot be accused of having failed to address the question, even if there are many critics of the approach adopted by the World Bank to the measurement of global poverty and some who doubt whether such measurement is actually possible.

What have been the key features of the World Bank approach? There are three key ingredients. First, crucial to the exercise is the increasing, although still limited, availability of high-quality data from household surveys. The World Bank uses the available evidence from household surveys to count the number of people living in households where consumption per person falls below the poverty line. Here it should be noted that there was an early switch from the income measure used by Chenery and colleagues to a consumption-based measure, and now "consumption per capita is the preferred welfare indicator for the World Bank's analysis of global poverty" (World Bank 2015, 31). The implications of employing a consumption-based definition, and of the fact that income continues to be used in some countries, are discussed in the section "Assessment: Household Surveys and Population Data," below.

The second key feature of the World Bank approach is that the poverty line is set in a way that reflects the national poverty standards set in the poorest countries for which national poverty lines are available: "the World Bank has elected to monitor global poverty by the standards that apply in the very poorest countries of the world" (World Bank 2015, 36). At the outset, drawing on the national poverty lines set nationally by 33 countries, Ravallion et al. (1991, 6) based their estimates of poverty in developing countries on two proposed per capita lines: $0.76 a day and $1.02 a day. The latter, which they found to be "more representative" (Ravallion, Datt, and van de Walle 1991, 348), became widely accepted as the basis for $1 a day per person (see also Chen, Datt, and Ravallion 1994). As described below, this poverty line later became $1.08 (see Chen and Ravallion 2001), $1.25 (see Chen and Ravallion 2010 and Ravallion, Chen, and Sangraula 2009), and in 2015, $1.90 a day. This approach introduces an important distinction: between poor *people* and poor *countries*. This distinction has been emphasized in studies of global inequality (see, for example, Bourguignon and Morrisson 2002 and Milanovic 2005, 2012, and 2016). Poor countries are typically identified according to gross national income (GNI) per head, a macroeconomic measurement from the national accounts, as in the World Bank classification of countries shown in box 1.1. Poor countries are the basis for setting the World Bank poverty line, but there are two further requirements: it is based on countries *for which national poverty lines are available,* and the variable employed is, in line with the consumption-based approach, *private consumption per capita.*

Box 1.1 World Bank Classification of Countries (Economies)

The World Bank classifies countries into three groups according to their gross national income (GNI) calculated using the World Bank Atlas method: low-income, middle-income, and high-income countries.

The classification is revised each year, so countries can move between groups. For the 2016 fiscal year, the following apply:

- Low-income economies are defined as those with an annual GNI per capita of $1,045 or less in 2014.
- Middle-income economies are those with an annual GNI per capita of more than $1,045 but less than $12,736.
- High-income economies are those with an annual GNI per capita of $12,736 or more.

(In addition, lower-middle-income and upper-middle-income economies are separated at an annual GNI per capita of $4,125.)

Part I and Part II Countries

The World Bank also distinguishes between:

Part I Member Countries, which are mostly developed countries that contribute to the resources of the International Development Association (IDA), which is the part of the World Bank Group that provides long-term

(continued next page)

Box 1.1 (continued)

interest-free loans (credits) and grants to the poorest of the developing countries.

Part II Member Countries, which are mostly developing countries, some of which also contribute to the resources of IDA.

Note: The term *country*, used interchangeably with *economy*, does not imply political independence but refers to any territory for which authorities report separate social or economic statistics.

The World Bank Atlas method of calculating GNI in U.S. dollars uses the *Atlas* conversion factor instead of simple exchange rates. The *Atlas* conversion factor for any year is the average of a country's exchange rate for that year and its exchange rates for the two preceding years, adjusted for the difference between the rate of inflation in the country and international inflation; the objective of the adjustment is to reduce any changes to the exchange rate caused by inflation.

The third key element is that the consumption per head recorded in household surveys is assessed across countries in terms of purchasing power, where this depends on domestic price indexes and on the international comparison of purchasing power. In the latter case, Chenery and colleagues used the findings from the 1975 round of the United Nations (UN) International Comparison Program (ICP) to express national currency amounts in terms of internationally comparable dollars (taking the United States as the reference country). In simple terms, this means that the poverty line applied in India is not obtained by converting U.S. dollars into rupees at the exchange rate, but that there is an additional adjustment to allow for the fact that the purchasing power in India is different. In 2011, for example, the exchange rate was such that one obtained 46.67 Indian rupees for a U.S. dollar, but the results of the ICP exercise for 2011 showed that 14.98 rupees would have been sufficient to buy the same basket of goods and services as $1 in the United States. Such "purchasing power parity (PPP)" exchange rates are based on the substantial investment that has been made in collecting and analyzing the price data necessary to compare purchasing power in different countries. Since 1970 there have been eight rounds of ICP data collection, the most recent to date being that for 2011 (World Bank 2014).

The measurement of extreme poverty, as described above, is in effect based on a *tripod*, whose three legs are shown schematically in figure 1.1:

(i) household surveys furnishing evidence about household consumption per head (or, in some cases, income per head), (ii) an International Poverty Line based on national lines in the poorest countries for which such lines are available, and (iii) domestic price indexes and purchasing power parities. These three legs are the major subjects of the analysis that follows, and they are the aspects that have featured most in the World Bank's presentation of the extreme poverty calculations. However, as drawn, the tripod would fall over without the aid of a fourth leg, shown dashed because it is mostly behind the scenes. This involves the estimates of total population per country. Population figures are widely used in all areas of economic and social policy but are commonly taken as unproblematic. As discussed in the section "Assessment: Household Surveys and Population Data," there needs to be careful scrutiny of these estimates. The extreme poverty figure is often stated in terms of a percentage of the total population, but it is the absolute number of human beings that is our ultimate concern, and, to know this, we have to have good population estimates.

Updating the Global Poverty Count

The adoption of the MDGs in 2000 gave prominence to the World Bank poverty count as the vehicle for monitoring progress. Goal 1 of the MDGs was "to halve, between 1990 and 2015, the proportion of people

Figure 1.1 Measuring Global Poverty: A Tripod (with an Additional Leg)

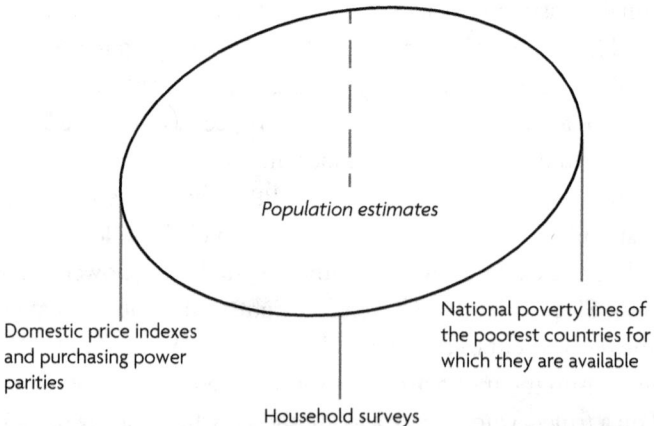

Population estimates

Domestic price indexes
and purchasing power
parities

National poverty lines of
the poorest countries for
which they are available

Household surveys

whose income is less than US$1 a day," and the estimates of the World Bank became central. The goal was stated in terms of "income"; but, as noted above, the World Bank monitoring has been based on consumption. Centrality of the World Bank extreme poverty numbers led, in turn, to efforts to upgrade the estimates. There has, for instance, been a considerable investment in improving the statistical base, extending the number of household surveys used in the data compilation. The work of the World Bank's poverty and inequality program has made an invaluable contribution.

Here, attention is focused on revisions to the underlying method of calculation. The period following the adoption of the MDGs saw a number of revisions to the World Bank estimates, and the PPP per capita poverty line rose from $1.02 a day to $1.08 a day (Chen and Ravallion 2004, 2007) to $1.25 a day (Ravallion, Chen, and Sangraula 2009). The last of these was described as a "major revision," and it generated considerable debate. The revised estimates implied an upward revision to the global poverty figures: "our new calculations . . . imply that 25% of the population of the developing world, 1.4 billion people, were poor in 2005, which is 400 million more . . . than implied by our old International Poverty Line based on national lines for the 1980s and the 1993 ICP" (Chen and Ravallion 2010, 1621). At the same time, the revisions raised the baseline figures and the authors stressed that the rate of progress in poverty reduction was little affected. In their analysis, it is important to distinguish the measurement of the level of poverty from the monitoring of poverty over time: "the trends over time and regional profile are robust to various changes in methodology, though precise counts are more sensitive" (Chen and Ravallion 2010, 1577).

The disconcerting effect on the level of extreme poverty of this major $1.25 revision led many people to seek understanding, notably Angus Deaton in his 2010 Presidential Address to the American Economic Association (the first president, at least in recent times, to take poverty as the subject of the address). The important point to emerge from this debate is that there had been changes in *two* of the three legs of the tripod. While attention had concentrated on the purchasing power comparisons, there had also been changes in the derivation of the International Poverty Line from the national lines. It was based on an entirely new compilation of national poverty lines that was updated and considerably extended (Ravallion, Chen, and Sangraula 2008, 2009), and on a different method of calculation. In the earlier revision, from $1.02 to $1.08, in addition to incorporating the results of the 1993 ICP, Chen and Ravallion had adopted the practice of taking the median of the lowest ten national poverty lines in the set of countries considered. The $1.25 revision involved a new method for deriving the global line from national poverty lines, based on the mean of the national poverty lines for the poorest 15 countries for which national poverty lines were available in an extended set of 75 developing countries.

The Sustainable Development Goals (SDGs)

The UN MDGs have been superseded by the SDGs. In September 2015, the Heads of State and Government and High Representatives, meeting at UN Headquarters in New York from September 25 to 27, 2015, agreed on a new set of global goals, and committed themselves to their achievement by 2030. The SDGs—summarized in box 1.2—built upon the MDGs and sought to address their unfinished business. The new goals

---

Box 1.2 2015 Sustainable Development Goals

1. No poverty
2. Zero hunger
3. Good health and well-being
4. Quality education
5. Gender equality
6. Clean water and sanitation
7. Affordable and clean energy
8. Decent work and economic growth
9. Industry, innovation, and infrastructure
10. Reduced inequality
11. Sustainable cities and communities
12. Responsible consumption and production
13. Climate action
14. Life below water
15. Life on land
16. Peace, justice, and strong institutions
17. Partnerships for the Goals

Source: United Nations Sustainable Development Goals website: https://sustainabledevelopment. un.org/?menu=1300.

and targets came into effect on January 1, 2016, and are a guide to development effort over the next 15 years.

The first of the seventeen SDGs are:

Goal 1.1: By 2030, eradicate extreme poverty for all people everywhere, currently measured as people living on less than $1.25 a day.

Goal 1.2: By 2030, reduce at least by half the proportion of men, women, and children of all ages living in poverty in all its dimensions according to national definitions.

Goal 1.3: Implement nationally appropriate social protection systems and measures for all, including floors, and by 2030 achieve substantial coverage of the poor and the vulnerable.

Goal 1.4: By 2030, ensure that all men and women, in particular the poor and the vulnerable, have equal rights to economic resources, as well as access to basic services, ownership and control over land and other forms of property, inheritance, natural resources, appropriate new technology, and financial services, including microfinance.

Goal 1.5: By 2030, build the resilience of the poor and those in vulnerable situations and reduce their exposure and vulnerability to climate-related extreme events and other economic, social, and environmental shocks and disasters.

Essential to the process is the monitoring of progress toward these goals. It is the monitoring of Goal 1.1 by the World Bank that is the concern of chapter 1 of this Report. The remaining elements of Goal 1 refer to issues that are discussed in chapter 2 or that concern the policy instruments by which poverty may be tackled.

The 2015 Point of Departure

In October 2015, the World Bank published a new set of extreme poverty estimates from 1990 to 2012 (Ferreira et al. 2015, 2016), which represent the point of departure for the present Report.[3] The 2015 estimates make use of the results from the 2011 ICP to make purchasing power adjustments, and set a new International Poverty Line at $1.90 PPP-adjusted a day per person. This section is devoted to an explanation of the main changes. Its aim is expository, spelling out what is involved for a general readership, and highlighting the aspects that are particularly relevant for the future monitoring of the SDG goal set by the United Nations. It should be stressed that the section is purely descriptive. The Commission was not asked to evaluate the procedures by which the World Bank arrived at the October 2015 estimates.

How do the 2015 poverty estimates of the World Bank differ from those that preceded them? The first difference—significant symbolically, if not quantitatively—is that the estimates now cover the world as a whole, rather than being confined to low- and middle-income countries. Whereas the study by Chen and Ravallion (2010) is entitled "The *developing world* is poorer than we thought. . . ," the 2015 World Bank estimates are contained in an article with the title "A *global count* of the extreme poor in 2012" (Ferreira et al. 2015, 2016, italics added). High-income countries are now regarded as within scope, reflecting the reference in SDG Goal 1.1 to "extreme poverty *for all people everywhere*" (italics added). There has been a shift in perspective to what Ravallion and Chen (2013) call "truly global" poverty measures. As they argue, while it may previously have been appropriate to focus on the developing world, the world distribution of income is changing in major respects. The need for a global reach is, moreover, underlined by increasing concerns about the deprivations faced by migrants and refugees entering high-income countries (the extent of extreme poverty in these countries is discussed further below).

Quantitatively, the differences in the poverty estimates arise for the same reasons as with past revisions. The 2015 estimates are based on an enlarged set of countries and years for which household survey data are available. The estimates applying the $1.25 standard described by Chen and Ravallion (2010) were based on 675 surveys spanning 115 countries and the years 1979 to 2006. The 2015 estimates of Ferreira et al. are based on 1,165 surveys covering 132 countries over the years 1990 to 2012. The future role of improved data coverage is the subject of the following section. In this section, the Report concentrates on the other two legs of the tripod: the PPP adjustment and the use of national poverty lines to set the poverty standard.

Purchasing Power Parity (PPP) Adjustments

The new global poverty estimate is close to that obtained by applying the previous methods. For the overlapping year 2011, the global poverty head count ratio is 14.1 percent (983 million people), compared with 14.5 percent (1,011 million people) in the earlier estimates (Ferreira et al. 2016, 166). At the same time, the rise in the poverty threshold in terms of PPP dollars from $1.25 at the prices of 2005 to $1.90 at the prices of 2011 is a large one, and has understandably given rise to the reaction that the World Bank has raised the bar. Adjusted solely for consumer price changes in the United States, a threshold of $1.25 in 2005 would have been raised only to $1.44 (Ravallion 2016, 15), an increase of 15.2 percent. Why has the U.S. dollar figure for the global poverty threshold risen so much?

The first point to be considered is that the new (2015) World Bank poverty estimates make use of the most recent round of the ICP, that relating to 2011 prices, in place of the 2005 ICP round. The 2011 ICP exercise concluded that, comparing the findings with those in the 2005 round, on average, prices in the developing world are lower than previously found, relative to those in the United States. Such a change led to a significant revision of the view taken of global economic magnitudes, such as gross domestic product (GDP). As summarized in the report on the 2011 Program, "the relative shares of the three Asian economies—China, India, and Indonesia—to the United States doubled, while Brazil, Mexico, and Russia increased by one-third or more" (World Bank 2014, 81). The report goes on to say that "some of the large differences in the Asian economies and developing economies in general can be attributed to the changes in the methodology used for the two comparisons." The economies were larger because a given value in local currency was, with the lower prices represented by the 2011 PPPs, a larger amount in international purchasing power measured with the United States as the benchmark. For the same reason, "the spread of per capita actual individual consumption as a percentage of that of the United States has been greatly reduced, suggesting that the world has become more equal" (World Bank 2014, 89).

The implications for global poverty measurement of the new PPPs have been much discussed (see, among others, Deaton and Aten 2015; Dykstra, Kenny, and Sandefur 2014; Inklaar and Rao 2014; Ravallion 2014). One way that the impact may be seen is by comparing the values of the different ICP conversion factors applied to a given year (2005). For India, the calculation goes as follows (see figure 1.2):

1. The conversion factor in 2005 was 15.60 local currency units (LCUs, Indian rupees in this case) per international dollar according to the 2005 PPP conversion factor, private consumption (that is, household final consumption expenditure). This implies that an International Poverty Line of $1.25 in 2005 corresponded to 19.50 rupees (point ❶ on the left-hand axis in figure 1.2).
2. The 2011 ICP conversion factor (LCU per international dollar) for private consumption extrapolated back to 2005 (World Bank table PA.NUS.PRVT.PP on the World Bank website)[4] is 10.43, which means that $1.25 corresponded to a poverty line in 2005 of 13.04 rupees (point ❸ on the left-hand axis in figure 1.2).

The move from ❶ to ❸ in figure 1.2 represents a reduction of a third, and it can be expected to reduce substantially the estimated number in poverty in 2005. (Points ❷, ❹, and ❺ in figure 1.2 are discussed below.) The impact on India was one of the larger, but for 65 countries there was a reduction in excess of 20 percent. These were nearly all developing and Middle East and North Africa (MENA) countries, including Bangladesh, the Arab Republic of Egypt, Guatemala, Jordan, Kenya, Madagascar, Myanmar, Pakistan, the Philippines, Saudi Arabia, Sri Lanka, Thailand, and Zambia.

The new ICP is important here not only because it changed the relative position of rich and poor countries but also because it changed the relative position of different developing countries: "the ICP 2011 reversed some of the increase in inequality between poor and rich regions in ICP 2005, but it did not reverse the 2005 changes on a country-by-country basis" (Deaton and Aten 2015, 10). They went on to say that "the reduction in Africa in 2011 undid much less of the 2005 increase than was the case in India, so that, just as the ICP 2005 'Asianized' poverty, the ICP 2011 will 'Africanize' it" (Deaton and Aten 2015, 10). There is a distinct regional pattern to the revisions, with larger effects in Asia and smaller effects in Africa and Latin America and the Caribbean.

At a country level, the adoption of the 2011 ICP conversion factors changed the poverty line in local currency around the world: out of 167 countries for which the 2005 value may be compared with the

Figure 1.2 The Impact of Change from 2005 ICP-Based Estimates to 2011 ICP-Based Estimates on the Poverty Line in India Measured in Rupees

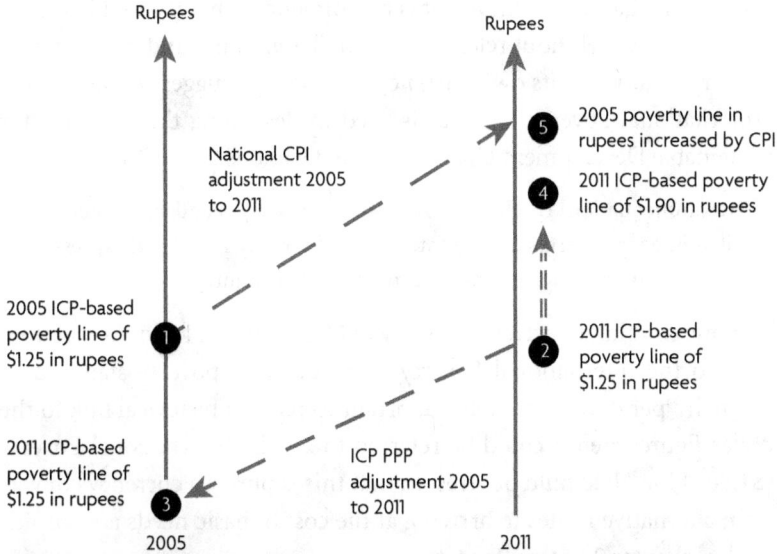

Note: The points 1 to 5 are defined as follows:

1. ICP2005 gives for 2005 15.60 local currency units per 2005 PPP dollar, implying that an International Poverty Line of $1.25 becomes *19.50 rupees* (1.25 times 15.60) in 2005.
2. ICP2011 gives for 2011 14.98 local currency units per 2011 PPP dollar, implying that an International Poverty Line of $1.25 in 2011 would become *18.73 rupees* (1.25 times 14.98).
3. ICP2011 series gives a 2005 figure of 10.43 local currency units per 2011 PPP dollar, implying that an International Poverty Line of $1.25 applicable in 2005 would be *13.04 rupees* (1.25 times 10.43).
4. Using again the ICP2011 figure for 2011 (as at step 2) 14.98 local currency units per 2011 PPP dollar, but taking the International Poverty Line of $1.90, yields *28.45 rupees* (1.90 times 14.98).
5. Just adjusting by the increase in CPI (65.5 percent) between 2005 and 2011 means that 19.50 rupees in 2005 (point ❶) would be increased to become *32.27 rupees* in 2011.

The two lines joining ❶ to ❺ (slope increase 65.5 percent) and ❸ to ❷ (slope increase 43.6 percent) are NOT parallel. If the CPI increase had been the same as the increase in the new ICP, then the top line would become parallel to the bottom line, but the point ❺ would not coincide with ❹, since the ratio of $1.90 to $1.25 exceeds the increase in the ICP in the case of India.

2011 value extrapolated backward, only 63 had a change of less than 10 percent (or were unaffected). One of the unaffected countries was the United States, as the benchmark. This obvious fact in turn evokes an obvious question: Why do we *continue* to quote the International Poverty Line in terms of U.S. dollars? For the measurement of global economic magnitudes, as is the primary purpose of the ICP, the United States may be an appropriate benchmark, but it is not apparent why the global poverty objective should be stated in terms of the currency of a country where relatively few people live below the extreme poverty line. To this end, and to underscore the global political legitimacy that the extreme poverty line has now achieved, it is recommended that it should be cited in *general terms* without reference to a dollar amount, and given in each country in terms of its own currency per day. The suggested name is the "International Poverty Line," as is used in describing the indicator for Sustainable Development Goal 1.1 (United Nations 2016, 39):[5]

> Recommendation 1: The global extreme poverty standard should be cited in general terms as "the International Poverty Line," and expressed in each country in terms of the currency of that country.

The presentation of extreme poverty in Nigeria in 2011 should therefore refer to the International Poverty Line, and to a poverty standard of 151 naira per day.[6] If it is felt important to retain a historical link to the dollar figure, then it could be referred to as "the International Poverty ($1.90) Line." It should be stressed that this is purely a currency conversion; alternative routes to arriving at the cost of basic needs are considered in chapter 2 of this Report.

The reader may at this point be thinking that no answer has been given to the question: How has the poverty line, when expressed in dollars, become $1.90 in place of $1.25? This brings us to the second leg of the tripod—the link with national poverty lines.

National Poverty Lines Revisited

In arriving at the poverty line to be applied in the estimates for 2011 based on the 2011 ICP, the World Bank considered a number of possible approaches (see Basu 2015; Ferreira et al. 2015, 2016). The approach after experimentation remained close to that employed in the $1.25 revision, basing the poverty standard on the national lines in operation in the set of 15 countries used in 2005 and uprating their national poverty lines according to the increase in the national consumer price index (CPI), and then applying the new ICP2011 to calculate the poverty line in international dollars. For all 15 countries, this process, taking the unweighted mean of the resulting $PPP poverty lines, gives $1.88, which, rounded up to $1.90, represents an increase over $1.25 of 52 percent. It is the $1.90 figure that the World Bank determined in 2015 should be the new International Poverty Line.

To illustrate in the case of one of the 15 countries—Tanzania—there are the following stages for calculating the daily poverty line per person (see table 4 in Ferreira et al. 2016):

1. The 2005 poverty line for Tanzania per day denoted in PPP2005 was $0.63PPP, which converted into LCUs by multiplying by the ICP2005 conversion factor of 482.45 gives 303.94 LCUs (shillings) a day; this figure in shillings a day is the way in which, if Recommendation 1 were to be adopted, the International Poverty Line would be communicated.

2. Moving forward, the CPI had increased from an index of 100 in 2005 to 169.9 in 2011, giving an LCU poverty line of 516.4 shillings a day when increased for domestic inflation; if only domestic inflation were to be taken into account, this would be the 2011 International Poverty Line in local currency.

3. But there is a new 2011 ICP, with a higher conversion factor of 585.52, so that the new poverty line for Tanzania in international dollars is reached by applying to the CPI increase of 1.699 an adjustment factor of 482.45 divided by 585.52 (equal to 0.82), giving a figure in PPP2011 of $0.88PPP per day ($0.63 times 1.699 times 0.82), or an increase over the corresponding 2005 figure of some 40 percent ($0.88 divided by $0.63).

4. If the increase in Tanzania alone had been taken as the basis for updating the International Poverty Line, then the 40 percent increase would have taken it to $1.25 to $1.75. In fact the average increase for the 15 countries was higher,[7] taking it to $1.90, an increase of 52 percent; this increases the poverty line in local currency in Tanzania to 561.9 shillings per day.

The World Bank also considered alternative approaches, such as those proposed by Kakwani and Son (2016), Sillers (2015), and Jolliffe and Prydz (2016). In each case, they lead to values close to $1.90: "most of the alternative approaches that have been proposed for updating the International Poverty Line to 2011 PPPs end up generating lines that are either exactly or very close to $1.90 a day" (Ferreira et al. 2016, 164). The World Bank's chief economist referred to this as "a strange alignment of the stars." At the same time, he recognized that we cannot rely on this being the case with any future new ICP exercise: "we will not always have the good fortune to be able to use different methods and still arrive at virtually the same line" (Basu 2015, 2).

Composition of the Population in Extreme Poverty

It is not just the total living in extreme poverty that is of concern. As the World Bank clearly recognizes, the composition of the population is important. This is analyzed in terms of regional composition and of the country-level changes. Here again it is important to distinguish between poor countries and people in poverty. As Devarajan and Kanbur emphasize, "the terrain of development has shifted significantly. . . . Strong growth in a number of large developing countries has moved them from [low-income countries] LICs to [lower-middle-income countries] LMICs (Devarajan and Kanbur 2013, 16). But they go on to caution that, "even within countries that have exited from the LIC category, significant numbers of people languish in poverty." According to Sumner (2012), twenty years ago 90 percent of the world's poor lived in LICs; today, 70 percent of the world's poor live in MICs.[8]

The effect of the move from a $1.25 line based on the 2005 ICP to a $1.90 line based on the 2011 ICP is to reduce the estimated total number of people living in extreme poverty in 2011 from 1,011.4 million to 983.3 million (Ferreira et al. 2016, table 5), a reduction of 28 million. Leaving aside the MENA region, for which estimates are not given,[9] the net change was the result of a combination of increases and decreases by region. There were increases in East Asia and Pacific (plus 12.3 million), Europe and Central Asia (plus 9.0 million, from the low value of 2.4 million), and Latin America and the Caribbean (plus 7.7 million). There were larger absolute decreases in South Asia (minus 37.3 million) and Sub-Saharan Africa (minus 22.2 million).

At the level of individual countries, the absolute effects are obviously smaller, but the proportionate changes can be substantial, as is shown by a scatter plot in Ferreira et al. (2016, figure 2, panel A). (From the results in PovcalNet, taking those for the most recent years, where available, it is possible to make comparisons for 103 countries, excluding 32 high-income countries.) There is considerable variation by region in the impact on the poverty rates. There is also considerable variation *within* regions. In Sub-Saharan Africa, for example, the poverty rate in Niger in 2011 rose by 9.5 percentage points and that in Nigeria in 2009 fell by 8.6 points, bringing their poverty rates close together, whereas they had been more than 20 percentage points apart. The poverty rate in Kenya in 2005 fell by 9.8 percentage points, to 33.6 percent, whereas that in The Gambia in 2003 rose from the latter percentage to 45.3 percent. These are not isolated cases, and a sizeable fraction of countries saw change in their estimated rates of extreme poverty. Out of the 103 countries where comparisons can be made, a quarter (26) saw a change of more than 5 percentage points. There were 11 countries where the poverty rate changed by more than 10 percentage points: 7 upward and 4 downward (Angola, Comoros, Liberia, and Mauritania). Beneath the surface, therefore, the new October 2015 World Bank estimates led to changes in poverty assessments at the national level that are of concern. For this reason, when considering future monitoring, the section below on "Assessment: Monitoring over Time" stresses the need for coherence between global and national level poverty estimates. Assessments of the progress made with the MDGs have emphasized the extent of country heterogeneity (for example, Bourguignon et al. 2010), and one has to be confident that this heterogeneity is measured with sufficient accuracy and is not the result of statistical artifacts.

Taking Stock: The Different Moving Parts

The aim of this presentation of the October 2015 changes in the method of counting global poverty has been to bring out a number of the key elements that feature in the subsequent discussion.

Examining the different elements shows that there are several changes happening at once, and that it is essential to view them in conjunction. The different elements are summarized in the case of India by figure 1.2, where the right-hand axis shows the implications for the new poverty line in 2011 measured in local currency. The move to the 2011 PPP would, in 2005, have led to a substantially lower rupee poverty line in that year (13.03 rupees in place of 19.50 rupees). However, this was to a considerable extent offset by the upward movement in the time series for the ICP2011 conversion factor, so that by 2011 the rupee value of the $1.25 international dollar poverty line becomes 18.73 rupees (point ❷ on the right-hand axis in figure 1.2), and with the new $1.90 international dollar line, rises to 28.45 rupees (point ❹ in figure 1.2). The upward movement in the conversion factor reflects the fact that domestic inflation was faster in India than in the benchmark country (the United States). At the same time, the upward movement shown by the ICP2011 conversion factor was less than domestic inflation recorded by the national CPI. If the rupee figure for 2005 is increased by the increase in the CPI between 2005 and 2011 (World Bank code FP.CPI. TOTL) the resulting figure is 32.27 rupees (point ❺ in figure 1.2). Note the steeper slope.

The case of India is not atypical, and illustrates well the importance of differences in domestic inflation rates (which means that particular attention has to be paid to how well this is measured). The reader looking at figure 1.2 may also wonder whether it would not have been simpler in future to move directly from point ❶ to point ❺. Would it not be better to have fewer moving parts? This is indeed the approach taken up in the section "Assessment: Monitoring over Time," below.

Assessment: Household Surveys and Population Data

The Commission was asked to take the 2015 estimates as its point of departure and to assess how the process may be carried forward to monitor progress up to 2030 in achieving the SDG Goal 1.1. In describing the 2015 estimates in the previous section, two core issues have been highlighted. First, how should the World Bank react when there are further revisions to the PPPs? Should it go through the process of updating? What are the respective roles of the PPPs and the domestic CPIs? Second, how far should account be taken of the national poverty targets in assessing Goal 1.1? These targets enter Goal 1.2, but should they influence the UN/World Bank poverty standard applicable to Goal 1.1? These two issues are taken up in the next section. But first, the third leg of the tripod needs closer examination: the household surveys that underlie the calculations. It is the existence of household surveys for individual countries that has allowed a global poverty estimate to be made and it is the multiplication of such surveys that has allowed greater accuracy to be achieved in monitoring progress. The 1990 World Development Report estimate of global poverty was based on single household surveys for 22 countries (World Bank 1990). A quarter of a century later, in 2015, the World Bank had access to more than a thousand surveys (World Bank 2015, 4).

Despite the considerable improvements in coverage and data access that have taken place, problems remain. A global poverty measure should cover everyone on the planet. In this respect, there is a difference from the initial World Bank estimates, which were intended to cover only developing countries (Part II Member Countries). There are at least four ways in which people may be missing from the PovcalNet statistics underlying the global poverty count: (i) the country (or territory) in which they live may not be covered by PovcalNet, (ii) their country may be covered but PovcalNet may not include a current household survey providing data on household consumption, (iii) the household survey used in PovcalNet may not cover them (including cases where coverage is not national), and (iv) people may be stateless or in transit between states.

Country Coverage
The data contained in PovcalNet 2011 cover 148 countries, of which 34 are classified as high income (as of July 1, 2013) and are taken as having zero extreme poverty (this assumption is discussed further below). For five countries where there was a large difference between the PPP adjustment and recorded domestic inflation, the 2011 PPP-based estimates were not used (instead the 2005 PPP was used), but they are included in the estimates using PovcalNet 2005.[10] For a further five countries (Algeria, Egypt, Iraq, Syria, and Yemen) country-level poverty estimates based on 2011 PPPs were not available in the 2011 round because of inexplicably large deviations between CPI and PPP inflations, outdated or major ongoing revisions to latest surveys, and ongoing conflicts. The PovcalNet website refers to 170 countries, but subtracting the 5+5 countries just identified, and allowing for the 12 separate entries for rural or urban populations for countries already counted, gives a total of 148 countries in PovcalNet 2011. Adding the five covered by PovcalNet 2005 gives a grand total of 153 that enter the 2011 global poverty estimates. (For Argentina and the Federated States of Micronesia, the results cover only the urban population.)

With 153 national estimates, PovcalNet does not cover all countries in the world. But it is not clear how far it falls short. How many countries there are in the world is not a question that is easily answered.

The United Nations had (in January 2016) 193 members and 2 permanent observers. (The World Bank had 188 members.) But this is not a complete list of economies. The World Bank has a list of 215 economies, and there were at the time 214 entries in the World Development Indicators (WDI) database (excluding aggregates).[11] There are 249 codes in the International Organization for Standardization (ISO) 3166-1 list. The difference between the 195 covered by the UN and the 249 in the ISO list includes Kosovo, population 1.8 million, and Taiwan, China, population 23.5 million. Of these, Kosovo is included in PovcalNet, but Taiwan, China is not covered. A major part of the difference between the 195 UN members and the 249 of the ISO list lies in the fact that the ISO list also includes Antarctica, and 45 inhabited (and 6 uninhabited) dependent territories.[12]

Behind these different numbers lie many deep-seated political disputes and claims. Here the only concern is whether there are significant numbers of people who are missing from statistics underlying the global poverty count. The countries in PovcalNet in 2011 and the five covered by PovcalNet 2005 contained some 6.5 billion people, or 93 percent of the world population (World Development Indicators). Adding the five countries included in PovcalNet for which there were no data (Algeria, Egypt, Iraq, Syria, and Yemen) brings the total to 6.7 billion, or some 300 million short of the total world population. In some cases, the population of individual country units is small, as with dependent territories; and there does not seem a high priority for seeking to extend coverage.[13] But, of the "missing" 300 million, about 70 percent live in nine economies with populations in excess of 10 million in 2011: Afghanistan; Cuba; the Democratic People's Republic of Korea; Myanmar; the Republic of Korea; Saudi Arabia; South Sudan; Taiwan, China; and Zimbabwe. While there are evident difficulties in some cases, in others there are reasonable hopes of extending the geographic coverage, and this forms part of Recommendation 6 later. In identifying priorities, taking together the absence of data in PovcalNet and the omission from PovcalNet, particular attention should be paid to the MENA region, where of the 19 countries in the region 6 appear in PovcalNet 2011 and 4 are covered by PovcalNet 2005, meaning that the country coverage is only about a half.

Global and National Poverty Estimates

The headline figure for monitoring Goal 1.1 is a global one, accompanied by regional breakdowns. But considerable interest attaches to the estimates at a country level, and these provide a direct link with the implementation of policy that is relevant both to the World Bank internally and to external agencies. At present, there appears to be a disjunction between the estimates for individual countries contained in the global poverty figures and the poverty estimates made at a national level. This is evident from the explanation of the Independent Evaluation Group as to why they focused on the latter:

> The evaluation will use the national poverty line adopted at the country level as the primary threshold for income-based poverty. It does this for two reasons. The first is driven by the nature of the evaluation: it is centered on improving the Bank's support to client countries at the level of the country program. The basis of this dialogue is thus the respective national poverty lines. The second is practical: much of the country-specific analytical work and dialogue is based on the national poverty line, without reference to international poverty lines. (World Bank 2013, 10)

As stressed at the beginning of this Report, it is important to place the global poverty estimate for each country alongside the national poverty estimates, so as to ensure closer engagement between those responsible for monitoring the global goals and those directly concerned with policy—whether from the country in question or from international agencies. Hence, the proposal is made here for annual National Poverty Statistics Reports (NPSR), one of the primary purposes of which is to build such a bridge. There has to be coherence between the global assessment and the experience on the ground. This is particularly important in view of the degree of country heterogeneity of performance, which "calls for more detailed country-specific analysis of the policy and structural determinants of well-being and poverty" (Bourguignon et al. 2010, 38). Potential contents of such NPSR are set out in box 1.3.

There are two elements of the national poverty calculation that are of particular interest for the NPSR, and both are illustrated for the case of Ghana in figure 1.3, panels a and b. The first is the (upper) official poverty line (OPL) adopted by the government of Ghana,

Box 1.3 National Poverty Statistics Reports

In this box, we describe possible contents for the recommended National Poverty Statistics Reports (ideal length—two pages).[a]

Sheet 1

1. International Poverty Line in national currency	zzz rupees per day (for most recent year)
2. International poverty head count ratio and number	zz.z percent and number of people (for most recent year and up to 5 comparable previous years)
3. National official poverty line, or line widely employed (and brief description of method of construction)	zzz rupees per day (for same year as 1)
4. National poverty head count ratio	zz.z percent (for same years as 2, where available)

Graph of 2 and 4.

Text discussion of the development of global poverty head count in light of the national estimates, of the other indicators, and of the economic and social circumstances of the country.

Sheet 2

World Bank portfolio of complementary indicators, including nonmonetary indicators (see chapter 2)	aa.aa to zz.zz

a. Countries to be included even where there are no World Bank poverty estimates.

which is shown in international dollars (ICP2011) on the left-hand axis in figure 1.3a, and as a percentage of mean per capita consumer expenditure on the right-hand axis. While poverty lines were initially selected as ratios of mean consumption, those shown in figure 1.3a are nutrition-based poverty lines (2,900 Calories per day per equivalent adult).[14] In 1998/99 the newly derived upper OPL was 63.7 percent of the mean consumption level (Statistics Ghana 2000, 5). In subsequent years, the OPL fell as a proportion of mean consumption, but rose significantly in terms of international dollar purchasing power (*ICP 2011* [World Bank 2014]), and after a rebasing in 2012/13 had reached a figure approaching ICP2011$4.00 a day. The second element consists of the national estimate of the extent of poverty,

Figure 1.3 National Poverty Calculation, Ghana

a. National official poverty line (OPL) in $PPP 2011 per day, Ghana

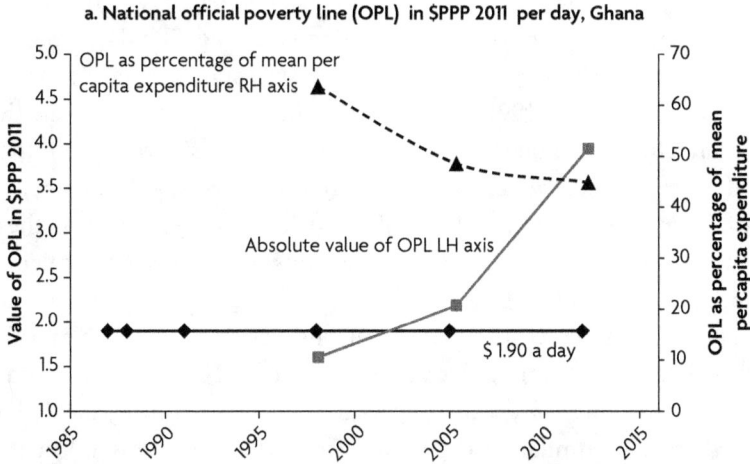

Source: Official Poverty Line (OPL), Upper Line: from Statistics Ghana 2000, 5; 2007, 5; 2014, 7. The figures are converted to international dollars using 2011PPP data from World Bank table PA.NUS.PRVT.PP. Account has been taken of the introduction of the Third Cedi in July 2007. The OPL as a percentage of mean consumption expenditure per person is from the same sources.

Note: In 1998/99 the national official poverty line was $1.60 (left-hand axis) in terms of international dollars and 64 percent of mean per capita expenditure. LH = left-hand; PPP = purchasing power parity; RH = right-hand.

b. Head count ratios in Ghana: Comparison of PovcalNet and national estimates

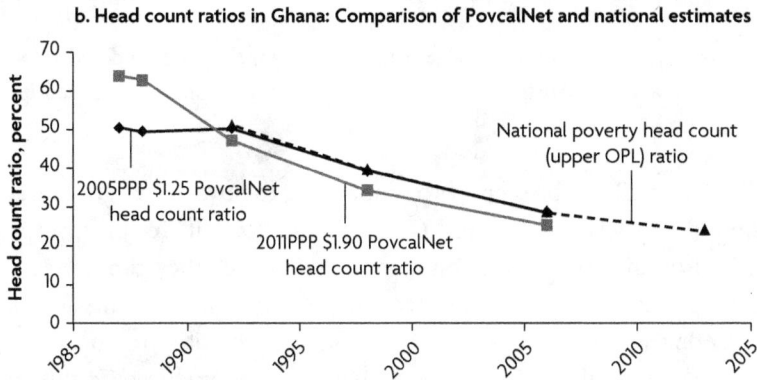

Source: PovcalNet estimates from World Bank website. National poverty head count from Statistics Ghana 2007, table A1.2; 2014, 9 (note rebasing of poverty line).

Note: In 1992, the head count ratio according to the national poverty estimates was 52 percent, whereas according to the PovcalNet estimates it was 51 percent on a 2005 ICP (International Comparison Program) basis and 47 percent on a 2011 ICP basis. OPL = Official Poverty Line; PPP = purchasing power parity.

compared with the global estimates for Ghana contained in PovcalNet. Figure 1.3b shows the findings for Ghana based on the upper OPL. These are derived from the Ghana Living Standards Survey (GLSS), which has been conducted for six rounds so far (1987/88, 1988/89, 1991/92, 1998/99, 2005/06, and 2012/13) (see Statistics Ghana 2014). The questionnaires were, however, significantly different after the second round (Coulombe and McKay 1995); hence, results are comparable only for the last four rounds, and it is these that are shown in figure 1.3b. Two versions of the PovcalNet calculations are shown, one based on the 2011 ICP and one on the earlier 2005 ICP. For the years in common, the national estimates and the PovcalNet 2005 estimates are very close, but the 2011 revision appears to have introduced a greater departure. At the same time, the downward trend is similar in the period from 1992 to 2006, and in this sense the comparison is a reassuring one.[15]

These considerations lead to:

Recommendation 2: There should be National Poverty Statistics Reports (NPSR) for each country, giving the Global Poverty estimates, explaining the local currency value of the International Poverty Line and the relation to the official poverty line(s) in that country (where they exist), considering how the trends in poverty measured according to the International Poverty Line relate to those shown by national statistics, and incorporating a set of World Bank Complementary Indicators, as proposed in chapter 2 of this Report.

The NPSR can be seen as accompanying the two-page "Poverty and shared prosperity at a glance" (P and SP) sheets that are currently produced by the World Bank on a country basis, or they can be seen as separate. In either case, the focus of the NPSR is different, as is the intended audience. The NPSR should be accessible to the general reader not familiar with the World Bank and its practices. To this end, there needs to be more explanatory text and fewer graphs; and there should be clear warnings about the margins of error that surround the estimates.

The NPSR would have a clear focus. The proposed *first sheet* is concerned with the international poverty estimate and its relation to national poverty estimates, covering in both cases the changes over time, comparing the most recent estimate with earlier comparable estimates (maximum of five). The text would discuss the reasons for the observed changes over time, and for any differences—in both level and trend—between the International Poverty Line estimates and the national estimates.[16] To give just one example, the P and SP sheet for Fiji in April 2016 shows that for 2008 the national estimate of the head count ratio was 35.2 percent but that the head count ratio using the $1.90 poverty line was only 1.9 percent. Such a large difference needs more explanation than is given. The proposed *second sheet* covers the portfolio of Complementary Indicators discussed in chapter 2 of this Report. These include not only a Shared Prosperity indicator, but also nonmonetary indicators. Again there should be text discussion of the differences, if any, in the trend in the monetary and nonmonetary indicators—a subject that is often evoked by commentators.

The NPSR would be less data-heavy. The first page of the April 2016 P and SP sheet for Cambodia contains 23 numbers plus more than 30 data points on graphs; the Key Indicators of National Data on the second page have 184 numbers. Such a volume of numbers can scarcely be absorbed "at a glance." The proposed first sheet for the NPSR would have fewer than 20 numbers and one graph; the second sheet, covering the Complementary Indicators, would have some 25 numbers. This, together with the textual commentary, should make the NPSR—despite the forbidding name—accessible to a wider audience.

In the case of the national poverty lines, the contents would build on a long-established activity. For more than 25 years, the World Bank has been assembling information about national poverty lines (see Ravallion, Datt, and van de Walle 1991), and this is now extensive in its coverage. For the historical material, it would be good if this information could be open to external scrutiny that is not at present possible. As noted by Allen (2013, 7), "many poverty lines are taken from World Bank staff reports in the 1980s, and many of these are either unavailable or provide too few details to be useful." For more recent years, the proposed NPSR can build on the valuable summaries of national poverty calculations that are now made available by the World Bank.[17] The NPSR can draw on similar compilations by other bodies, such as the Economic Commission for Latin America and the Caribbean (ECLAC).

It should be made clear what is *not* recommended. There is no proposal to use the collection of data on national poverty lines so as to revisit the $1.90 line. Earlier in this Report, it was seen that the $1.90 line was reached only as a result of an "alignment of stars," which in 2015 allowed different possible methods to generate a similar figure. It does not seem wise to assume that such celestial assistance will be on hand in the future. More fundamentally, the initial motivation for the World Bank procedure, making use of the poverty lines adopted within poor countries to set the global standard, was an obvious starting point in 1990. However, circumstances have changed, and the $1.90 has acquired an independent political status.

Those Missing from Household Surveys

Both global and national poverty estimates are typically based on information obtained from household surveys, and the content of these surveys is the subject of much of this section. However, first consideration must be given to those who are missing from household surveys: "one of the most fundamental inequalities is between those who are counted and those who are not" (United Nations 2014, 19). In the present context, those who are not counted are those who are omitted from the sampling frame for the household survey and those who are covered but are not respondents to the survey. In statistical terms, these omissions matter to the extent that those omitted are more likely or less likely to be living in extreme poverty. If the poverty rate is the same among the missing population as among those covered, then the poverty estimate obtained by applying the rate for those covered to the whole population is accurate. If the PovcalNet extreme poverty rate is estimated at 20 percent, then this can be applied to the whole recorded population of the country, not just to that part represented by the surveyed population. There are, however, good reasons to expect those missing from the survey data to differ in their poverty incidence (Evans 1995). Moreover, the total recorded population figure itself may be open to question, and this is the subject of the next subsection.

Why are people missing? At the top end of the scale, the well off may be less willing to take part in surveys, and therefore are underrepresented. In that case, it would not be appropriate to apply a rate of 20 percent to those not responding to the survey; zero might be the better assumption.

Extreme poverty would be overstated, both in absolute numbers and as an overall rate. At the other end of the scale, those in refugee camps are not typically covered by household surveys, and are much more at risk of extreme poverty. In their case, it would not be appropriate to apply a rate of 20 percent, and the existing practice would understate extreme poverty. For example, in Colombia the stock of internally displaced persons is more than 10 percent of the population, and a study for 2005 showed that the poverty rate among this group was 95 percent compared to a national poverty rate of 50 percent (Ibañez 2008).

In what follows, it is important to distinguish between underrepresentation (those who are covered by the survey but where response rates are lower) and noncoverage. In the former case, it is possible to make ex post corrections by reweighting the respondents, and this is a common practice in both household surveys and population censuses. For example, there may be good grounds for supposing that urban slum dwellers are underrepresented (Carr-Hill 2013), in which case this can be addressed by oversampling or by ex post stratification. However, where a whole category—such as the institutionalized elderly or pastoralists—are missing from the survey, then it is not simply a question of multiplying up the observed frequencies.

Those not covered may include (see Carr-Hill 2013):

1. Those resident in a household but not treated as a member—this applies particularly to servants, in both rich and developing countries;
2. Foreign officials or military;
3. People living in institutions, including hospitals, care homes, prisons, military barracks, factory barracks, religious orders, schools, and universities;
4. The homeless;
5. Those living in refugee camps;
6. Mobile populations, including nomads/pastoralists and guest workers, and those in the course of migration; and
7. Those living in war zones or dangerous areas.

Not all of those in categories listed above are unrecorded: for example, a young person may be away at school but recorded as a family member. A household survey may include a migration module that tracks internally displaced persons. However, people in the categories listed are at risk of being underrepresented and in many cases they are indeed missing.

The groups listed above are all potentially important in developing countries. Even in the case of (3), where one tends to think more naturally of developed countries, there are significant institutionalized populations in countries that feature in the poverty calculations. The percentage of the elderly who are institutionalized in Europe and the United States is about 5 percent, but it is about 3 percent in Mexico and 2 percent in Chile (ODI 2015, 4), which is higher than in Spain (1.3 percent). The prison population is 0.71 percent in the United States, but 0.58 percent in Kenya, 0.4 percent in El Salvador, and 0.34 percent in Chile (ODI 2015, 6). For others of the groups, there are good reasons to expect their prevalence to be higher in the case of developing countries, such as where there is rapid urbanization and greater flows of workers in a changing labor market. The significance of the last category (7)—those in dangerous areas—is illustrated by the report of the Sri Lanka Household Income and Expenditure Survey in 2009/10 that the survey had failed "to cover the entire Northern province as Mannar, Kilinochchi and Mullaithivu districts were out of reach for survey due to massive mine clearance and [resettlement]" (Sri Lanka Department of Census and Statistics 2011, 2).

In order to assess the scale of the problem, there are two requirements. The first is the estimation of the total missing population, relevant to the population total—see below. Overall global totals are not easy to assess. For the groups of nomads/pastoralists, refugees, military, hospitals, and prisons, Carr-Hill (2015, table 1) gives a minimum of 185 million and a maximum of 253 million, but the addition of other categories would undoubtedly lead to considerably higher figures. The second is an assessment of the proportion of the missing population living in extreme poverty, in order to correct the total calculation. Here the statistical requirements are even more challenging. While it is likely that the incidence of extreme poverty is high in some of the categories, such as those living in refugee camps or the homeless, other groups may be quite heterogeneous, as was found for instance in the study of migrant workers in Vietnam by Pincus and Sender (2008).

There are a number of possible sources of information. These include separate surveys or counts, use of administrative data, and exploiting new technology and data sources. For example, in the case of Afghanistan, the national household survey stratifies on the nomadic population, with the same instrument that aims to enumerate the Kuchi (largely nomadic) population. It may be necessary to employ statistical methods different from those used to date. As was pointed out in the UN *Handbook on Poverty Statistics*, "administrative files provide a first line of potentially useful information in this connection, especially in those instances where attention is paid by policy-makers to disadvantaged groups and where officials are required to monitor conditions and report on actions taken in this area" (Kamanou, Ward, and Havinga 2005, 209). Assessing the quantitative impact of adjustments for the missing population would depend on cooperation at the country level, including from high-income countries (on inflows of migrants and refugees). It would require additional funding.

To sum up, it is recommended:

> Recommendation 3: There should be an investigation of the extent to which people are "missing" from the global poverty count, and proposals made for adjustments where appropriate at the national level for survey underrepresentation and noncoverage by surveys; more generally, the World Bank should carry out a review, in conjunction with other members of the UN statistical system, of the fitness for purpose of the baseline population data for each country, and the methods used to update from the baseline to the years covered by the global poverty estimates.

The first part of this recommendation is important for two reasons. First, as the total living in extreme poverty falls over time, the missing population will become proportionately more significant. Second, the circumstances of the missing groups in a number of cases differ qualitatively from those of the general population: there is a categorical as well as a consumption difference. And a number of the groups—such as refugees, the homeless, and those living in war zones—have a particular claim on our compassion.

The need for improved total population data (the second part of Recommendation 3) is taken up below.

Improving Population Data

The process of estimating global poverty has been described in terms of three legs of the tripod, but there is the fourth leg of population data. The addition of a leg might give the image of greater security, but in fact this additional leg is also a source of concern. The 2012 estimate of 896.7 million is reached by multiplying the proportions in extreme poverty in each country by the population of that country and then adding to arrive at a grand total for the world as a whole. The process is then reversed, dividing 896.7 million by the relevant population (in some cases that of the developing world, in others the total world population) to arrive at the percentage living in extreme poverty. Errors in the population figures potentially affect the measurement of the scale of the problem and the geographical composition of those living in extreme poverty.

Population estimates are important for a wide variety of uses. Many economic and social indicators are expressed in per capita terms—like GDP per capita—or as rates in the population. The World Bank is just one of many users. This raises questions for the coordination of statistical activity among international agencies. The World Bank does not have responsibility for population statistics: it is a user of these statistics. Action has to be taken by the UN Statistical Commission. However, it does not follow that the World Bank should use the data "sight unseen." Any users of data drawn from sources not under their control should first ask whether they are fit for the specific purpose for which they are to be employed. In the present context, verification of the quality of the inputs is part of the responsibility of the World Bank in assembling the global poverty estimates. Of course, the suppliers of the population data have a much greater understanding of the field, and duplication of effort must be avoided, but the use of data cannot be a one-way process. Users, such as the World Bank, should be engaged in improving the population data for use in the global poverty estimates—hence the second part of Recommendation 3. An example of the "fit for purpose" test would be the existence of adequate decompositions of the population data by the subgroups in which the World Bank is interested, such as by age or disability status.

The need for such scrutiny of the population data is already apparent from the discussion in the previous paragraphs of those who are missing from household surveys, and similar considerations apply to censuses of the population. The potential impact may be illustrated by the case of a country where the census is carried out to the highest professional standards (and where the requirement to conduct a population census is embedded in the Constitution): the United States. The U.S. Census Bureau has long been engaged in measures to improve coverage. The report on the 2010 census of population (U.S. Department of Commerce

2012) based its measure of coverage on a comparison of the census numbers with those derived from a "dual system estimate." The dual system estimate is based on a post-enumeration survey that is in turn used to generate statistical estimates of the population total. The difference between the total so generated and the census count is the "net undercount." For the 2010 census, the net undercount turned out to be extremely small: both figures gave a total U.S. population of 300.7 million, the difference being 36,000 (U.S. Department of Commerce 2012, table 3). However, this is a *net* figure: there are both pluses and minuses. The Census Bureau showed that there were in fact 284.7 million correct census enumerations. In the remaining 16 million cases, there were either erroneous enumerations (10 million) or whole-person census imputations (6 million). A substantial number of those erroneously enumerated (8.5 million) were duplicates, typically on account of second homes. The loss of 16 million was almost exactly counterbalanced, when it came to the net figure, by the 16 million who were found to be missing. Some of the missing may have been covered by the whole-person imputations, but even if all were subtracted this would still leave 10 million. The importance of there being both additions and subtractions arises from the fact that these affect different groups of people. The U.S. analysis of the 2010 Census showed for example that there was an estimated net *undercount* for renters of 1.09 percent, but a net *overcount* for owner-occupiers of 0.57 percent (U.S. Department of Commerce 2012, 2). There was a significant net overcount for Non-Hispanic Whites (0.84 percent), but significant undercounts for Hispanics (1.54 percent), Non-Hispanic Blacks (2.07 percent), and American Indians on Reservation (4.88 percent) (U.S. Department of Commerce 2012, 15, table 7). If the incidence of poverty and deprivation differs systematically across the groups affected, then it is the 16 million adjustment that is relevant rather than the (close to zero) net undercount.

The U.S. experience, in a country with best-practice census methods, is a salutary warning. What can be said about the sources of population data around the world? There are good reasons to believe that similar issues arise across all countries. As it was put by Kamanou, Ward, and Havinga,

Problems can arise, however, where some sections of the population do not belong to a defined housing unit or are periodically confined to institutions, such as hospitals, nursing homes, asylums and prisons. Others not listed may not have any fixed abode and thus regularly sleep [or "doss down"] on the streets and in common public areas like parks and railways stations. Even countries like the USA have encountered these problems in census inquiries, and census officials around the world continue to face difficulties in correctly enumerating sub-groups like the homeless and illegal immigrants. This problem invariably results in the significant undercount. (2005, 228)

Of particular relevance in many developing countries is the role of migration in leading to undercounting (Bhalla and McCormick 2009). In the case of Pakistan, for example, Gazdar (2003, 5) comments on the problems with the enumeration of international immigrants "who might be refugees, or whose residential status in the country might be considered semi-legal or illegal. The affected group might also include some legal migrants who nevertheless feel discriminated against."

The discussion above has been framed in terms of population censuses; but this is not the only source of population data, and a number of countries have abandoned decennial or quinquennial censuses in favor of using register or other administrative data. Such data have also an important role in extrapolation from the most recent census. (It should be noted that the concern here is not with predicting the future, but with establishing the present, population.) The possible margins of error are examined by the World Bank (2015), which cites the example of Bangladesh, where, prior to the 2011 population census, the projected population for that year was some 150 million according to the Bangladesh Bureau of Statistics, but 164 million according to the UN WPPP 2008 revision. (The 2011 census gave a result close to the former figure.) Moreover, the projections made for a given year change over time. The U.S. National Research Council (2000, 42) study of population projections noted that "the estimate of the world population in 1950 changed 17 times—13 times upward and 4 times downward—in U.N. *Demographic Yearbooks* published from 1951 to 1996." These revisions to the population estimates cause in turn revisions to the poverty estimates. These may be significant, as emphasized by the World Bank (2015). In the case of Bangladesh, for example, the number of people estimated to be living in extreme poverty in 2011 was 71 million when population data from the WDI 2011 or earlier were employed, but

65 million on the basis of population data from the WDI 2014 and later (World Bank 2015, 232, figure 6.1).

The review by the U.S. National Research Council (2000) of population projections found that the average absolute error in country population projections five years ahead was 4.8 percent. The World Bank suggests (2015, 232) that this is a reasonable basis for assessing potential error in the poverty counts and notes that, at present levels, this would mean that some 50 million people would be misclassified. The National Research Council (2000, 44) also discusses the direction of the errors, observing that these vary by region: "for most of these regions, projections have been too high rather than too low. . . . Notably large biases on the high side appear for Latin America and the Caribbean."

Quality and Coverage of Survey Data

The way in which key variables are measured in household surveys raises many issues, and there is an extensive literature (see for example United Nations 2005). Here the specific concern is with the ambition of achieving consistency of approach across countries. As has been argued by Deaton and Dupriez (2011, 161), "our plea is mostly for greater harmonization across countries. We realize that surveys are used for different purposes in different countries, and that a survey that works in one country may be useless in another. Nevertheless, greater standardization is certainly possible in some cases, not only in data collection, but in the reporting and documentation of survey design." In their study of the reliability of food data, for example, Smith, Dupriez, and Troubat (2014, 48) found "great variety across surveys in data collection methods and thus in both reliability and relevance."

In order to address this issue, it is suggested that the World Bank should take the lead in a joint statistical working group concerned with the measurement of household variables that are key to the estimates of poverty, particularly household consumption:

> Recommendation 4: The World Bank should take the lead in a standing Joint Statistical Working Group for household consumption statistics, with a remit to set guidelines for the measurement of household consumption, to examine the relation between consumption and income, and to investigate the relation between household survey, national accounts, and other data sources.

It is understood that this could build on work already underway in the World Bank on this subject,[18] and that there is a parallel process under the auspices of the Intersecretariat Working Group on Household Surveys under the UN Statistical Commission. Possible items for the agenda are noted later in this Report, but an important element is the expansion of the remit to include the relationship between household surveys and national accounts. It should build a bridge between two branches of statistics that are often treated as separate silos. In this respect, it could be similar in its remit to that of the Canberra Group for household income statistics established by the UN Statistical Commission (Expert Group on Household Income Statistics 2001). It is essential that the group include leading experts with a variety of perspectives and experience of the issues.

The issues to be addressed are conceptual as well as technical. The first to be considered here is indeed the fundamental choice between consumption and income as indicator of household poverty status.

Consumption or Income

"Consumption per capita is the preferred welfare indicator for the World Bank's analysis of global poverty" (World Bank 2015, 31). On this standard of living approach, it is in terms of consumption per head that household poverty is measured in the UN/World Bank indicator. This is not an uncontroversial choice, and there are alternative approaches, as discussed in chapter 2 of this Report. Welfare could be governed by the right to resources. This would have different consequences. On a standard of living approach, zero is not an option. People cannot physically survive for any length of time without access to food and shelter. But it is quite conceivable that people have no right to resources. Even while limiting attention to consumption, it can be questioned whether a per capita calculation is more appropriate than one that allows for the differing needs of different people within the household (such as variation with age) or for the possible benefits from shared consumption (via an equivalence scale that varies with household size and composition, as employed in many national poverty calculations). Again this is an issue left to chapter 2.

Consumption is defined as the *use* of resources whether acquired through purchase (expenditure) or through household production or provided from outside the household, such as by relatives, charities, or the government. So that, in a given period, a person may buy food, clothing, and other goods; may eat food grown at home; may receive a gift from a relative; and may receive medical attention free from a publicly employed doctor. All of these sources of consumption should in principle be covered. It is immediately clear that the implementation of such an extensive measure poses serious data problems, and these are taken up below.

First, it is necessary to address the fact that for a significant minority of countries, the global poverty measure is based not on consumption but on *income*. A number of these are high-income countries (see box 1.1), where extreme poverty is taken to be zero (as discussed further below). For a number of other countries, such as Mexico, there are both income and consumption data. There are, however, 17 non-high-income countries where there are only (recent year) income data, of which all except Malaysia and Micronesia are in the Latin American and Caribbean region. Income data are employed for a variety of reasons. Income may be the basis for national poverty estimates, and may, at a national level, be judged a more appropriate basis. It may be a question of data availability. In Malaysia, the expenditure survey (the Household Expenditure Survey) is carried out only every five years (2009 and 2014), whereas the Household Income Survey is more frequent (2009, 2012, and 2014). PovcalNet contains annual income data for Brazil, but the Household Budget Survey (Pesquisa de Orçamentos Familiares) was conducted less frequently: in 2002–3 and 2008–9.

The first best would be for all estimates to be based on consumption, as the World Bank's preferred measure of living standards. This should certainly be the case where both sources are available. However, it is less clear that high priority should be given to replacing the income surveys by (not currently available) consumption data. The resource costs would be substantial. The provision of consumption data to PovcalNet by national statistical agencies would compete with the demands on their resources that follow from the recommendations later in this Report. This seems to be a case where the second best should be accepted, with the estimates continuing to be based on a mix of consumption and income data.

In adopting such a position, it has to be acknowledged that the use of income data is likely to lead to a higher estimated poverty count. In the case of Mexico in 2012, for example, where both data are available, on an income basis, the proportion below $1.90 a day is 5.9 percent, but on a consumption basis, applying the same poverty line, the figure falls to 2.7 percent (from PovcalNet). The global poverty estimate is not just a second best, but also an overstatement; moreover, the overstatement applies particularly to Latin America and the Caribbean, where income surveys are more frequent, distorting the measured regional composition of the global poor. At the same time, the extent of the difference should not be over-stated. Chen and Ravallion (2004, 13) examined the poverty rates in surveys for 27 countries where both consumption and income data were available, and "found only . . . a statistically insignificant difference . . . consumption had a lower mean but also lower inequality." Using the $1 a day line, the mean head count ratio was 17.8 percent using consumption and 21.2 percent for income.[19]

The position with regard to income data should nonetheless be kept under review, and the World Bank should investigate further methods of adjustment to the results obtained from income surveys. Recent proposals in this direction have been made, for example, by Lahoti, Jayadev, and Reddy (2015). Using 120 cases where both income and consumption data are available (in the World Income Inequality Database of UNU-WIDER) on quintile shares,[20] they estimated the relation between the quintile shares in the two sources, and adjusted to ensure that the shares added to 100 percent. Before such a method can be applied with confidence to the PovcalNet, a wider assessment is necessary of the potential error introduced at the different stages. The authors helpfully supply confidence intervals for the adjustment factors (Lahoti, Jayadev, and Reddy 2015, table 3), but this is only one element in calculating the impact on the estimated poverty rate.

Estimating Consumption from Expenditure

If household surveys contained information on expenditure (plus home production and transfers), on income (again including the value of home production and transfers), and on the change in assets between the beginning and end of the relevant period, then consumption could be estimated either using the first variable or as the difference between the second and third. In reality, few surveys contain all the information required. Indeed, in a number of countries the early national accounts relied solely on the expenditure side (for example, for Nigeria, see Okigbo 1962 and Atkinson 2016). As a result, consumption is commonly estimated from expenditure alone, and this is the subject of the present subsection. The word "estimated" should be stressed. Consumption cannot simply be equated with measured expenditure, even when allowance is made for home production and transfers.

In estimating consumption from recorded expenditure, the first issue concerns the nature of the record. To begin with, *who* is making the report? Ideally, all members of the household should report spending. In practice, responses may only be available from adults, or even only from a primary respondent, such as the head of household. Next one has to ask about the nature of the response. How far is it based on retrospective recall, and how far on prospective recordkeeping? The diary method, requiring respondents to maintain a continuous record of all spending has evident advantages, but inevitably involves some degree of retrospection. Dutifully itemizing each gin and tonic as it is consumed may be good for recordkeeping, but may make for a less enjoyable evening. The second issue concerns the length of the recording period. Both memory and willingness to maintain a diary impose limits on the period that can be selected. Short periods, such as seven days, raise the issue of irregular purchases. While expenditure may be more smooth than income, spending is less smooth than consumption. Different periods could be adopted for different categories of goods, with a longer period for goods or services that are expected to be purchased less frequently. The third issue concerns the timing of the reporting period. Where the period is less than a year, timing may be of critical importance, particularly where there is a strong seasonality to income and home production. As expressed by the World Bank, "when livelihoods are closely linked with agriculture, well-being will also follow the seasonal pattern . . . with relatively better off periods around harvest time and lean seasons, typically post planting when stocks have dwindled" (World Bank 2015, 195).

These may be considered arcane points of limited practical importance. However, experience has shown that they can be highly significant.

A well-known example is that of India, which is described by Gibson as follows:

> Between 1989 and 1998, the National Sample Survey (NSS) in India experimented with different recall periods for measuring expenditure, replacing the previously used 30-day recall period with a 7-day recall for food and a one year recall for infrequent purchases. The shorter recall period raised reported expenditure on food by around 30 percent and on total consumption by about 17 percent. As Deaton (2005, p. 16) points out, "because there are so many Indians close to the poverty line, the 17 percent increase was enough to reduce the measured head count ratio by a half, removing almost 200 million people from poverty." (Gibson 2005, 136)

More generally, differences in survey design and implementation can affect the comparability of poverty estimates over time. The example of Cambodia given by Gibson is instructive:

> Three socio-economic surveys were carried out in Cambodia during the 1990s to measure living standards and monitor poverty. Despite this active investment in data gathering, all supported by international donors, each survey was inconsistent with previous and subsequent surveys so no firm evidence exists on whether poverty rose or fell. The initial 1993–94 survey had a very detailed consumption recall list (ca. 450 items). . . . The second survey in 1997 used only 33 broadly defined items in the consumption recall, and was fielded at a different time of the year. Consumption estimates from this survey were adjusted upwards (and poverty rates downwards) by up to 14 percent for rural households to correct for a perceived under reporting of medical expenses. . . . The apparent fall in the head count poverty rate from 39 to 36 percent between 1993 and 1997 is reversed if this adjustment is not applied. The third survey in 1999 used 36 items in the consumption recall and was in conjunction with a detailed income and employment module. It was again conducted in different months than the earlier surveys. But this time, it was randomly split into two rounds, with half the sample in each. Greater efforts to reconcile consumption and income estimates at a household level in the second round led to dramatic changes in poverty estimates. In the first round, the head count poverty rate was 64 percent, and in the second round it was only 36 percent. The dramatic fall in the poverty rate came from higher recorded expenditures and lower inequality in the second round. No robust poverty trend for the 1990s can be calculated from these irreconcilable data. (Gibson 2005, 137)

These issues—the nature of the report, the length of the recording period, and the timing in the year—are among the many that should feature on the agenda for the Joint Statistical Working Group for household consumption statistics proposed in Recommendation 4. Other important items include (i) the length/division of the item list; (ii) the treatment of purchases, notably food consumption, away from home; (iii) the treatment of home production; (iv) imputations, including those for the rent of owner-occupied housing; (v) the identification and treatment of outliers; and (vi) the treatment of collective consumption individually consumed, such as health care and education. In its work, the Group has three principal tasks. The first is to set guidelines for best practice. Since the guidelines have to be applicable to all countries, this task will involve balancing the theoretical ideal with the reality of what can be achieved with the available statistical resources. The second is to recommend methods that can be adopted ex post to harmonize existing surveys to bring them closer to the guidelines, taking account of the potential conflict between international comparability and consistency over time in the national findings. The third is to advise on the likely implications of departures from the guidelines and on the methods that can be adopted to assess the likely magnitude of the errors. From the standpoint of the World Bank's responsibility for monitoring global poverty, this requires that particular attention be paid to departures that would affect the measurement of changes over time. As has been stressed in a number of studies (for example Gibson 2015), particular attention should be paid to the changes in consumption patterns following greater urbanization, such as increased consumption of food away from home.

A number of the items listed above may be seen as leading to a more complete measure of the resources at the disposal of the household. This may change the picture: in the case of social transfers in kind "developing countries with high coverage of free education and health-care services, such as South Africa, and Costa Rica, provide a living standard for those with low consumption levels that is very different from countries where similar populations have to pay for services" (Evans 2015).[21] This is evidently important, although the extent of individual benefit is not easily determined, and the valuation of the services cannot be based on the cost of supply.[22] At the same time, it should be noted that, if the definition of consumption becomes more extensive, then the associated poverty line has to be reexamined. The International Poverty Line, and the national poverty lines in which it originated, was drawn in the context of a particular definition of consumption. It would be wrong to change only one side of the calculation.

Inequality within Households

The statistic for global poverty is typically stated as x million people living in poverty, but the correct statement is that there are x million people living *in households* that are in poverty. What the World Bank statistics capture is the number of households in poverty, treating the household as a statistical unit. No account is taken of the unequal distribution within the household (on within-household inequality, see for example Folbre 1986, and Woolley and Marshall 1994). Neither conceptually nor practically can the data available to calculate global poverty provide evidence about the intrahousehold distribution. Conceptually, there is the problem of allocating the benefits from shared purchases and home resources. Practically, there is the problem of collecting information on individually consumed goods (intensified when the survey is based on a single household member respondent). In view of this, the statement in the *Global Monitoring Report 2015/2016*, for example, that "poverty remains unacceptably high, with an estimated 900 million people in 2012 living on less than $1.90 a day" (World Bank Group 2016, 1) should refer instead to the "900 million people in 2012 *who are in households* living on less than $1.90 per person a day."

How much does this matter? If the conceptual problems in defining individual consumption could be overcome, would the resulting figure for the number of people with individual consumption below the poverty line be higher? If, in a two-person household, one person consumes $1.80 and the other consumes $2.20, then the household as a whole has consumption per person above $1.90, thus missing the person who is actually below. Taking account of the additional inequality within the household spreads out the distribution, and for a certain class of poverty measures the poverty rate necessarily rises (Ravallion 1998; Haddad and Kanbur 1990, 869). This class includes the poverty gap (discussed further in chapter 2 in the section "Enriching the Analysis of Those in Economic Poverty"). But the class does not include the head count. While the household head count is an understatement in the two-person example just given, it would not be if the poorer person has $1.50, causing both to be counted as poor on a household basis, rather than just one as on an individual basis.

Empirical evidence about what happens within the household is limited. In the case of income, it is possible to allocate certain categories of income, such as earnings, to individuals, but there remains the need to make assumptions about other sources, such as the profits from a family business. Studies of this kind for the United Kingdom of the distribution between women and men have found that "the bottom of the individual distribution is dominated by women" (Sutherland 1997, 20). Recent research for the European Union (Corsi, Botti, and D'Ippoliti 2016, table 3) reported that, measured in terms of individualized income, the proportion below 60 percent of the median was double (about 40 percent) for women than for men (about 20 percent). On the side of consumption, studies have been made of variables such as individual calorific intake. In a survey of rural Philippines, Haddad and Kanbur found that measures of the adequacy of individual calorie intake, compared to assuming receipt of the average of individual adequacy, led to a head count ratio that was in fact lower (for the reason given above), on this basis (Haddad and Kanbur, 1990, table 4 columns 2 and 5), but that the poverty gap was understated by 18.4 percent (1990, table 4 columns 3 and 6).

It is not, however, easy to observe individual consumption within the household. This has led to an extensive literature that seeks to infer such consumption from the aggregate behavior of the household on the basis of assumptions about the intrahousehold allocation (see, for example, Browning, Chiappori, and Weiss 2014 and Chiappori and Meghir 2015). The most commonly employed set of—strong—assumptions involve a collective decision-making model, with efficient allocations and caring preferences,[23] which allow the implicit preferences and sharing rules to be identified. Based on such modeling of sharing rules, Lise and Seitz (2011), for instance, find for a subset of working age households in the United Kingdom that consumption inequality was considerably understated, although to a declining extent over the period 1970 to 2000, so that both level and trend would be affected. Using a sample of couples from the U.S. Panel Study of Income Dynamics 1999 to 2009, and applying revealed preference restrictions to obtain bounds on the sharing rule, Cherchye et al. (2015, 2005) find that "11% of our child-less couples have incomes below a two-person poverty line, but taking the individual allocations of resources within households into account, our bounds show that 15% to 18% of individuals are below the corresponding poverty line for individuals. Moreover, it turns out that poverty is more prevalent among women in childless couples than among men in childless couples." Their approach provides a definite weakening of the assumptions required, but "there is still a long and important agenda in this research" (Chiappori and Meghir 2015, 1415).

The analysis of within-household inequality is an exemplification of the way in which measurement and economic theory are intimately bound together. It is no accident that many of the pioneers of economic measurement were also known for their mastery of economic theory: Richard Stone being a prime example. In the present case, the measures of within-household inequality described in the previous paragraph depend essentially on a theoretical model where it is assumed that household decisions are efficient: no alternative would be preferred by all members of the household. Such an assumption allows for a variety of theoretical models that have been proposed. At the same time, it is open to criticism on at least two grounds.

To begin with, the collective decision-making framework does not allow models of inefficient bargaining, and readers might not be surprised by the notion that households may get trapped in outcomes where at least one could be better off without making the others worse off. One such model is that of Basu (2006), where, in a two-person household, the household maximizes the weighted average of their individual welfares, where the weights depend on the decisions taken. It is not just the potential wage of the wife that matters but also whether she actually has her own earnings. Basu shows how the dynamics of such a model may generate inefficient outcomes. (See also Ulph 2006; Konrad and Lommerud 2000; and Woolley and Chen 2001.)

Second, the literature is largely based on the standard assumption of utility maximization, whereas alternative approaches to household behavior may yield different predictions. In particular, the capability approach—discussed in chapter 2—is relevant not only to normative evaluation of outcomes but also to the positive explanation of household behavior. The potential richness of such an approach is demonstrated by Sen (1990) in his analysis of "Gender and cooperative conflicts." He builds on the household production approach but with the key difference that production is not a purely technical matter: "technology is not only about equipment and its operational character-istics but also about the social arrangements that permit the technology to be used and the so-called productive processes to be carried on" (Sen 1990, 463). "The nature of 'social technology' has a profound effect on relating production and earnings to the distribution of that earning between men and women and to gender divisions of work and resources" (Sen 1990, 465). He goes on to argue that the determination of the social technology is a balance between conflict and cooperation: "although serious conflicts of interests may be involved . . . the nature of the family organization requires that these conflicts be molded in a gen-eral format of cooperation, with conflicts treated as aberrations or devi-ant behavior" (Sen 1990, 481).

Pursuit of this research is indeed promising as a route to learn more about inequality within the household, but it is likely to be some time before the results can be applied to poverty measurement on a regular basis, and the presentation of the method would need to be transparent. The estimates of global poverty should therefore continue to refer to people living in households with consumption below the poverty line. At the same time, concern about intrahousehold inequality—and the World Bank's wider Gender Cross-Cutting Initiatives—underlines the need to look, in chapter 2 of this Report, not just at the decomposition of global poverty by gender but at nonmonetary dimensions that may be more readily measured on an individual basis.

Extreme Poverty in High-Income Countries

In the World Bank global poverty count, high-income countries are assumed to have zero extreme poverty, described as "a useful simpli-fying assumption that appears to closely approximate the correct esti-mate" (Ferreira et al. 2016, 160). At the same time, the adoption of a truly global approach to poverty measurement certainly implies that high-income countries should come within the scope of inquiry, and there have been a number of recent studies suggesting that there are significant numbers in the United States living on incomes below $2.00 a day (Shaefer and Edin 2013; Edin and Shaefer 2015; Chandy and Smith 2014). (See the review by Jencks [2016].) Chandy and Smith, for example, estimate that some 2 percent of the U.S. population had incomes below $2.00 a day in 2011 (Chandy and Smith 2014, 10, table 1, more extensive measure of income). However, not only do they demonstrate major differences according to the definition of income and the treatment of zero/negative responses, but also the marked differences in the case of the United States between low income and low consumption (Chandy and Smith 2014, figure 5). The consumption function does not appear to pass through the origin: "the range of consumption levels for those reporting zero or close to zero income is not only wide but indistinguishable from the equivalent range for those reporting income levels up to 20 dollars of income per person per day" (Chandy and Smith 2014, 14). Using consumption data from the U.S. Consumer Expenditure Survey for the fourth quarter of 2011, they find that only 0.07 percent (or 0.09 percent when using a more selective definition of consumption) of the U.S. population were below $2 a day.

High-income countries should be seen as within scope, and as raising significant issues. First, observation of the extreme bottom of the distribution in rich countries raises issues about the definition of both "consumption" and "income." Should soup kitchens and food banks be regarded as providing consumption of equal value to purchases made freely in a supermarket? Should income from begging be regarded as equal in value to a welfare check? Is money received from selling plasma, as described by Edin and Shaefer (2015, 93), equivalent to a paycheck? The qualitative nature of the transaction, and the degree of agency, need to be taken into account. This may lead to consumption financed by certain kinds of income being discounted by a factor less than 1 that takes account of the conditions on which it is obtained, or even discounted altogether. Second, Recommendation 3 concerning the missing population is relevant, particularly with regard to high-income countries facing substantial in-migration. As emphasized by the International Movement ATD Fourth World (2015, 1), "Europe is confronted with an unprecedented flow of refugees fleeing war and destitution," and many are suffering a high level of deprivation. Moreover, looking ahead to 2030 and the probable impact of climate change on the risks of weather disasters, it is likely that these will not be confined to developing countries. Third, the case of the United States underlines the importance of monetary indicators being accompanied by non-monetary indicators. To take just one example, there is evidence from the study of Case and Deaton (2015) of rising mortality among middle-aged white non-Hispanics between 1999 and 2013. As the authors say, "concurrent declines in self-reported health, mental health, and ability to work, increased reports of pain, and deteriorating measures of liver function all point to increasing midlife distress" (Case and Deaton 2015, 15078).

Errors: Sampling and Nonsampling

The final set of issues considered in this section concern the reliability of the estimates. There are multiple potential sources of error. Most people think of sampling error, arising from the fact that the underlying household survey data are drawn for a sample of the population. The results from household surveys are typically quoted with associated estimates of the standard errors, but rather surprisingly this is not the case for the World Bank poverty estimates.[24] In the United Kingdom, the proportion living in households with equivalized disposable incomes below 60 percent of the median in 2013/14 is reported as 15.2 percent with a 95 percent confidence interval of 14.5 to 15.9 percent. In Tanzania, the poverty rate, according to the basic needs poverty line in 2011/12, derived from the Household Budget Survey, is given as 28.2 percent with a 95 percent confidence interval of 24.6 to 31.8 percent (Tanzania National Bureau of Statistics 2014, 158). In contrast, no such confidence interval is given for the World Bank figure for 2012 of 12.73 percent of the world's population or a total of 896.7 million.[25] Indeed, giving the estimate with two decimal places gives a quite misleading impression of precision.

The Global Poverty estimate is, of course, a more complex statistic than a national poverty estimate derived from a single household survey. The total is reached by combining information from more than one thousand surveys, each with its own design features. It is not suggested in this Report that the World Bank should embark on the (laborious) calculation of a confidence interval for the Global Poverty total. Rather, attention should be drawn to the fact that the estimate is based on samples, and the possible impact illustrated by reference to particular national calculations. It would be good to include, for example, 95 percent confidence intervals for the estimates at a national level (derived from PovcalNet) for rural India or for Nigeria. Such illustrations would, on their own, be sufficient to alert users to the fact that the figures are only approximate estimates.

In any case, at a global level sampling error may be much less of concern than nonsampling error. This may also be true at the national level. According to Banda, "if not properly controlled nonsampling error can be more damaging than sampling error for large-scale household surveys" (Banda 2003, 7-4). What is nonsampling error? Nonsampling error has been well described by the U.S. Department of Commerce:

> Nonsampling error is a catch-all term for errors that are not a function of selecting a sample. It includes errors that can occur during data collection and the processing of survey data. For example, while an interview is in progress, the respondent may make an error answering a question, or the interviewer may make an error asking a question or recording the answer. Sometimes interviews fail to take place or households provide incomplete data. Other examples of nonsampling error . . . include matching error, modeling error [where data are imputed] and classification error. Unlike sampling error, nonsampling error is difficult to quantify. (U.S. Department of Commerce 2012, 9)

The last sentence should be noted. There seems to be a degree of ambivalence concerning nonsampling error. On the one hand, it is stated—as above—that it is difficult to quantify. On the other hand, to quote the U.S. Census Bureau (2015, 8), "the Census Bureau recommends that data users incorporate information about nonsampling errors into their analyses, as nonsampling error could impact the conclusions drawn from the results."

In making Recommendation 5, nonsampling error receives therefore particular attention:

> Recommendation 5: The World Bank poverty estimates should be based on a "total error" approach, evaluating the possible sources, and magnitude, of error, particularly nonsampling error and the error introduced by the process of determining the International Poverty Line.

How should such information about nonsampling error be incorporated? Here there is an extensive literature on "total survey error"—see, for example, the review by Groves and Lyberg (2010). This dates back at least to the article by Deming (1944, 359), in which he set out a "classification of factors affecting the ultimate usefulness of a survey." His list of 13 factors includes, in addition to sampling error, variability in response, interviewer bias, imperfections in questionnaire design, post-survey changes in the survey population, late reports, processing errors, and errors of interpretation. Much of the subsequent literature has been concerned with fleshing out this approach, and amplifying the different concepts. The 2004 text *Survey Methodology* (Groves et al. 2004), for example, "is organized around a total survey error framework, with an attempt to link the steps of survey design, collection, and estimation into the error sources" (Groves and Lyberg 2010, 856). They go on to note "that two separate inferential steps are required in surveys—the first inference is from the response to a question for a single respondent and the underlying construct of interest to the measurement. The second inference is from an estimate based on a set of respondents to the target population" (Groves and Lyberg 2010, 857).

What does this mean in terms of World Bank practice? The concrete proposal made here is that there should be a checklist of potential sources of nonsampling error—drawing on the literature that has followed the original Deming proposal—and that attempts are made for a selection of countries to assess their likely direction and magnitude. From the discussion in this section, there are a number of obvious candidates for inclusion on the checklist, and these are shown in table 1.1, which also contains a number of issues raised in the next section.[26]

In some cases, the possible direction and size of the error has been discussed earlier, but the table should be seen primarily as a work program, with the final column to be completed on the basis of country studies. To take one example, considerable work has been conducted on differential nonresponse. Korinek, Mistiaen, and Ravallion (2006 and 2007) have investigated the bias due to unit nonresponse in the U.S. Current Population Survey 1998–2004, where compliance declines monotonically with income. They conclude that "the poverty rate tends to be over-estimated, though the impact is small up to poverty lines normally used in the U.S." (Korinek, Mistiaen, and Ravallion 2006, 52). Or, to take a different example, where the sampling frame excludes certain

Table 1.1 Illustrative Checklist for Nonsampling Errors

	Source of error
1	Incomplete country coverage
2	Incomplete measurement of consumption/measurement error
3	Use of income in place of consumption
4	Population missing from sampling frame
5	Survey differential nonresponse
6	Inaccurate or out-of-date population totals
7	Errors in the determination of the poverty line
8	Standard error of PPP indexes to calculate baseline local currency poverty line
9	Surveys not comparable over time
10	Extrapolation of out-of-date survey data
11	Bias in domestic CPI to update local currency poverty line
12	Differential inflation for the poor
13	Rural/urban and other geographical differences
14	Use of equivalence scale in place of per capita calculation

Note: CPI = consumer price index; PPP = purchasing power parity.

categories of people whose poverty rate is known to be higher, such as the example of displaced persons in Colombia, then a potential corrective factor can be calculated. Reference has been made earlier in this section to the possible margins of error in the country population totals. Later in the next section, there is discussion of the potential biases that may cause the rate of domestic inflation to be overstated by the consumer price indexes that are employed. As is summarized there, approximate formulae can be applied to estimate the possible size of such biases. Or, to give another example discussed in the next section, there is evidence that certain categories of income may be underrecorded in household surveys. The later recommendation is against making blanket adjustments, but it would be useful to explore the consequences for the poverty estimates if such a correction were made: for example, for the understatement of informal sector self-employment income.

To sum up, both nonsampling and sampling errors need to be taken into account. Nonsampling error, however, is likely to be of greater significance in the present context. What is more, in the case of some sources of nonsampling error, the direction of the bias may be determined. For example, where consumption per head is measured with a multiplicative error assumed independent of the true value, and the density is rising, the head count ratio with the error-contaminated distribution exceeds that in the error-free distribution to an extent that depends on the density and the elasticity of that density (Chesher and Schluter 2002, 367). The possible quantitative impact is illustrated by the calculation of Gibson (2005) for Papua New Guinea, where "a proportionate error was added to the survey data on consumption, x, so that the error-ridden indicator was x · (0.5 + v) where v was a uniformly distributed random number distributed between zero and one. The error-ridden indicator has the same mean level of consumption, but all poverty statistics are biased upwards" (Gibson 2005, 144). The biased head count ratio was 40.0 percent, compared with a survey value of 37.4 percent, which appears modest, although the poverty gap was proportionately more affected.

Equally, allowance has to be made for uncertainty surrounding the poverty line. If the head count ratio is written as the proportion $F(z/y)$ below z/y, where F is the cumulative distribution, z is the poverty line, and y is the mean per capita consumption, then there is uncertainty both about $F()$ and about z/y. For any given potential spread of the poverty line, the impact on the head count ratio of that spread depends on the slope of the cumulative distribution, obviously being greater in densely populated parts of the distribution. The elasticity of the head count ratio with respect to the poverty line is equal to (minus) the growth elasticity of poverty reduction—a concept that has been much discussed in the literature (for example, Kakwani 1993; Ravallion and Chen 1997; Bourguignon 2003).[27] Estimates of the growth elasticity have varied, but even relatively low values for the elasticity imply that the poverty estimates are potentially quite sensitive to where the line is drawn.[28]

One potentially important ground for uncertainty about the location of the poverty line is associated with the PPP basis for the international comparisons. The local currency value of the baseline poverty threshold has been obtained by applying the ICP purchasing power adjustments, which are themselves estimates with an associated confidence interval. Standard errors for the price ratios have been derived by Deaton (2012) for both the bilateral and the multilateral cases. As he explains, intuitively the magnitude depends on the extent of relative price variability and can be approximated using the logarithm of the ratio of the Laspeyres to Paasche price indices. Deaton and Aten (2015, 17) find that "the resulting relative standard errors are large, 20 to 30 percent for United States to India or China comparisons."

The considerations outlined above may cause some readers to wonder why they have read so far. As it has been expressed by one member of the Advisory Board, "the margin of uncertainty for the global poverty estimates is so large that there must be serious questions about whether they are worth doing in anything like their current form." There are at least two rejoinders. The first is the obvious point that, if the World Bank were to vacate the territory, then the public debate would not disappear. It would be conducted using estimates that are even less securely based. The second is that the primary function of the estimates is to monitor *changes* in global poverty. The total figure of 896.7 million is important in terms of securing political support, but the achievement of the SDGs depends on the number being reduced.

The question that has therefore to be asked concerns the accuracy with which the World Bank estimates measure the *changes over time*. In the case of sampling error, the standard error of the difference between the estimates for two years depends on the degree to which they are correlated. To the extent that they are positively correlated, the confidence interval surrounding the measured change is reduced.[29] In the case of nonsampling error, there may well be positive error correlation, as where there are "fixed effects." The error associated, for example, with incomplete population coverage may remain relatively fixed, in the absence of special factors, such as civil unrest or mass in-migration. The error associated with the purchasing power adjustment (to arrive at the local currency poverty line) would be constant in terms of the location on the cumulative distribution. Variations in methodology have been found to affect levels of poverty to a greater extent than the changes over time. Two recent studies of the measurement of poverty in India found that, although the proposed changes in methodology affected the recorded levels of poverty, the decline in the head count ratio over time was little changed: "whether we use the new methodology or the old, it is found that decline in the percentage of population in poverty is roughly of the same magnitude" (India Planning Commission 2011, 4). The later report, by Rangarajan (2014, 69), similarly concluded that, with the new methodology proposed, the reduction in poverty "is not very different." The title of Chen and Ravallion's 2010 article on global poverty, with new data and new price surveys from the 2005 ICP, was "The Developing World Is Poorer than We Thought, but No Less Successful in the Fight against Poverty."

There may therefore be grounds for believing that changes over time are less sensitive to error, or to changes in methodology, than the absolute levels. At the same time, there are arguments in the opposite direction. The year-on-year estimates may be affected by bias in the domestic price indexes used to update the poverty line. Or there may be an interaction between the fixed effect and the poverty reduction associated with a particular rate of growth: drawing the poverty line at a higher level may be associated with a higher (or lower) growth elasticity of poverty. Or, to give a different example, as the overall poverty rate falls, the problem of missing groups will become proportionately more significant. It is therefore necessary to consider individually the different sources of error, and this is the main message of the total error approach.

This Report therefore advocates that the World Bank should adopt a total error approach to robustness, where all potential sources are considered in conjunction. This could be institutionalized through the appointment of a "devil's advocate." Suppose that the World Bank estimates of extreme poverty for 2022 show a sizeable fall compared with 2012. A unit within the World Bank could then be tasked with seeking to disprove that progress has in fact been made. It would investigate whether there is a combination of different errors, operating in the same direction, which could reverse the direction of change. By generating such a confidence interval, the devil's advocate would formalize a process that is commonly adopted in a more informal manner.

To sum up, the users of these estimates for the purpose of monitoring change over time, while not despairing, should keep concerns about reliability at the forefront of their minds. They are certainly not matters to be relegated to footnotes. Indeed, the identification of potential sources of error should be the first stage in the process of producing new estimates. Moreover, explicit discussion of possible sources of error is important not only because it provides a necessary note of caution but also because it points to areas where investment in improving data quality may be most productive. Should attention be focused on the training of field workers? Should priority be given to raising response rates? Are there design features that cause respondent fatigue? As is argued in chapter 3, there needs to be increased investment in data, but one needs to know what form that investment should take.

Assessment: Monitoring over Time

The essence of the monitoring exercise is to establish the extent of progress toward reducing extreme poverty. For this, current information is required to compare with the 2011 baseline. At a country level, the World Bank publishes poverty figures only for years for which there is a household survey (Ferreira et al. 2015, 26), but in order to reach a global total an estimate has to be made for all countries for all years. In what follows, the task is therefore discussed in terms of making estimates for all countries for all years; moreover, given the priority attached to the SDGs, it is assumed that there is annual monitoring. In other words, every year is a reference year.[30]

This implies that there are two types of poverty estimate for the latest reference year: those based on a survey for the year in question (a "new survey estimate") and those based on the extrapolation of a survey for an earlier year (referred to here as "shadow estimates"). The calculations differ in form. The new survey estimate involves applying to the new data the International Poverty Line (converted to LCUs) updated to the year in question; the shadow estimates apply to the data for a previous year, say t, the poverty line for year t divided by $(1 + g)$ where g is the proportionate growth of constant price consumption per capita between year t and the current year. (The division of the poverty line by $(1 + g)$ is equivalent to everyone receiving a proportionate increase of g.) The estimated reduction in poverty depends in the latter case solely on g; in the former case, it depends on the new data and on the updating of the poverty line.

This procedure raises a number of issues. Some, such as the use of population projections to establish the total populations, have already been evoked and are not discussed further. Attention is focused on the availability over time of household survey data, the methods used to extrapolate from the most recent survey (determination of g), the updating of the poverty line via domestic indexes of consumer prices, and the use of PPPs.

Coverage and Comparability over Time

The availability of household survey data to monitor change over time depends on (i) surveys having been conducted at the relevant dates, (ii) the microdata being made available by the national statistical agency (or other body) in an appropriate form, and (iii) the surveys being sufficiently comparable.

The issue of availability is quite limiting. To give a recent example, the World Bank study, *Poverty in a Rising Africa*, identified 180 surveys in Africa over the period 1990–2012, but only 148 were available in the World Bank's microdata library and could be included (Beegle et al. 2016, 51). Moreover, a number of these did not include a consumption aggregate with which to measure poverty, and others had not yet been vetted. As a result, there were only 113 out of 180 surveys that could be used to analyze poverty trends (Beegle et al. 2016, 51, n7).

How far is availability, specifically with respect to PovcalNet and the global poverty figures, subject to the control of the World Bank? While historically PovcalNet sourced surveys directly, it is understood that the present practice is for PovcalNet to obtain all new additions from the World Bank's regional databases—with the exception of data obtained from the Luxembourg Income Study Database (LIS Database) covering high- and middle-income countries.[31] To manage the interaction between regional databases and PovcalNet, there is a technical working group (Global Poverty Technical Working Group [GPWG]) whose members are drawn primarily from the Development Economics Vice Presidency (Research and Data teams) and Poverty and Equity Global Practice. The responsibilities of the working group, spelled out in a formal protocol, are to assure the quality of data that enter PovcalNet from the regional databases (that is, establish standards, check consistency with official data, document, and so on) and address technical issues related to data quality and welfare measurement. The protocol establishes the following basic principles:

1. Surveys to be included in the PovcalNet have to be "official surveys," collected by national agencies and used for official statistics, or drawn from the LIS Database.
2. Surveys must meet a number of criteria (being nationally representative, and having proper documentation), and certain key statistics, such as the poverty rate, must replicate national statistics and divergences explained and documented.

3. Any exceptions to the above are granted only after extensive consultations within the GPWG members, often including detailed checks
   on the microdata.

This appears an excellent basis for managing the coverage issue.
Presumably (c), for example, explains the acceptance in two cases of
data limited to the urban population. It would, however, be good to have
a more explicit statement of the criteria, covering for instance the basis
on which choices are made when there is more than one eligible survey,
and the extent to which use is made of data from administrative registers
in conjunction with household surveys (as is increasingly the case with
the European Union Statistics on Income and Living Conditions
[EU-SILC] statistics in the EU). In the case of (a), the restriction to "official" surveys is open to debate, since there may be alternative sources
from academic or research institutions of equal or superior quality.

Inclusion in PovcalNet or the microdata library does not in itself ensure
that the surveys are consistent over time. Comparability is a matter of
degree, so that judgments may differ, but the *Poverty in a Rising Africa*
study sets out three reasonable criteria. The sample should be nationally
representative (see [b] above); the surveys should have been carried out at
periods of the year that are comparable in terms of seasonality, and the
instrument for recording expenditure (diary or recall) and the reporting
period should remain consistent. Application of these criteria to the data
for African countries from 1990 to 2012 meant that, of 113 surveys for
which data are available, in only 78 cases were they comparable with at
least one other survey for that country (Beegle et al. 2016, figure 1.4). For
South Africa, there are two pairs of comparable years, but the pairs cannot
be linked. Guinea and Mali each carried out four surveys, but none were
deemed comparable. When the criteria for comparability are applied,
there were on average just 1.6 poverty estimates per country over the
period 1990 to 2012 (Beegle et al. 2016, 33). This does not provide a satisfactory basis for monitoring trends over time in global poverty. Nor is the
problem limited to Africa. As is noted by Serajuddin et al. (2015, 3),

> during the ten year period between 2002 and 2011, among the 155 coun-
> tries for which the World Bank monitors poverty data using the WDI
> database, 29 countries do not have any data point and 28 countries
> have only one poverty data point. Thus, in over a third of the world's

developing or middle income countries there is essentially no meaningful way of monitoring poverty or shared prosperity for that specific period.

The gaps in coverage—specifically the countries without a single data point—were cited by the president of the World Bank in his speech of October 15, 2015, in which he pledged "to work with developing countries and international partners to ensure that the 78 poorest nations have household-level surveys every three years, with the first round to be completed by 2020."

The step from availability to comparability is one that the World Bank is taking seriously, but it is one where greater transparency would be welcome:

> Recommendation 6: The World Bank should make public the principles according to which household survey data are selected for use in the global poverty count; and there should be an assessment at national level of the availability and quality of the required household survey data, and a review of possible alternative sources and methods of ex post harmonization.

The imposition of criteria for comparability, together with restrictions on availability, has the effect of reducing survey coverage. The setting in place of an agreed set of principles for selection may, however, facilitate the addition of surveys, extending coverage, if it facilitates post-survey harmonization. Moreover, there may be scope for increased collaboration with other bodies that carry out similar harmonization procedures. Reference has already been made to the LIS Database. The Organisation for Economic Co-operation and Development (OECD) has a major database, and the EU-SILC data framework now covers more than 30 countries. The World Bank is already working closely, in the case of Latin America and the Caribbean, with CEPALSTAT, the statistical department of ECLAC, and SEDLAC (Socioeconomic Database for Latin America and the Caribbean), which is a joint venture of the Center for Distributive, Labor and Social Studies (CEDLAS), at the National University of La Plata in Argentina, and the World Bank's Poverty and Gender Group for Latin America and the Caribbean Region. They provide time series of inequality and poverty indicators for a majority of countries in the region—although few Caribbean countries are covered.

Filling the Gaps: Household Surveys and National Accounts

Where there is no survey for the relevant year, "the country-level poverty count is estimated by extrapolating consumption or income from national accounts" (Ferreira et al. 2016, 159). More precisely, the extrapolation underlying the "shadow estimates" uses the growth rate of household final consumption expenditure (HFCE) per capita at constant prices (or GDP per capita in the case of Sub-Saharan Africa). Underlying this procedure is the assumption that the national accounts provide a good estimate of the *rate of growth* (g) of consumption per capita (no assumption is required about the *level*) applicable to household surveys. There are a priori grounds for doubts about this assumption. As was noted by Ravallion (2003, 646), "the two types of data to be compared here could hardly be more different in the way they are obtained." Whereas the survey data are derived from household responses, the national accounts figures are the outcome of a process that involves estimation of the aggregate flows in the economy and their reconciliation. In addition, the underlying definitions differ. The national accounts are drawn up in the context of international standards set by the UN System of National Accounts, although these definitions are followed to varying degrees, and are subject to revisions in the light of changes in these standards. Household surveys tend to be operated at a national level, and are much subject to national concerns and practices. It is not therefore surprising if the resulting measured growth rates turn out to be different.

"There is an urgent need for a serious research program for reconciliation between NAS [national accounts] and HES [household expenditure survey] data" (Srinivasan 2010, 150). In the case of India, the relationship between the two sources was part of the remit of the Rangarajan Expert Group, which explored a number of sources of the difference, concluding that "there are infirmities in both sets of estimates" (Rangarajan 2014, 44). The necessity of reconciling household survey information with the national accounts has been recognized in the work of international and national statistical agencies (see for example Fesseau, Wolff, and Mattonetti 2013 and Mattonetti 2013 on the work of an OECD-Eurostat Expert Group). These efforts are clearly important for the World Bank. At the same time, the World Bank's interest in the household survey–national accounts interface is quite specific, and requires an approach focused on the lower part of the distribution, specifically—looking ahead to chapter 2—to the bottom 40 percent.

Two major reasons for the differences between household survey consumption (income) and the national accounts aggregates are (i) that the two sources record different amounts for the same variables, and (ii) that the two sources differ in their definitions. To start with the former, there are well-rehearsed reasons (for example, differential nonresponse or systematic underrecording) why reported consumption expenditure in surveys may fall short, when aggregated, of the national accounts total. This has led some researchers to adjust upward total consumer expenditure as reported in household surveys (for example, Sala-i-Martin and Pinkovskiy 2010) to match a chosen national accounts aggregate (which may be HFCE or may be gross domestic income [GDI] or gross national product [GNP]). It is not, however, clear that such an adjustment is appropriate here for several reasons. First, it assumes that all error arises on the side of the surveys, whereas "there can be no presumption that the NAS [national accounts] is right and the surveys are wrong" (Ravallion 2003, 647). Second, the Global Poverty goal has been set with household survey data in mind, and a different political objective might have been set if the application of the adjustment had been known in advance. Third, the application of a correction at the level of total consumer expenditure seems too gross when the concern is focused on those at the bottom of the distribution.

A more nuanced approach seeks to adjust the household survey data by addressing the reasons for the possible shortfall. This is well illustrated by the database assembled for Latin America and the Caribbean by CEPALSTAT, whose estimates of overall inequality and poverty have been summarized by Bourguignon (2015). The corrections proceed by first considering differential nonresponse by households and, among survey participants, nonresponse by item. Imputation of missing items, and weighting for nonresponse, can narrow some of the gap. They then compare reported incomes by category and apply an upward correction where the household survey total falls short. In broad terms, self-employment income is increased by a factor of 2 and property income by a factor of 3. Such adjustments change not only the total but also the distribution. Indeed, it is assumed in the Latin American case that the property income uplift applies only to the top 20 percent (which would not necessarily be valid in countries where older households have substantial savings for retirement). The detailed research that has been conducted by CEPALSTAT is of considerable interest; however, adjustments that may be reasonable when applied to overall income inequality are not necessarily appropriate for the measurement of global poverty. While the more nuanced procedure meets the third of the objections raised in the previous paragraph, the first and second objections remain. Moreover, the experience with income measures does not immediately carry over to consumption expenditure. There are good reasons for not undertaking this final upward adjustment of income by categories: "the agreement is rather wide that such a procedure should be avoided when measuring poverty" (Bourguignon 2015, 569). (To avoid any doubt, this does not rule out the first stages of corrections for differential nonresponse and for item nonresponse.)

In advising against proportionate adjustments to income categories, it is not being suggested that research on this topic should be abandoned. Indeed, such studies provide a good example of supplementary information that is valuable in appraising the quality of the data. As noted in the previous section, it would be useful to explore the consequences for the poverty estimates if such corrections were made: for example, for the understatement of informal sector self-employment income.

The second source of differences—those that arise from differing definitions—may be seen by comparing the two sources. A number of components of the national accounts are readily recognizable as categories of consumption that should appear in a household survey—see table 1.2 (based on Havinga, Kamanou, and Viet 2010, table 9.3).

In considering the definitions in table 1.2, it is important to note first that "actual final consumption" includes social transfers in kind, such as health care and education, and that these items are not easily valued in the hands of the household and may not actually be received. There is certainly no counterpart in the typical household survey. This means going back up table 1.2 to the national accounts aggregate two rows up ("final consumption expenditures").[32] But this, too, includes items that have no counterpart, such as FISIM, so that it is therefore more appropriate to subtract these, going further back up the table.

Table 1.2 Linking Household Survey (HS) and National Accounts (NA) Concepts of Consumption

Goods and services purchased for final consumption
+ Goods and services provided by employer
+ Own-produced consumption, including imputed rent on owner-occupied dwellings
+ Goods and services bartered for consumption
+ Current private transfers in kind
= HS definition of final consumption
To this is then added
+ Financial intermediation services indirectly measured (FISIM)
+ Insurance service charges
= NA household final consumption expenditures
+ Social transfers in kind from government and nonprofit institutions serving households
= NA Actual household final consumption

The issues raised above lead to the recommendation:

Recommendation 7: The World Bank, in conjunction with national statistical agencies and other statistical bodies, should explore the construction of an annual national accounts–based indicator of household living standards, as measured by consumption defined in a way that matches as far as possible household survey practice.

Such a household standard of living indicator would differ from HFCE in the coverage of consumption, excluding the nonprofit sector serving households, and—in line with the earlier discussion—social transfers in kind and the imputed value of financial services consumed. All of these contribute to the observed discrepancy between the two sources (Deaton 2005). Such a new national accounts measure should be constructed not only with regard to its future evolution, but also in the form of a historical time series. A long-run perspective reaching back in time is necessary in order to understand the underlying drivers of a country's record on poverty.

The household consumption series should be constructed in both current and constant prices. In the latter case, there are potential differences in the deflator employed. The deflator applied in the national accounts typically behaves in a different way from the consumer price index, and there may be significant divergences.[33] To give an example from the European Union, between 2005 and 2011 the national accounts deflator for the EU27 (27 Member States) increased by 8.9 percent, whereas the Harmonised Index of Consumer Prices rose by 15.4 percent—a difference of more than 1 percent per year (Atkinson, Guio, and Marlier 2015, 23). For the purpose of the proposed indicator, consumer prices are the relevant deflator; this is discussed further below. Again the construction of long-run time series is important in terms of understanding the historical record.

Up-to-Date Data

So far, the procedure for updating to the current reference year has been under the microscope, but there are those who are more ambitious and who have urged us to consider monitoring poverty in the same way that GDP is monitored—on an up-to-the-present basis (Chandy 2013). A move could be made in this direction by accelerating the processing of survey data, and progress has been made toward this goal. But that would still leave a significant lag, whereas it has been suggested that global poverty estimates would not have to wait for household surveys if the World Bank were to generate "provisional" estimates via identifying and tracking indicators that correlate with poverty levels reported in surveys and that can be or are already being monitored on a more regular basis.[34] Such provisional poverty estimates would be in line with the experiments being made in the EU and several Member States with the "nowcasting" of income distribution and poverty rates. As described by the U.K. Office for National Statistics,

> nowcasting is an increasingly popular approach for providing initial estimates of such [distributional] indicators. Unlike forecasting, which relies heavily on projections and assumptions about the future economic situation, nowcasting makes use of data that are already available for the period of study. Although, at the time of producing these statistics, detailed survey data on household incomes are not yet available . . . , a lot is known about various individual components of household income, as well as other factors that affect them. . . . This information is then used to adjust income survey data for recent years to reflect the current period. (U.K. Office for National Statistics 2015, 2)

Using these techniques, an EU project was able to produce by August 2015 estimates of the extent of poverty up to 2014 for ten countries (Rastrigina, Leventi, and Sutherland 2015).

The application of this nowcasting approach is not uncontroversial. In the United Kingdom, the Department for Work and Pensions (DWP) has entered its reservations.[35] Doubts also arise from the Bank's experience with the related exercise of interpolating between household surveys, reviewed by the World Bank (2015, 208–212). Whereas the use of quarterly labor force survey data in the case of Morocco (Douidich et al. 2013) provides a satisfactory basis for the extrapolation/reverse extrapolation of household survey results, the same method applied to Sri Lanka (Newhouse et al. 2014) showed significant discrepancies. The World Bank (2015, 212) concludes that "survey-to-survey imputation approaches to generate higher-frequency data based on two survey sources do not necessarily work well in all contexts." It should also be noted that techniques developed to forecast income (for instance, those based on labor force surveys or income tax information) may be less applicable to nowcasting consumption. Indeed, given the relative smoothness of consumption (Deaton 1987), the exercise may not be worth pursuing (although volatility may be greater in lower-income countries).

The development of nowcasting techniques for global poverty estimates may therefore be premature, but the potential of obtaining more current data should be explored further by the World Bank, experimenting with different approaches in different countries and recognizing that a uniform method may not be appropriate. This research should encompass the mounting of limited surveys for the purpose of monitoring. The scope for a limited survey is illustrated by the World Bank's recent use of the SWIFT (Survey of Well-being via Instant and Frequent Tracking). This new "quick" household survey instrument uses 15 to 20 questions to collect poverty correlates, such as household size, ownership of assets, or education levels, and then converts them to poverty statistics using estimation models (Yoshida et al. 2015). (SWIFT does not collect direct income or consumption data.) The effectiveness of this approach depends crucially on the modeling, where the SWIFT project has made use of the approach developed by Elbers, Lanjouw, and Lanjouw (2002 and 2003). As discussed in chapter 2, it would be possible to include in the quick survey a question about the subjective assessment of poverty. Finally, other data sources should be contemplated, such as the Gallup World Poll, already being used by the World Bank. The World Poll covers most countries of the world every year, including more than two-dozen countries in Africa, with a sample of about 1,000 in each country, and asks identical questions throughout the world. The surveys are available on a timely basis.[36]

An alternative is to hold scaled-down consumption surveys between the regular household surveys. As suggested by Olson Lanjouw and Lanjouw (2001, 40), it may be possible to monitor poverty using an "abbreviated, low-cost survey—that is, purposefully creating data that are not comparable in order to lower the cost of collection." The scaled-down survey would collect information on the consumption of a limited range of goods and services, which would be linked to the consumption of those goods in the baseline household survey. The *change* in the consumption of the limited range of goods would then be used to project the change in the poverty count. Modeling is still involved, but the step from up-to-the-present survey to imputation would be smaller.

> Recommendation 8: There should be an investigation for a small number of countries by the World Bank of alternative methods of providing up-to-date poverty estimates using scaled-down surveys, or the SWIFT or other surveys, plus modeling, where the appropriate methods may vary across countries.

The proposal is for a small-scale set of experiments, in order to assess whether the gain in currency would justify the costs of such an exercise.

National Consumer Price Indexes (CPIs)

Where there *is* new survey information, the counterpart of the updating procedure is the adjustment of the poverty cutoff in LCUs beyond the baseline 2011 figure. As is explained below in the section dealing with PPPs, it is recommended that this should be based throughout the period on the domestic CPI. The construction of consumer price indexes is a matter of wide interest in economic management, and the World Bank is in general a "user," via the WDI, of the CPI series originating from the International Financial Statistics data files of the International Monetary Fund. CPIs have indeed long been controversial, which is scarcely surprising since they are employed in ways that affect the incomes of households: for example, via wage bargaining, social security benefits uprating, and index-linked government securities. The 2012 survey by the ILO (in conjunction with FAO) of

169 countries showed that in 91 percent of countries the CPI was used for the indexation of wages and pensions, and for rents and contracts in 88 percent of countries (ILO 2013, 2). For this reason, the methods chosen, and the adequacy of the measurement, have been the subject of close scrutiny, often involving outside evaluation, such as in the United States by the Boskin Commission (Boskin et al. 1996, 1998).

The issues regarding the construction of the CPI are highly relevant to the estimates of global poverty and will acquire still greater importance if the World Bank adopts Recommendation 10 below, which means that reliance would be placed on the domestic CPI to update the poverty line up to 2030. As the World Bank has observed, "although most countries have well-established statistical systems in place for collecting relatively high-frequency price data, the quality of CPI data varies significantly across countries . . . and suffers from many potential sources of error" (World Bank 2015, 243). There can be considerable differences between different indexes, and the best choice is not always evident, as is illustrated by the fact that the World Bank 2015 poverty estimates make use of the WDI series on the CPI for 104 countries, but replace them by other national CPIs for 20 countries and by other indexes for 8 countries, as well as using subnational CPIs for China and India (Ferreira et al. 2016, table 3).

A CPI is a measure of the change over time in the price level faced by households in their role as consumers. There are two key ingredients: (i) price quotations for individual commodities for two different dates, which are aggregated using (ii) commodity weights typically derived from household surveys. The total value of the expenditure is then compared at the two different dates, the weights being held constant. If the prices at the initial date are set at unity, then the total value at the later date provides a measure of the change in the overall level of prices faced by consumers. As has long been recognized, the conclusions drawn can depend crucially on the choice of weights, where there is a variety of possibilities. For this reason, there has been a succession of international conventions, which are summarized in the *Consumer Price Index Manual* published by the ILO in conjunction with other international organizations including the World Bank (ILO et al. 2004). This has been supplemented by the UN *Practical Guide to Producing Consumer Price Indices* (United Nations 2009).

The first international standards for CPIs were established in 1925 by the Second International Conference of Labour Statisticians (ICLS). These standards referred to "cost of living" indexes rather than CPIs, and later meetings of the ICLS distinguished between a CPI defined simply as measuring the change in the cost of purchasing a given "basket" of consumption goods and services, as described above, and a cost of living index defined as measuring the change in the cost of maintaining a given standard of living, or level of utility. For this reason, the Tenth ICLS in 1962 decided to adopt the more general term "consumer price index" to embrace both concepts. The utility interpretation has led to a substantial theoretical literature that is not reviewed here (see, for example, Diewert 1983).

The textbook account of the choice of form for the CPI typically opens by contrasting Laspeyres weights from the initial year with the use of Paasche weights from the final year, making the point that use of Laspeyres weights "tends to overstate the rise in the cost of living by not allowing any substitution between goods to occur" (Diewert 1998, 48).[37] This "substitution bias" gives too much weight to goods or services whose relative prices have increased, and it matters because Laspeyres weights are widely used in official price indexes. Indeed, the situation is aggravated by the fact that the weights commonly relate not to the initial year but to an earlier reference year (referred to in the ILO Manual as a Lowe index). As is noted by Beegle et al. (2016, 37), "CPI weights are often many years old. As of July 2012, for example, 13 percent of the African population was living in countries in which the CPI basket was based on data from the 1990s (or earlier)."

Substitution bias is only one of the potentially serious issues confronting the construction of the CPI. There is substitution not only between products but also between sources. A product or service may be supplied from within the household, and failure to allow for home production may influence recorded inflation. The 2012 ILO survey of 169 countries shows that 37 percent failed to cover own production (ILO 2013, 5). There may have been a shift toward purchasing food outside the home; indeed this may have been a switch toward a relatively more expensive source where other factors—such as location of employment—determine the choice (this is an example of a situation where an approach to household behavior based on capabilities may be illuminating—see chapter 2). In terms of purchased consumption, there may have been shifts in the outlets: "with the advent of discount retail stores in some countries in Africa, failure to adjust where the price data are collected is expected to lead to an overestimate of inflation" (Beegle et al. 2016, 36).

Substitution also involves new products and the related issue of quality change, issues that received considerable attention in the Boskin Report and commentaries (Diewert 1998; Deaton 1998). There are equally long-standing issues concerning seasonal goods and durable goods, including housing. For fuller discussion of these issues, and the theoretical specification, see ILO et al. 2004. There are, however, also major issues concerning the empirical information that furnish the content of the CPI. Of the 169 countries surveyed by the ILO in 2012, 97 percent made use of data on weights drawn from household expenditure surveys. Indeed the initial purpose of many household budget surveys was to provide an input into the construction of CPI: in the United Kingdom, where the Family Expenditure Survey (and its successors) have been in continuous annual operation since 1957, it "originates from a recommendation of the Cost of Living Advisory Committee . . . that an enquiry should take place into the pattern of expenditure of private households as a source for the weighting pattern of the Index of Retail Prices" (U.K. Department of Employment and Productivity 1968, v).

The derivation of the weights raises many of the same issues as discussed earlier and these are not re-rehearsed. There is however one key issue, usually raised under the heading of "plutocratic bias," which refers to the fact that, when aggregating across households, the CPIs typically weight households according to their total consumption (Prais 1959; Muellbauer 1977). As Beegle et al. (2016, 37) observe, "plutocratic weights are the natural choice in the deflation of economic aggregates, such as national accounts, but not generally the first choice for measuring poverty and welfare." This introduces the question of "price indexes for the poor," to which a separate subsection is devoted below.

When attention is turned to the price quotations, it may be seen that two crucial dimensions are the degree of commodity detail and the extent of coverage of different outlets. Here there is a great deal of variation. In the case of Africa, Beegle et al. (2016, 36) note that Statistics

South Africa "regularly collects 65,000 price quotations from 27,000 outlets [whereas in] other African countries, the number of CPI quotations ranges from 1,150 (São Tomé and Príncipe) to 51,170 (Ethiopia)." Again, there is an issue of the distributional dimension of the price quotations. Prices may vary across outlets, which cause differences from those faced by the poor, and this is taken up below.

To sum up this discussion of the domestic CPI, it is evident that there are many potential shortcomings to the domestic CPI that should lead the World Bank to be cautious as a user of these statistics. In particular, for a variety of reasons, there are concerns that the domestic CPI may overstate the rate of inflation and hence cause the poverty line to be uprated by too much. What, as a user, should the World Bank therefore be recommending? Opinion is divided, as is neatly illustrated by the commentaries on the Boskin Report in the United States. Deaton (1998, 37) opens by saying that he "is now prepared to believe that, in some sense, the rate of growth of the Consumer Price Index likely overstates the rate of increase of the cost of living, suitably defined, provided that enough emphasis is laid on the 'in some sense' and 'suitably defined.'" But he goes on to cast doubt on our ability, in a context of heterogeneous consumers, to determine the extent and direction of the bias, and states that "it is unclear whether there are any sound measures that [could] improve the Consumer Price Index that: a) are not already in process; b) will not require large increases in funding; and c) will do much to improve matters in the short run" (Deaton 1998, 37). He concludes that, "if the Consumer Price Index is so hard to measure . . . the government should be more careful about its use" (Deaton 1998, 44).

Being more careful about its use includes, in the case of poverty monitoring by the World Bank, attaching greater prominence to the health warnings surrounding the accuracy of the estimates. It is in this respect that the contrasting contribution of Diewert (1998) is highly relevant. He makes estimates, on the basis of a series of assumptions, of the likely bias arising from substitution, at both elementary (combining price quotations to form prices for commodity aggregates) and commodity level, outlet substitution, quality change, and new goods, where in each case "bias" is defined as the difference between the Laspeyres index, commonly employed, and the Fisher index, obtained by taking the geometric mean of the Laspeyres and Paasche indexes.[38] For example, the formula he gives for the approximate substitution bias is equal to one half the Laspeyres index times the variance of the price changes. Taking in the U.S. case an annual rate of inflation of 2 percent, and making an assumption about the variance of price changes, he concludes that the annual upward bias, taking account of both elementary and commodity substitution, would be some 0.5 percentage points. Estimated outlet bias is 0.41 percentage points and that due to quality change 0.49 percentage points. These estimates relate to the United States in the 1990s, and the magnitudes may be quite different in other contexts, but they both provide a warning as to the potential magnitude of the biases and indicate an approach that can be adopted in the present application. Applying the formulae described above, calculations can be made—for a selection of countries—in order to explore the potential bias relative to the averaged Fisher index. The work of Diewert furnishes an example of the "positive" approach to nonsampling error advocated in the previous section, "Assessment: Household Surveys and Population Data."

Prices and the Poor

There are two respects in which a "price index for the poor" would depart from the national CPI: (i) the weight attached to different goods and services, and (ii) the price quotations applied when measuring inflation. Both differences—in the weights and in the price quotations for goods of comparable quality—are potentially significant; and this may involve bringing together from different sources. For example, in their study of Côte d'Ivoire, Grootaert and Kanbur (1994) combine price data from the ICP with expenditure share data from the Living Standards Measurement Survey.

The potential difference that could arise from the application of specific price indexes for the poor may be seen from countries that construct price indexes based on a budget for basic needs. In the case of Bangladesh, such a Basic Needs Price Index (BNPI) has already been incorporated into World Bank estimates, and the BNPI shows a higher rate of price increase: 85.8 percent over the period 2005 to 2010, compared with 44 percent according to the official CPI series reported in the WDI (Ferreira et al. 2015, 62). Updating from 2005 to 2010 on this basis would make a considerable difference to the estimated poverty rate: using the CPI, the poverty rate is estimated to fall from 50.5 percent in

2005 to 24.6 percent in 2010, whereas with the BNPI the fall is much more modest—to 43.3 percent (Giménez and Jolliffe 2014, figure 1). This strongly suggests that the use of special price indexes for the poor should be explored for all countries. It would allow examination as to whether the rate of inflation is generally higher for the poor, and would provide a better basis for assessing the impact of food price shocks.

To sum up the conclusions regarding domestic CPIs:

> Recommendation 9: The World Bank, as a user of consumer price indexes (CPIs), should, in conjunction with the responsible international bodies and with the national statistical agencies, seek to improve the quality of the domestic CPI, with particular reference to those aspects most relevant to global poverty measurement; this should include examination of the likely magnitude of any bias, and exploration of special price indexes for the poor.

Purchasing Power Parity (PPP) Adjustments

The account given earlier in "The 2015 Point of Departure" explained the role of adjustments for purchasing power parity. The October 2015 World Bank estimates are based on the results of the International Comparison Program (ICP) for 2011. The World Bank is a key player in the ICP and has housed its Global Office. The PPPs are required for a variety of purposes, notably to measure the size of economies, independently of the use for global poverty measurement. According to the OECD, "there is a growing demand for PPPs from a variety of other users, including government agencies, universities, research institutes, public enterprises, private firms, banks and individuals."[39] The discussion in this Report proceeds therefore on the assumption that the next round of the ICP for a benchmark year of 2017 will take place with a rolling program such that the results can be expected around 2020.

Once new PPPs become available, the World Bank has to decide how to use them for the computation of global poverty. In the past, there has been a presumption that the Bank would incorporate the new PPPs into its poverty measures. At the time that the results of the 2011 ICP became available, there were strong arguments for their inclusion in revised global poverty figures. These arguments were based on two distinct elements. The first is the specific argument that the previous ICP round in 2005 had been the subject of considerable criticism and it was believed that the 2011 PPPs were of higher quality (Deaton and Aten 2015). In concrete terms, the 2005 PPPs were considered to have overstated relative prices in developing countries, causing the local currency equivalent of $1.25 to be overstated, and hence the poverty count to be overstated. The second argument was a different and generic one: relative prices across countries are subject to change over time, and any change should be taken into account as soon as possible in setting internationally comparable poverty lines.

In the future, the first of these arguments may be applicable if the ICP results become progressively more reliable as further rounds are conducted. If there is a further round of results from the ICP before 2030, as is currently planned for benchmark year 2017, there will undoubtedly be pressure on the World Bank to adopt the new PPPs, on the grounds that these will represent an improvement over those available from the 2011 exercise. However, as argued in the previous paragraph, such a step would combine two changes: a (better) adjustment for price changes and a recasting of the view about relative living standards in different countries. This takes us to the heart of the problem: underlying the application of the PPPs is the fact that these are influenced by factors other than the evolution of the national CPIs. The objective of the PPP exercise is to set the purchasing power in an international context, and the PPP applied to a particular country reflects what has happened to prices in other countries. It is, for instance, quite possible that there has been no change in any domestic price, but the PPP adjustment leads to a change in the local currency poverty line.

Rebasing with a new set of PPPs would, almost inevitably, change the poverty line in individual countries in terms of domestic purchasing power, as seen in the second section in this chapter. The case for making such a change is that we, collectively, have revised our view of the appropriate poverty line in the light of changes in the global situation. However, whereas it may be right to make such a revision at the end of a policy-relevant period such as 2030, it is not evident that such a revision is justified in an intervening year. As shown earlier, the adoption of a new set of PPPs led to major changes in the International Poverty Line expressed in local currencies. Of 167 countries for which the comparison can be made, only 63 had a change less than 10 percent. This in turn means that there is a changed relationship with the national poverty lines and national poverty estimates. As illustrated by the case of Ghana in figure 1.3b, the move to the 2011 ICP changed both the level of the poverty head count ratio and the extent of the downward trend. Given the importance attached in this Report to ensuring coherence between global and national poverty estimates, a repeat of such an upheaval is not to be recommended. Of course, it is possible that the impact of a future new ICP would be less, and not lead to significant changes in the relation. But that argument is double-edged: if the impact is minor, then a realignment can be postponed.

The grounds for not making a further set of PPP corrections are reinforced by the fact that the PPP adjustment is, without doubt, the least transparent part of the global poverty calculation. It is not always easy to explain the direction, let alone the extent, of the change that is induced in the poverty count. Considerable suspicion is generated by these revisions. For these reasons, this Report shares the view of Deaton that the poverty lines should be "regularly updated using domestic price indexes. Rebasing, using updated PPP rates, would be done infrequently" (Deaton 2003, 353). As he says, there is a parallel with the rebasing of the national accounts: "while such re-basing is desirable, it cannot be done too often" (Deaton 2003, 364). In the case of national accounts, the most recent revisions of the UN System of National Accounts have been at an interval of 15 years (from 1993 to 2008), which is not very different from the effective gap proposed here (19 years from 2011 to 2030).

In sum, there are two different objectives. The first is to maintain the purchasing power associated with each country's poverty line; the second is to maintain the comparability of poverty lines across countries. The recommendation here is that updating to 2030 should focus on the first objective:

> Recommendation 10: The global poverty estimates should be updated up to 2030 on the basis of the International Poverty Line for each country set in local currency, updated in line with the change in the national CPI or, where available, national index of prices for the poor; the estimates would not be revised in the light of new rounds of the ICP.

Recommendation 10 may be seen as undermining one major reason for conducting the ICP process. However, it should be seen more as a

breathing space. There is little doubt that, come 2030 and the establishment of new global goals, the PPPs will have an important role to play
in the setting of these goals. In particular, as argued above, there is a
strong case for developing specific national price indexes for the poor,
and the same case can be made for the PPPs, following the lead of
Deaton and Dupriez (2011).

PPPs for the Poor

How would the construction of PPPs for the poor make a material difference to the measurement of global poverty? Such new PPPs would
differ in two ways (as already noted above in the case of CPIs). First, the
"expenditure share difference" means that the prices collected in the
ICP exercise would be weighted differently to reflect the budgets of
those below (or close to) the poverty line. Second, separate "poverty-
specific price data" would be collected, to allow for the differences in the
prices paid by the poor. The first of these elements is investigated by
Deaton and Dupriez (2011), who make use of data from 62 household
surveys to examine the expenditure pattern of households at or near the
poverty line. (As they discuss, there are also differences between the
expenditure shares in the surveys and those in the national accounts.)
From this analysis, they find that "the substitution of poverty weights
for plutocratic national accounts weights will not, in and of itself, make
a large difference to global poverty counts" (Deaton and Dupriez 2011,
157). This result, and the work of the Asian Development Bank (ADB
2008), is cited by the World Bank in concluding that the construction of
PPPs for the poor "is not a major concern for cross-country comparisons of poverty" (World Bank 2015, 244).

There remains, however, the second element: differences in the prices
paid by the poor. There has been an extensive literature in developed
countries on this topic (see, for example, Caplovitz 1968) where the presumption has been that the poor face higher prices, since they purchase
smaller quantities, have less access to low-cost outlets, and face higher
charges for financial transactions. The poverty-specific surveys carried
out by the Asian Development Bank, covering 16 countries in Asia and
the Pacific, tended to show the reverse: in general, poverty-specific price
data were lower than the 2005 ICP Asia Pacific survey prices" (ADB
2008, 44). The price data were obtained by specifying types of goods

Figure 1.4 Percentage of Prices from Poverty-Specific Surveys below Prices from ICP

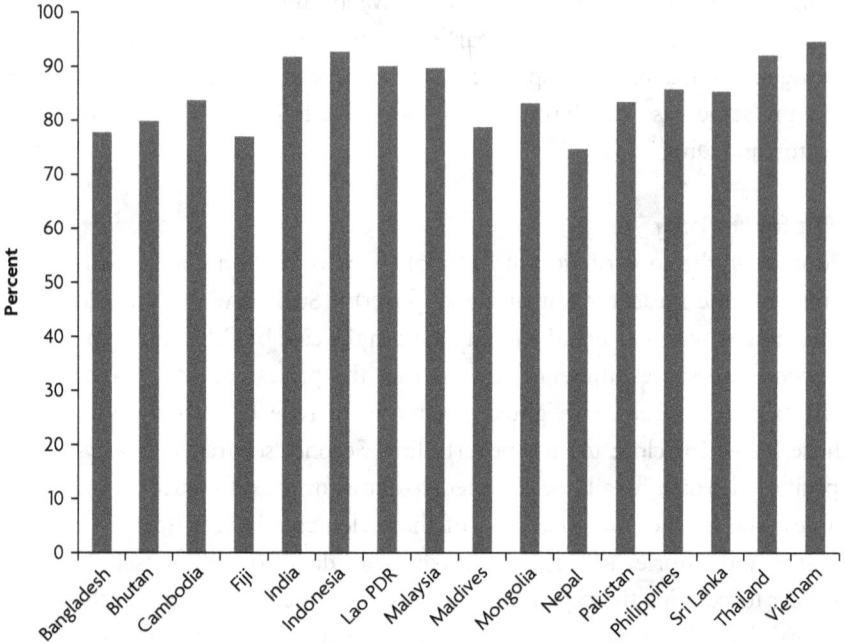

Source: ADB 2008, table 16.
Note: In Bangladesh, 78 percent of prices from the poverty-specific surveys were below the prices from the International Comparison Program (ICP).

that tended to be bought by the poor and collecting the data in shops and markets thought to be frequented by the poor. Figure 1.4 shows that the percentage of prices that were lower ranged from 75 percent in Nepal to over 90 percent in India, Indonesia, Thailand, and Vietnam. These results relate to a particular part of the world, and may depend on certain features of the analysis, such as the treatment of different quantities used in the price surveys,[40] but suggest that the second ingredient in PPPs for the poor is potentially important.

The effect of the two elements on the PPP calculations is shown in figure 1.5. It should be stressed that the results refer to the *relative* PPPs for different countries; the PPPs have been normalized with Malaysia = 1. The first column shows the impact of the use of expenditure shares appropriate for the poor (but with the same price quotations).

Figure 1.5 ADB Analysis of ICP for the Poor, 2005

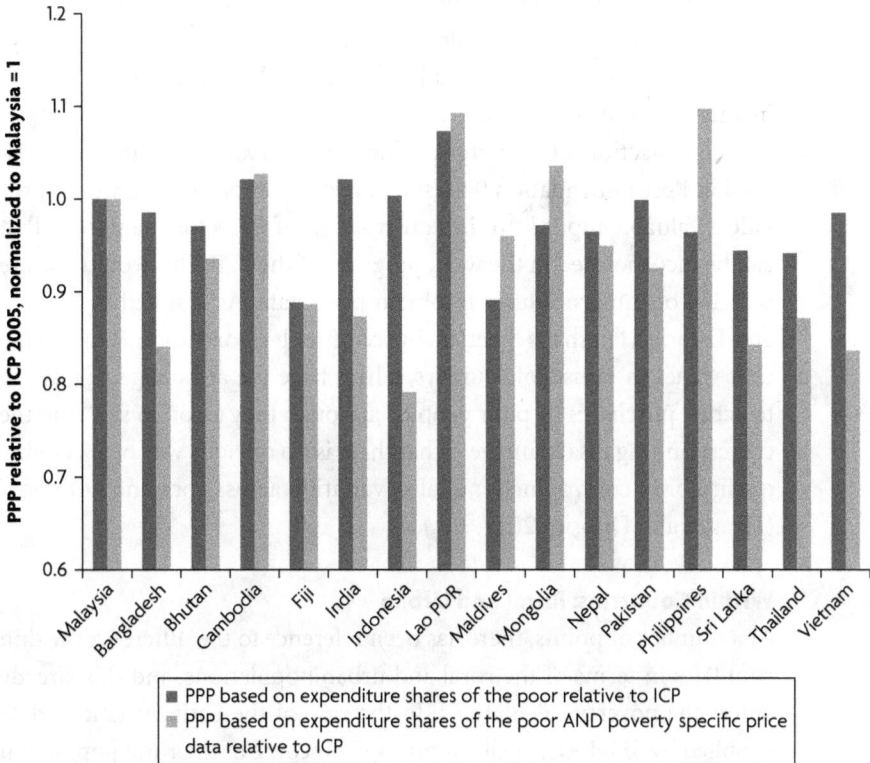

PPP relative to ICP 2005, normalized to Malaysia = 1

Malaysia, Bangladesh, Bhutan, Cambodia, Fiji, India, Indonesia, Lao PDR, Maldives, Mongolia, Nepal, Pakistan, Philippines, Sri Lanka, Thailand, Vietnam

■ PPP based on expenditure shares of the poor relative to ICP
▨ PPP based on expenditure shares of the poor AND poverty specific price data relative to ICP

Source: ADB 2008, tables 24 and 25.
Note: In the case of Bangladesh, the use of the expenditure shares of the poor would change the purchasing power parity (PPP) figure by little (by 1.5 percent) relative to that for Malaysia, but the use of poverty-specific price data (and use of the expenditure shares of the poor) would reduce it by 16 percent. ADB = Asian Development Bank; ICP = International Comparison Program.

It is true that, with the exception of Fiji and the Maldives, this change would leave all countries within 10 percent of the Malaysian value. The maximum change among the 14 countries is that from the Lao People's Democratic Republic to Thailand, where there is overall a 14 percent change. For the largest countries, there is no difference (Indonesia and Pakistan), and only 1.5 percent in Bangladesh and 2.1 percent in India. Addition of the second element—the use of poverty-specific price data—does, however, lead to larger differences. Five countries—Malaysia (normalized to 1), Cambodia, Lao PDR, Mongolia, and the Philippines—are now 1 or above, whereas Bangladesh, Indonesia, Sri Lanka, and Vietnam are below 0.85. The Asian Development Bank concludes that "the application of the new PPPs based on poverty-specific price survey data is likely to alter the estimates of poverty incidence" (ADB 2008, 65).

The collection of poverty-specific price survey data, already envisaged in Recommendation 9 for the development of the CPI, would provide a valuable input into the construction of PPPs for the poor if that can be incorporated in the work program of the ICP. This would require scrutiny of the procedures to obtain price data. As is noted by Deaton and Dupriez, "perhaps a better source of such information is to use the unit values in household surveys, which have the advantage of relating to actual purchases by poor people," although they go on to say "that the corresponding disadvantage is that there is no obvious way of specifying quality, or of controlling for quality variation across poor and nonpoor" (Deaton and Dupriez 2011, 161).

Within Countries: Rural and Urban

At a number of points, there has been reference to the differences within countries in terms of the rural and urban populations, and this already enters the poverty calculations. In the case of the Latin American data supplied by SEDLAC, in all countries the income of the rural population is reduced by 15 percent. The World Bank estimates differentiate for China, India, and Indonesia between the rural and urban populations (and the estimates for Argentina and the Federated States of Micronesia refer only to the urban population). These show a clearly higher poverty rate in rural areas. The head count poverty ratios in Indonesia in 2010 were higher by half in rural areas (19.8 percent rural vs. 12.0 percent urban); in India in 2011/12 the rural rate was nearly double (24.8 percent rural vs. 13.4 percent urban). In China in 2010, rural head count ratio was at the rate of 21.3 percent, whereas urban poverty was close to zero (0.7 percent). For the world as a whole, the World Bank's *Economic Premise* profile shows that the rural population accounted for 58.4 percent of the total population, but 77.8 percent of those living in households in extreme poverty (Olinto et al. 2013, figure 7). Applying the Multidimensional Poverty Index, Alkire et al. (2014) found that 85 percent of those who were poor on this basis lived in rural areas.

There are evident structural reasons to expect that rural poverty rates will decline as the development of the economy leads to migration from the rural to urban sector. Rural residents face less competition for land and employment, raising their economic possibilities, and they can benefit from remittances from those who have left. At the same time, there may be negative forces. The pattern of out-migration may be such that those remaining are less able to cope with threats to their natural resources: "rural communities usually rely heavily on secure and equitable access to land, fisheries and forests, which are a source of food and shelter, the basis for social, cultural and religious practices and a central factor for economic growth" (United Nations 2012, 15). The operation of informal rules depends on a degree of stability that may not survive high rates of out-migration, and may only slowly be replaced by formal governance. Much internal armed conflict takes place in rural areas where the state is absent and armed groups can easily hide (Kalyvas 2006).

It has been seen earlier that the rural/urban distinction may be important with regard to differential movements in prices. The World Bank has rightly sought to avoid the use of price indexes that are limited to urban areas and given preference to those with national coverage. For example, in the calculation for Cambodia the World Bank replaces the official CPI, which covers only the capital city, by an index that has broader coverage of the country (Ferreira et al. 2015, annex 1). The same applies to Lao PDR, where the official price index only covered urban areas. More complex—and part of a wider issue—is the situation where the data are richer: there is full national coverage, but separate price indexes can be applied for rural and urban areas, as in China, India, and Indonesia, as part of separate poverty estimates for rural and urban populations. The price index question is then more complex in that allowance has to be made, not just for the difference in the rate of inflation but also for the differences in price levels, "where we have good evidence from many countries that urban prices are higher than rural prices" (Deaton and Dupriez 2011, 139). Increased coverage is likely to involve the extension of price collection: many middle-income countries do not at present collect rural price data. The discussion now turns more generally to ask whether the extreme poverty estimates should be made separately for rural and urban areas for countries other than the present three countries.

The first challenge is that of definition. There is no internationally agreed basis for drawing the distinction. The UN, in its advice on the definition, states that "because of national differences in the characteristics that distinguish urban from rural areas, the distinction between the urban and the rural population is not yet amenable to a single definition that would be applicable to all countries or, for the most part, even to the countries within a region."[41] The definitional problem is exacerbated when account is taken of the fact that people and place may be differently defined. This is most evident in the case where people may be resident in areas defined as urban but themselves not be registered as urban residents. This applies with the Chinese *hukou* system, and may be one explanation for the low rate of recorded urban poverty in that country.

Countries differ significantly in their approach. According to the Indian Government website, the "rural sector" means any place that meets the following criteria: (i) population of less than 5,000, (ii) density of population less than 400 per square kilometer, and (iii) more than 25 percent of the male working population is engaged in agricultural pursuits.[42] "Rural" may be defined as the complement of "urban." In Colombia, the rural population consists of people living outside the boundaries of the municipal capital; in Chile, urban areas are defined as those with housing of more than 2,000 inhabitants, or between 1,001 and 2,000, with 50 percent or more of its population economically active dedicated to secondary and/or tertiary activities (Tresoldi 2013). As noted by the International Fund for Agricultural Development (IFAD 2011, 294, note 21) in its report on rural poverty, these differences matter: "in many situations, areas defined as urban have rural characteristics in terms of occupations (e.g. reliance on agriculture), and also in terms of level of infrastructure and services. Such characteristics may even extend into bigger cities. In some regions – particularly Latin America, this can lead to significant undercounting of the rural population and of the rural poor."

The country definitions of rural and urban are also subject to change over time. There can be political pressures, such as those related to funding of local governments, that lead districts to seek reclassification, and this may lead to major shifts. In the case of China, for example, Goldstein (1990, 675) has described how in the 1980s, "many localities have been added to the city and town rosters, through annexation to existing urban places or through reclassification, greatly expanding the number of such localities, the number of persons living in urban places, and the number of urban residents who are engaged in agricultural activities."

The second challenge is that of the availability of data. While it may be possible to disaggregate population census data, and administrative data, in considerable geographical detail, this may not be feasible with household surveys where the limitations of coverage and sample size considerations prohibit poverty estimates being operationalized at this level.

Can these challenges be overcome in a way that means that an indicator can be constructed on a comparable basis that distinguishes the extent of extreme poverty between urban and rural residents? Such figures have indeed been presented by the World Bank. The *Economic Premise* figures cited above came from "the first attempt to report poverty profiles at the global scale," and were presumably based on the national definitions of rural/urban available in the underlying household surveys. The IFAD *Rural Poverty Report 2011* based its estimates on national poverty incidence studies: in effect the rural poverty rate is obtained from an internationally comparable poverty rate for the whole country by multiplying by the ratio of rural to urban poverty found in the national studies. It is this latter step that depends on assumptions that do not seem necessarily valid, notably (i) that within a country the ratio of the poverty rates remains constant as the poverty threshold is varied, and (ii) that across countries the rural and urban poverty lines are drawn in a comparable fashion. With regard to the latter, Ravallion, Chen, and Sangraula (2007) report that the ratio of the urban line to the rural line tends to be higher in poorer countries.

Such national study–based calculations may be informative at a national level, and should form part of the National Poverty Statistics Reports. They may form an adequate basis for an overall poverty profile at the national level. The question to be addressed here, however, is whether there should be a major investment in making separate estimates of rural and urban poverty in each country (or the majority of countries) as a basis for the global poverty estimate. It is not evident that the underlying assumptions have sufficient support to allow a reliable monitoring tool differentiated between rural and urban populations to be developed at this stage. To this must be added the substantial data requirements from a move to a rural/urban division within a wider range of countries. There is a need for separate cost of living indexes, but also for a PPP baseline, and the latter would involve substantial new data collection. In view of these considerations, no recommendation is made in this Report for further within-country disaggregation along geographical lines within the global poverty estimate.

Conclusions

In chapter 1, ten recommendations have been proposed regarding the monitoring of extreme poverty over the years up to 2030. These recommendations are reprinted below, not in order of appearance, but in a more logical order: raw materials (data), analysis, and presentation:

Raw Materials

Recommendation 6: The World Bank should make public the principles according to which household survey data are selected for use in the global poverty count; and there should be an assessment at national level of the availability and quality of the required household survey data, and a review of possible alternative sources and methods of ex post harmonization.

Recommendation 3: There should be an investigation of the extent to which people are "missing" from the global poverty count, and proposals made for adjustments where appropriate at the national level for survey underrepresentation and noncoverage by surveys; more generally, the World Bank should carry out a review, in conjunction with other members of the UN statistical system, of the fitness for purpose of the baseline population data for each country, and the methods used to update from the baseline to the years covered by the global poverty estimates.

Recommendation 9: The World Bank, as a user of consumer price indexes (CPIs), should, in conjunction with the responsible international bodies and with the national statistical agencies, seek to improve the quality of the domestic CPI, with particular references to those aspects most relevant to global poverty measurement; this should include examination of the likely magnitude of any bias, and exploration of special price indexes for the poor.

Recommendation 8: There should be an investigation for a small number of countries by the World Bank of alternative methods of providing up-to-date poverty estimates using scaled-down surveys, or the SWIFT or other surveys, plus modeling, where the appropriate methods may vary across countries.

In addition, looking ahead to 2030, it has been proposed that there be investigation of PPPs for the poor.

Analysis

Recommendation 10: The global poverty estimates should be updated up to 2030 on the basis of the International Poverty Line for each country set in local currency, updated in line with the change in the national CPI or, where available, national index of prices for the poor; the estimates would not be revised in the light of new rounds of the ICP.

Recommendation 7: The World Bank, in conjunction with national statistical agencies and other statistical bodies, should explore the construction of an annual national accounts–based indicator of household living standards, as measured by consumption defined in a way that matches as far as possible household survey practice.

Recommendation 4: The World Bank should take the lead in a standing Joint Statistical Working Group for household consumption statistics, with a remit to set guidelines for the measurement of household consumption, to examine the relation between consumption and income, and to investigate the relation between household survey, national accounts, and other data sources.

Presentation

Recommendation 1: The global extreme poverty standard should be cited in general terms as "the International Poverty Line," and expressed in each country in terms of the currency of that country.

Recommendation 2: There should be National Poverty Statistics Reports (NPSRs) for each country, giving the Global Poverty estimates, explaining the local currency value of the International Poverty Line and the relation to the official poverty line(s) in that country (where they exist), considering how the trends in poverty measured according to the International Poverty Line relate to those shown by national statistics, and incorporating a set of World Bank Complementary Indicators, as proposed in chapter 2 of this Report.

Recommendation 5: The World Bank poverty estimates should be based on a "total error" approach, evaluating the possible sources, and magnitude, of error, particularly nonsampling error and the error introduced by the process of determining the International Poverty Line.

The recommendations are primarily directed to the World Bank, but this Report has been written with the wider audience also in mind. The successful accomplishment of a number of the recommendations (such as that concerning population data) will only be possible with the active support of other UN and international organizations and the national statistical institutions. The Report has drawn on their valuable research. More generally, the Report has tried to engage with the academic and other independent researchers who have actively debated the World Bank approach.

The need for wide support is particularly important since the task faced by the World Bank in measuring extreme poverty is likely to become increasingly challenging. This Report has argued for the global poverty total to be stated with an explicit recognition of the likely margin of error, and this margin is likely to get *proportionately* larger as the total shrinks. It is already the case that the estimates are weakest in countries where the underlying statistical sources are the most stretched, and "extreme poverty is likely to become increasingly concentrated in fragile states" (USAID 2015, 28). Within countries, the potentially missing "hard to reach" groups will constitute an increasing fraction of the extreme poor. The Research Team of Beijing Normal University found that increasingly "the poor people have consisted of more heterogeneous individuals," noting that this "will challenge the present policy reduction policies that have mainly dealt with the problems of officially defined homogeneous groups" (Zhu 2015, 2). For all these reasons, it may be that the closer the world gets to achievement of the extreme poverty goal, the harder it becomes to establish whether it has been attained.

Notes

1. It should be stressed that this report is concerned with poverty monitoring, and does not consider the full range of the research activities of the World Bank dealing with poverty nor its academic publications on this subject.
2. See PovcalNet (database), World Bank, Washington, DC, http://iresearch .worldbank.org/PovcalNet/index.htm?1,0.

3. A valuable reference is provided by the June 2016 Special Issue on Global Poverty Lines of the *Journal of Economic Inequality*, edited by Lustig and Silber (2016). The Special Issue contains articles by Ferreira et al. (2016), Kakwani and Son (2016), Jolliffe and Prydz (2016), Klasen et al. (2016), and Ravallion (2016).

4. Deaton and Aten carry out the reverse operation, comparing the 2011 ICP figure for 2011 with that based on the 2005 ICP extrapolated forward to 2011. The latter extrapolations are no longer available on the World Bank website and we have taken the alternative approach using publicly available data.

5. An earlier draft of the Report proposed "Global Poverty Line," but "International" is more appropriate, because the line is based on comparisons at the national level.

6. The poverty line is defined in this report as *per day*, but in some countries national poverty lines are defined *per month*: for example, in Sri Lanka (Sri Lanka Department of Census and Statistics 2015, 1).

7. For example, for Mali the increase in the CPI was by a factor of 1.198, but the 2011 ICP conversion factor was lower at 221.87, compared with 289.68 according to ICP2005, implying an adjustment factor of 1.31, and an overall increase of some 57 percent. These calculations, and those in the text, are based on equation (1) in Ferreira et al. (2016, 154).

8. The same applies when we consider multidimensional poverty. Alkire, Roche, and Sumner find that "only a quarter of multidimensionally poor people and just one-third of severely multidimensionally poor people live in the world's poorest countries – meaning Low Income Countries (LICs) or Least Developed Countries (LDCs)" (2013, page 1).

9. The omission of the MENA regional numbers and of several country-level estimates from that region is a matter of concern. The reason given is the "low coverage and concerns with the aggregates" (Ferreira et al., 2016, page 167, note 44). This raises issues with regard to investment in data, while recognizing the reasons for it being difficult to secure adequate data in this region.

10. Bangladesh, Cabo Verde, Cambodia, Jordan, and Lao PDR.

11. See World Development Indicators (database), World Bank, Washington, DC, http://data.worldbank.org/data-catalog/world-development-indicators.

12. In the case of the United Kingdom, for example, the dependent territories include Anguilla, Bermuda, British Virgin Islands, Cayman Islands, Falkland Islands, Gibraltar, Montserrat, St. Helena, and the Turks and Caicos Islands.

13. For example, the total population in U.K.-dependent territories is some 350,000. There are in addition the Crown Dependencies of Jersey and Guernsey (the Channel Islands) and the Isle of Man, with a total population of 250,000. While it would be essential to include these territories in any study of international taxation, their inclusion is less necessary when estimating world poverty.

14. The definition of calorie units needs to be clarified, including the difference between a small c and a large C. Small calorie (cal) is the energy needed to increase 1 gram of water by 1°C at a pressure of 1 atmosphere; large

calorie (Cal), also called a kilocalorie, or the food calorie, is the energy needed to increase 1 kg of water by 1°C at a pressure of 1 atmosphere. So 1 Cal = 1,000 cal. Here Cal is used.

15. At the time of writing, the results of the 2012/13 Ghana household survey had not yet been incorporated into PovcalNet.

16. The P and SP sheets for countries in East Asia and the Pacific in April 2016 included the most recent national estimate of the head count ratio but no time series.

17. See the World Bank's Poverty web page, http://web.worldbank.org/WBSITE /EXTERNAL/TOPICS/EXTPOVERTY/0,,contentMDK:23109452~pagePK:148 956~piPK:216618~theSitePK:336992,00.html.

18. The World Bank, together with PARIS 21, has been responsible for the implementation of the International Household Survey Network (IHSN), established in 2004 following the Marrakech Action Plan for Statistics. The IHSN would be an important participant in the proposed Working Group.

19. As a result, they dropped the past practice in their estimates of rescaling the mean for income surveys.

20. See the United Nations University World Institute for Development Economics Research WIID database at https://www.wider.unu.edu/project/wiid---world-income-inequality-database.

21. For discussion of the impact on measured poverty of social transfers in kind, specifically health and education, in a range of middle-income countries, see Lustig 2015a and 2015b.

22. Government services are valued at the cost of supply in some national accounts, but, following the UN System of National Accounts 1993 and the European System of National Accounts (ESA1995), countries have increasingly adopted output indicators. There remain considerable problems in implementing such output measures, but progress has been made in their introduction into the national accounts (Atkinson 2005).

23. Efficiency refers to Pareto efficiency; and "caring preferences" require that each household member's decision function is an increasing function of the utilities of other household members.

24. Ravallion, Datt, and van de Walle (1991, table 2) do give a confidence interval for the proportion below $31 a month in 1985, of 27.9 to 39.2, but this refers to the extrapolation to countries for which no distributional data were available.

25. http://www.worldbank.org/en/topic/poverty/overview (dated April 13, 2016).

26. The kind of checklist envisaged is illustrated in the case of income distribution statistics by the box "Robustness of income distribution results to data imperfections" in the Canberra Report (Expert Group on Household Income Statistics 2001, 105). The Group recommends that all data should be accompanied by a Robustness Assessment Report, a recommendation that has been followed as part of a wider concern with data quality by a number of national statistical agencies and by the European Statistical System (see, for example, Eurostat 2011).

A valuable starting point in the case of poverty measurement is the World Bank training document "Poverty Indices: Checking for Robustness" (chapter 5), but it only includes some of the items in table 1.1.

27. A rise in z is equivalent in this context to an equal proportionate reduction in all incomes.

28. A related, but different, point is made by Gibson (2015), where he shows that, as incomes rise proportionately, the impact on the head count ratio depends on the extent of inequality within the poor population.

29. Use is made here of the approximate formula (see, for example, US Census Bureau (2015, page 16)), where the standard error of the difference squared is equal to the sum of the squared standard errors in each years, $s_1^2 + s_2^2$, minus $2r\,s_1 s_2$ (assuming the same sample size), where r is the correlation coefficient.

30. Reference years used at present in PovcalNet are 1981, 1984, 1987, 1990, 1993, 1996, 1999, 2002, 2005, 2008, 2010, 2011, and 2012.

31. The Luxembourg Income Study Database (LIS Database) includes household- and person-level data from countries in Europe, North America, Latin America, Africa, Asia, and Australasia. The Database includes datasets since 1968, organized into "waves" corresponding to regular intervals. The data refer to income, not expenditure. The differences with respect to measured inequality are discussed in the case of India by Vanneman and Dubey (2013).

32. There is also a case for extending the table downward, to allow for the subtraction of indirect taxes paid and the addition of subsidies. These are quantitatively significant in many countries, and often highly politically salient, and warrant fuller attention.

33. It should be borne in mind that the national accounts estimates of consumption often start from physical volumes of output, so that errors in the choice of price index may enter twice: through the conversion of the physical units to currency values and then via the adjustment of those current price values to constant prices—see Deaton 2005, 15).

34. An early example of a study seeking to make such forecasts is that by Mwabu et al. (2003) for Kenya, where use is made of information on GDP growth and the change in the Gini coefficient.

35. The DWP argues that "the published figures have always to date shown a very different picture. DWP believes this may have a negative effect on trust of the official statistics, work against coherence and confuse users" (U.K. Statistics Authority 2015, 20). A more recent assessment by the Office for National Statistics concludes that "while nowcasting may be subject to some limitations, ONS's view is that it has the benefit of producing timely estimates of household income and thus the potential to facilitate monitoring of the effects of recent changes in economic policies. Nowcasting is a more reliable approach than forecasting as it combines both actual data for components that are known. [This] suggests that it may have the potential to be a suitable approach to producing early estimates of key income indicators while waiting for survey

based estimates to become available" (Stoyanova and Tonkin 2016, 12). They do, however, go on to caution that "there remain considerable questions regarding the potential for nowcasting to produce reliable estimates for measures using thresholds, such as the At-Risk-of-Poverty rate."

36. Reference should also be made to alternative nonsurvey sources, such as satellite mapping—see Elvidge et al. 2009.

37. There is no discussion at this point of the—comparatively neglected—subject of the issues of aggregation at the most elementary level, where the prices of representative products are combined to yield a measure for each commodity group (see ILO et al. 2004, chapter 1, sections 1.120 to 1.146, and chapter 20). Reference is made below to the possible magnitude of the bias.

38. The Fisher index is often referred to as an "ideal" or "true" index, on the grounds that it can be derived, under certain strong assumptions, from utility-maximizing behavior (see ILO et al. 2004, chapter 17). This terminology is not used here, the index being regarded simply as an average.

39. See "The Eurostat-OECD Programme and the ICP—A Shared Commitment" on the OECD website, http://www.oecd.org/std/price-ppp/theeurostat-oecdppppro-grammeandtheicp-asharedcommitment.htm.

40. Both of these elements are addressed by Attanasio and Frayne (2006), who discuss the identification problem where the price paid depends on the quantity and provide evidence for Latin America. Their results for rural Colombia show that the price falls with the quantity purchased as a result of discounts for bulk purchasing, causing the poor to pay more. In the case of the Asian Development Bank study, the conversion from the larger amounts specified in the ICP to the smaller amounts in the poverty-specific surveys is achieved "using a pro rata adjustment, which assumes a linear relationship between quantity and price" (ADB 2008, 44).

41. See the United Nations Department of Economic and Social Affairs (UNDESA) website on "Population Density and Urbanization," para. 281, at http://unstats .un.org/unsd/demographic/sconcerns/densurb/densurbmethods.htm#B.

42. See the Indian Government's website at http://www.archive.india.gov.in/citizen /graminbharat/graminbharat.php.

References

ADB (Asian Development Bank). 2008. *Research Study on Poverty-Specific Purchasing Power Parities for Selected Countries in Asia and the Pacific.* Manila: Asian Development Bank.

Ahluwalia, M. S. 1974. "Income Inequality: Some Dimensions of the Problem." In *Redistribution with Growth,* edited by H. B. Chenery, M. S. Ahluwalia, C. L. G. Bell, J. H. Duloy, and R. Jolly. London: Oxford University Press.

Ahluwalia, M. S., N. G. Carter, and H. B. Chenery. 1979. "Growth and Poverty in Developing Countries." *Journal of Development Economics* 6: 299–341.

Alkire, S., M. Chatterjee, A. Conconi, S. Seth, and A. Vaz. 2014. "Poverty in Rural and Urban Areas: Direct Comparisons Using the Global MPI 2014." OPHI Brief 24, University of Oxford, Oxford, U.K.

Alkire, S., J. M. Roche, and A. Sumner. 2013. "Where Do the World's Multidimensionally Poor People Live?" OPHI Working Papers 61, University of Oxford.

Allen, R. C. 2013. "Poverty Lines in History, Theory, and Current International Practice." Department of Economics Discussion Paper 685, University of Oxford, Oxford, U.K.

Atkinson, A. B. 2005. *Atkinson Review: Final Report, Measurement of Government Output and Productivity for the National Accounts.* London: Palgrave Macmillan.

———. 2016. "The Distribution of Top Incomes in Former British West Africa." Unpublished.

Atkinson, A. B., A.-C. Guio, and E. Marlier. 2015. "Monitoring the Evolution of Income Poverty and Real Incomes over Time." CASE paper 188, London School of Economics.

Attanasio, O. P., and C. Frayne. 2006. "Do the Poor Pay More?" Paper presented at the 8th BREAD Conference, Ithaca, New York.

Banda, J. P. 2003. "Nonsampling Errors in Surveys." Expert Group Meeting to Review the Draft Handbook on Designing of Household Sample Surveys, December 3–5, United Nations Statistical Division, United Nations, New York.

Basu, K. 2006. "Gender and Say: A Model of Household Behaviour with Endogenously Determined Balance of Power." *Economic Journal* 116: 558–80.

———. 2015. "The Poverty Line's Battle Lines." Project Syndicate, Tuesday, February 16, 2016.

Beegle, K., L. Christiaensen, A. Dabalen, and I. Gaddis. 2016. *Poverty in a Rising Africa,* volumes 1 and 2. Washington, DC: World Bank.

Bhalla, A. S., and P. McCormick. 2009. *Poverty among Immigrant Children in Europe.* Basingstoke, U.K.: Palgrave Macmillan.

Boskin, M. J., chair, E. R. Dulberger, R. J. Gordon, Z. Griliches, and D. W. Jorgenson. 1996. *Final Report of the Commission to Study the Consumer Price Index,* U.S. Senate, Committee on Finance. Washington, DC: U.S. Government Printing Office.

Boskin, M. J., E. R. Dulberger, R. J. Gordon, Z. Griliches, and D. W. Jorgenson. 1998. "Consumer Prices in the Consumer Price Index and the Cost of Living." *Journal of Economic Perspectives* 12 (1): 3–26.

Bourguignon, F. 2003. "The Growth Elasticity of Poverty Reduction: Explaining Heterogeneity across Countries and Time Periods." In *Inequality and Growth: Theory and Policy Implications,* edited by T. Eicher and S. Turnovsky, 17–40. Cambridge, MA: MIT Press.

———. 2015. "Appraising Income Inequality Databases in Latin America." *Journal of Economic Inequality* 13: 557–78.

Bourguignon, F., and C. Morrisson. 2002. "Inequality among World Citizens: 1820–1992." *American Economic Review* 92: 727–44.

Bourguignon, F., A. Bénassy-Quéré, S. Dercon, A. Estache, J. W. Gunning, R. Kanbur, S. Klasen, S. Maxwell, J.-P. Platteau, and A. Spadaro. 2010. "The Millennium Development Goals: An Assessment." In *Equity and Growth in a Globalizing World*, edited by R. Kanbur and M. Spence. Washington, DC: World Bank.

Browning, M., P.-A. Chiappori, and Y. Weiss. 2014. *Family Economics.* New York: Cambridge University Press.

Caplovitz, D. 1968. *The Poor Pay More: Consumer Practices of Low-Income Families.* Free Press.

Carr-Hill, R. 2013. "Missing Millions and Measuring Development Progress." *World Development* 46: 30–44.

———. 2015. "Non-Household Populations: Implications for Measurements of Poverty Globally and in the UK." *Journal of Social Policy* Vol. 44: 255–75.

Case, A., and A. Deaton. 2015. "Rising Morbidity and Mortality in Midlife among White Non-Hispanic Americans in the 21st Century." *Proceedings of the National Academy of Sciences of the United States of America* 112: 15078–83.

Chandy, L. 2013. "Counting the Poor: Methods, Problems, and Solution behind the $1.25 a Day Global Poverty Estimates." Brookings Institution and Development Initiatives, Washington, DC.

Chandy, L., and C. Smith. 2014. "How Poor Are America's Poorest? U.S. $2 a Day Poverty in a Global Context." Policy Paper 2014-03, Brookings Institution, Washington, DC.

Chen, S., G. Datt, and M. Ravallion. 1994. "Is Poverty Increasing in the Developing World?" *Review of Income and Wealth* series 40: 359–76.

Chen, S., and M. Ravallion. 2001. "How Did the World's Poorest Fare in the 1990s?" *Review of Income and Wealth* series 47: 283–300.

———. 2004. "How Have the World's Poorest Fared Since the Early 1980s?" *World Bank Research Observer* 19: 141–70.

———. 2007. "Absolute Poverty Measures for the Developing World, 1981–2004." *Proceedings of the National Academy of Sciences of the United States* 104: 16757–62.

———. 2010. "The Developing World Is Poorer than We Thought, but No Less Successful in the Fight against Poverty." *Quarterly Journal of Economics* 125: 1577–1625.

Cherchye, L., B. De Rockz, A. Lewbel, and F. Vermeulen. 2015. "Sharing Rule Identification for General Collective Consumption Models." *Econometrica* 83: 2001–41.

Chesher, A., and C. Schluter. 2002. "Welfare Measurement and Measurement Error." *Review of Economic Studies* 69: 357–78.

Chiappori, P.-A., and C. Meghir. 2015. "Intrahousehold Inequality." In *Handbook of Income Distribution*, vol. 2B, edited by A. B. Atkinson and F. Bourguignon, 1369–1418. Amsterdam: Elsevier.

Corsi, M., F. Botti, and C. D'Ippoliti. 2016. "The Gendered Nature of Poverty in the EU: Individualized versus Collective Poverty Measures." *Feminist Economics* March: 1–19.

Coulombe, H., and A. McKay. 1995. "An Assessment of Trends in Poverty in Ghana, 1988–1992." PSP Discussion Paper Series 81, World Bank, Washington, DC.

Deaton, A. 1987. "Life-Cycle Models of Consumption: Is the Evidence Consistent with the Theory?" In *Advances in Econometrics*, Fifth World Congress, vol. 2, edited by T. F. Bewley. New York: Cambridge University Press.

———. 1998. "Getting Prices Right: What Should Be Done?" *Journal of Economic Perspectives* 12 (1): 37–46.

———. 2003. "How to Monitor Poverty for the Millennium Development Goals." *Journal of Human Development* 4: 353–78.

———. 2005. "Measuring Poverty in a Growing World (or Measuring Growth in a Poor World)." *Review of Economics and Statistics* 87: 1–19.

———. 2012. "Calibrating Measurement Uncertainty in Purchasing Power Parity Exchange Rates." International Comparison Program 7th Technical Advisory Group meeting, Washington, DC.

Deaton, A., and B. Aten. 2015. "Trying to Understand the PPPs in ICP 2011: Why Are the Results So Different?" Princeton University, Princeton, NJ.

Deaton, A., and O. Dupriez. 2011. "Purchasing Power Parity Exchange Rates for the Global Poor." *American Economic Journal: Applied Economics* 3 (2): 137–66.

Deming, E. 1944. "On Errors in Surveys." *American Sociological Review* 9: 359–69.

Devarajan, S., and R. Kanbur. 2013. "The Evolution of Development Strategy as Balancing Market and Government Failure." Working Paper 9: 12, Charles H. Dyson School of Applied Economics and Management, Cornell University, Ithaca, NY.

Diewert, W. E. 1983. "The Theory of the Cost of Living Index and the Measurement of Welfare Change." In *Price Level Measurement*, edited by W. E. Diewert and C. Montmarquette, 163–233. Ottawa: Statistics Canada. Reprinted in W. E. Diewert, ed. 1990. *Price Level Measurement*. Amsterdam: North-Holland, 79–147.

———. 1998. "Index Number Issues in the Consumer Price Index." *Journal of Economic Perspectives* 12 (1): 47–58.

Douidich, M., A. Ezzrari, R. Van der Weide, and P. Verme. 2013. "Estimating Quarterly Poverty Rates Using Labor Force Surveys: A Primer." Policy Research Working Paper 6466, World Bank, Washington, DC.

Dykstra, S., C. Kenny, and J. Sandefur. 2014. "Global Absolute Poverty Fell by Almost Half on Tuesday." Centre for Global Development blog: http://www.cgdev.org /blog/globalabsolute-poverty-fell-almost-half-tuesday.

Edin, K. J., and H. L. Shaefer. 2015. *$2.00 a Day: Living on Almost Nothing in America*. Boston: Houghton Mifflin Harcourt.

Elbers, C., J. O. Lanjouw, and P. Lanjouw. 2002. "Micro-level Estimation of Welfare." Policy Research Working Paper 2911, World Bank, Washington, DC.

———. 2003. "Micro-level Estimation of Poverty and Inequality." *Econometrica* 71: 355–64.

Elvidge, C. D., P. C. Sutton, T. Ghosh, B. Tuttle, K. E. Baugh, B. Bhaduri, and E. Bright. 2009. "A Global Poverty Map Derived from Satellite Data." *Computers and Geosciences* 35: 1652–60.

Eurostat. 2011. *Quality Assurance Framework of the European Statistical System*. Luxembourg: Eurostat.

Evans, M. 1995. "Out for the Count: The Incomes of the Non-household Population and the Effect of Their Exclusion from National Income Profiles." Welfare State Programme Discussion Paper WSP 111, London School of Economics, London.

———. 2015. Submission to Global Poverty Commission.

Expert Group on Household Income Statistics (The Canberra Group). 2001. Final Report and Recommendations. Ottawa: The Canberra Group.

Ferreira, F. H. G., S. Chen, A. L. Dabalen, Y. M. Dikhanov, N. Hamadeh, D. M. Jolliffe, A. Narayan, E. B. Prydz, A. L. Revenga, P. Sangraula, U. Serajuddin, and N. Yoshida. 2015. "A Global Count of the Extreme Poor in 2012: Data Issues, Methodology and Initial Results." Policy Research Working Paper 7432, World Bank, Washington, DC.

———. 2016. "A Global Count of the Extreme Poor in 2012: Data Issues, Methodology and Initial Results." *Journal of Economic Inequality* 14: 141–72.

Fesseau, M., F. Wolff, and M. L. Mattonetti. 2013. "A Cross-Country Comparison of Household Income, Consumption and Wealth between Micro Sources and National Accounts Aggregates." OECD Statistics Working Paper 2013/03, Organisation for Economic Co-operation and Development, Paris.

Folbre, N. 1986. "Hearts and Spades: Paradigms of Household Economics." *World Development* 14: 245–55.

Gazdar, H. 2003. "A Review of Migration Issues in Pakistan." Refugee and Migratory Movements Research Unit, University of Dhaka, Dhaka.

Gibson, J. 2005. "Statistical Tools and Estimation Methods for Poverty Measures Based on Cross-Sectional Household Surveys." Chapter 5 in *Handbook on Poverty Statistics: Concepts, Methods and Policy Use*. New York: United Nations Statistics Division.

———. 2015. "Poverty Measurement: We Know Less than Policy Makers Realize." Working Paper in Economics 8/15, University of Waikato, Hamilton, New Zealand.

Giménez, L., and D. Jolliffe. 2014. "Inflation for the Poor in Bangladesh: A Comparison of CPI and Household Survey Data." *Bangladesh Development Studies* 37: 57–81.

Goldstein, S. 1990. "Urbanization in China, 1982–87: Effects of Migration and Reclassification." *Population and Development Review* 16(4): 673–701.

Grootaert, C., and R. Kanbur. 1994. "A New Regional Price Index for Côte d'Ivoire Using Data from the International Comparisons Project." *Journal of African Economies* 3: 114–41.

Groves, R. M., F. Fowler, M. Couper, E. Singer, and R. Tourangeau. 2004. *Survey Methodology*. New York: Wiley.

Groves, R. M., and L. Lyberg. 2010. "Total Survey Error: Past, Present, and Future." *Public Opinion Quarterly* 74: 849–79.

Haddad, L. J., and S. R. Kanbur. 1990. "How Serious Is the Neglect of Intra-Household Inequality?" *The Economic Journal* 100: 866–81.

Havinga, I., G. Kamanou, and V. Q. Viet. 2010. "A Note on the Mis(use) of National Accounts for Estimation of Household Final Consumption Expenditures for Poverty Measures." In *Debates on the Measurement of Global Poverty*, edited by S. Anand, P. Segal, and J. E. Stiglitz, 238–245. Oxford, U.K.: Oxford University Press.

Ibañez, A. M. 2008. *Desplazamiento forzoso en Colombia: Un camino sin retorno hacia la Pobreza*. Bogotá: Ediciones Uniandes.

IFAD (International Fund for Agricultural Development). 2011. *Rural Poverty Report 2011*. Rome: IFAD.

ILO (International Labour Organization), IMF (International Monetary Fund), OECD (Organisation for Economic Co-operation and Development), UNECE (United Nations Economic Commission for Europe), Eurostat, and World Bank. 2004. *Consumer Price Index Manual: Theory and Practice*. Geneva: ILO.

ILO (International Labour Organization). 2013. *Methodologies of Compiling Consumer Price Indices: 2012 ILO Survey of Country Practices, Preliminary Results*. Geneva: ILO.

India Planning Commission. 2011. "Press Note on Poverty Estimates." Planning Commission, New Delhi.

Inklaar, R. C., and D. P. Rao. 2014. "Cross-Country Income Levels over Time: Did the Developing World Suddenly Become Much Richer?" GGDC Research Memorandum 151, University of Groningen, Groningen Growth and Development Centre, Groningen.

International Movement ATD Fourth World. 2015. Submission to the Global Poverty Commission.

Jencks, C. 2016. "Why the Very Poor Have Become Poorer." *New York Review of Books*, June 9.

Jolliffe, D., and E. Prydz. 2016. "Estimating International Poverty Lines from Comparable National Thresholds." *Journal of Economic Inequality* 14: 185–98.

Kakwani, N. 1993. "Poverty and Economic Growth with Application to Côte d'Ivoire." *Review of Income and Wealth* series 39: 121–39.

Kakwani, N., and H. Son. 2016. "Global Poverty Estimates Based on 2011 Purchasing Power Parity: Where Should the New Poverty Line Be Drawn?" *Journal of Economic Inequality* 14: 173–84.

Kalyvas, S. 2006. *The Logic of Violence in Civil War.* New York: Cambridge University Press.

Kamanou, G., M. Ward, and I. Havinga. 2005. "Statistical Issues in Measuring Poverty from Non-survey Sources." Chapter 6 in *Handbook on Poverty Statistics: Concepts, Methods and Policy Use.* New York: United Nations Statistics Division.

Klasen, S., T. Krivobokova, F. Greb, R. Lahoti, S. Pasaribu, and M. Wiesenfarth. 2016. "International Poverty Measurement: Which Way Now?" *Journal of Economic Inequality* 14: 199–225.

Konrad, K. A., and K. E. Lommerud. 2000. "The Bargaining Family Revisited." *Canadian Journal of Economics* 33: 471–87.

Korinek, A., J. Mistiaen, and M. Ravallion. 2006. "Survey Nonresponse and the Distribution of Income." *Journal of Economic Inequality* 4 (2): 33–55.

———. 2007. "An Econometric Method of Correcting for Unit Nonresponse Bias in Surveys." *Journal of Econometrics* 136: 213–35.

Lahoti, R., A. Jayadev, and S. G. Reddy. 2015. "The Global Consumption and Income Project (GCIP): An Introduction and Preliminary Findings." DESA Working Paper 140, United Nations Department of Economic and Social Affairs (UNDESA), New York.

Lise, J., and S. Seitz. 2011. "Consumption Inequality and Intra-household Allocations." *Review of Economic Studies* 78: 328–55.

Lustig, N. 2015a. "Inequality and Fiscal Redistribution in Middle Income Countries: Brazil, Chile, Colombia, Indonesia, Mexico, Peru and South Africa." Working Paper 410, Center for Global Development.

———. 2015b. "The Redistributive Impact of Government Spending on Education and Health: Evidence from 13 Developing Countries in the Commitment to Equity Project." Chapter 17 in *Inequality and the Role of Fiscal Policy: Trends and Policy Options,* edited by B. Clements, R. de Mooij, S. Gupta, and M. Keen. Washington, DC: International Monetary Fund.

Lustig, N., and J. Silber. 2016. "Introduction to the Special Issue on International Poverty Lines." *Journal of Economic Inequality* 14: 129–40.

Mattonetti, M. L. 2013. "European Household Income by Groups of Households." Eurostat Methodologies and Working Papers, Publications Office of the European Union, Luxembourg.

Milanovic, B. 2005. *Worlds Apart: Measuring International and Global Inequality.* Princeton, NJ: Princeton University Press.

———. 2012. "Global Inequality by the Numbers: In History and Now." Policy Research Working Paper 6259, World Bank, Washington, DC.

———. 2016. *Global Inequality: A New Approach for the Age of Globalization.* Cambridge, MA: Harvard University Press.

Muellbauer, J. N. J. 1977. "Community Preferences and the Representative Consumer." *Econometrica* 44: 979–99.

Mwabu, G., M. S. Kimenyi, P. Kimalu, N. Nafula, and D. K. Manda. 2003. "Predicting Household Poverty: A Methodological Note with a Kenyan Example." *African Development Review* 15: 77–85.

National Research Council. 2000. *Beyond Six Billion: Forecasting the World's Population.* Washington, DC: The National Academies Press.

Newhouse, D. L., S. Shivakumaran, S. Takamatsu, and N. Yoshida. 2014. "How Survey-to-Survey Imputation Can Fail." Policy Research Working Paper 6961, World Bank, Washington, DC.

ODI (Overseas Development Institute). 2015. *Exclusion in Household Surveys: Causes, Impacts and Ways Forward.* London: Overseas Development Institute.

Okigbo, P. N. C. 1962. *Nigerian National Accounts, 1950–57.* Enugu, Nigeria: Government Printer.

Olinto, P., K. Beegle, C. Sobrado, and H. Uematsu. 2013. *The State of the Poor: Where Are the Poor, Where Is Extreme Poverty Harder to End, and What Is the Current Profile of the World's Poor?* Economic premise 125. Washington, DC: World Bank.

Olson Lanjouw, J., and P. Lanjouw. 2001. "How to Compare Apples and Oranges: Poverty Measurement Based on Different Definitions of Consumption." *Review of Income and Wealth* 47: 25–42.

Pincus, J., and J. Sender. 2008. "Quantifying Poverty in Viet Nam: Who Counts?" *Journal of Vietnamese Studies* 3: 108–50.

Prais, S. J. 1959. "Whose Cost of Living?" *Review of Economic Studies* 26: 126–34.

Rangarajan, C. 2014. *Report of the Expert Group to Review the Methodology for Measurement of Poverty.* New Delhi: Planning Commission.

Rastrigina, O., C. Leventi, and H. Sutherland. 2015. "Nowcasting: Estimating Eevelopments in the Risk of Poverty and Income Distribution in 2013 and 2014." EUROMOD Working Paper series EM12/15, University of Essex, U.K.

Ravallion, M. 1998. "Poverty Lines in Theory and Practice." LSMS Working Paper 133, World Bank, Washington, DC.

———. 2003. "Measuring Aggregate Welfare in Developing Countries: How Well Do National Accounts and Surveys Agree?" *Review of Economics and Statistics* 85: 645–52.

———. 2014. "An Exploration of the International Comparison Program's New Global Economic Landscape." NBER Working Paper 20338, National Bureau of Economic Research, Cambridge, MA.

———. 2016. "Toward Better Global Poverty Measures." *Journal of Economic Inequality* 14: 227–48.

Ravallion, M., and S. Chen. 1997. "What Can New Survey Data Tell Us about Recent Changes in Distribution and Poverty?" *World Bank Economic Review* 11: 357–82.

———. 2013. "A Proposal for Truly Global Poverty Measures." *Global Policy* 4: 258–65.

Ravallion, M., S. Chen, and P. Sangraula. 2007. "New Evidence on the Globalization of Urban Poverty." *Population and Development Review* 33: 667–702.

———. 2008. "Dollar a Day Revisited." Policy Research Working Paper 4620, World Bank, Washington, DC.

———. 2009. "Dollar a Day Revisited." *World Bank Economic Review* 23: 163–84.

Ravallion, M., G. Datt, and D. van de Walle. 1991. "Quantifying Absolute Poverty in the Developing World." *Review of Income and Wealth* series 37: 345–61.

Ravallion, M., G. Datt, D. van de Walle, and E. Chan. 1991. "Quantifying the Magnitude and Severity of Absolute Poverty in the Developing World in the Mid-1980s." PRE Working Paper 587, World Bank, Washington, DC.

Sala-i-Martin, X., and M. Pinkovskiy. 2010. "African Poverty is Falling . . . Much Faster Than You Think!" NBER Working Paper 15775, National Bureau of Economic Research, Cambridge, MA.

Sen, A. K. 1990. "Gender and Cooperative Conflicts." In *Persistent Inequalities*, edited by I. Tinker, 123–49. Oxford, U.K.: Oxford University Press.

Serajuddin, Umar, Hiroki Uematsu, Christina Wieser, Nobuo Yoshida, and Andrew Dabalen. 2015. "Data Deprivation: Another Deprivation to End." Policy Research Working Paper No. 7252. World Bank, Washington, DC.

Shaefer, H. L., and K. Edin. 2013. "Rising Extreme Poverty in the United States and the Response of Federal Means-Tested Transfers." *Social Service Review* 87: 250–68.

Sillers, D. 2015. "Is $1.82 the New $1.25? Choosing the Next International Extreme Poverty Line." USAID Economics Brief, U.S. Agency for International Development, Washington, DC.

Smith, L. C., O. Dupriez, and N. Troubat. 2014. "Assessment of the Reliability and Relevance of the Food Data Collected in National Household Consumption and Expenditure Surveys." IHSN Working Paper 008, International Household Survey Network.

Sri Lanka Department of Census and Statistics. 2011. *Poverty Indicators: Household Income and Expenditure Survey, 2009/10*. Colombo: Ministry of Finance and Planning.

———. 2015. *Poverty Indicators*. Colombo: Ministry of Policy Planning Economic Affairs, Child Youth and Cultural Affairs.

Srinivasan, T. N. 2010. "Irrelevance of the $1-a-Day Poverty Line." In *Debates on the Measurement of Global Poverty*, edited by S. Anand, P. Segal, and J. E, Stiglitz, 143–53. Oxford, U.K.: Oxford University Press.

Statistics Ghana. 2000. *Poverty Trends in Ghana in the 1990s*. Accra: Statistics Ghana.

———. 2014. *Ghana Living Standards Survey Round 6 (GLSS 6): Poverty Profile in Ghana (2005–2013)*. Accra: Statistics Ghana.

Stoyanova, Sofiya, and Richard Tonkin. 2016. "Nowcasting Household Income in the UK: Financial Year Ending 2015." Paper prepared for the 34th IARIW General Conference, Dresden, Germany, August 21–27, 2016.

Sumner, A. 2012. "Where Do the Poor Live?" *World Development* 40 (5): 865–77.

Sutherland, H. 1997. "Women, Men and the Redistribution of Income." *Fiscal Studies* 18: 1–22.

Tanzania National Bureau of Statistics. 2014. *Household Budget Survey Main Report 2011/12*. Dar es Salaam: Ministry of Finance.

Tresoldi, J. C. 2013. "How Are Urban and Rural Areas Determined in Census Cartography in Latin America?" Available at: http://www.popclimate.net/indicators/view/31-%C2%BFhow-are-urban-and-rural-areas-determined-in-census-cartography-in-latin-america.

U.K. Department of Employment and Productivity. 1968. *Family Expenditure Survey*. London: HMSO.

U.K. Office for National Statistics. 2015. "Nowcasting Household Income in the UK: Financial Year Ending 2015." *Statistical Bulletin*, London.

U.K. Statistics Authority. 2015. *Monitoring Review Progress Report: Coherence and Accessibility of Official Statistics on Income and Earnings*. London: UK Statistics Authority.

Ulph, D. 2006. "Un modèle non-coopératif de Nash appliqué à l'étude du comportement de consommation du ménage." *Actualité économique: Revue d'analyse économique* 82: 53–86.

United Nations. 2005. *Handbook on Poverty Statistics: Concepts, Methods and Policy Use*. New York: United Nations Statistics Division, United Nations.

———. 2009. *Practical Guide to Producing Consumer Price Indices*. New York: United Nations.

———. 2012. *Final Draft of the Guiding Principles on Extreme Poverty and Human Rights*. New York: United Nations.

———. 2014. *A World That Counts*. Report by the Independent Expert Advisory Group on a Data Revolution for Sustainable Development. New York: United Nations.

———. 2016. *Report of the Inter-Agency and Expert Group on Sustainable Development Goal Indicators*. New York: Economic and Social Council, United Nations.

USAID (U.S. Agency for International Development). 2015. *Vision for Ending Extreme Poverty*. Washington, DC: USAID.

U.S. Census Bureau. 2015. *Source and Accuracy of Estimates for Income and Poverty in the United States: 2014 and Health Insurance Coverage in the United States: 2014*. Washington, DC: U.S. Government Printing Office.

U.S. Department of Commerce. 2012. "Census Coverage Measurement Estimation Report Summary of Estimates of Coverage for Persons in the United States." Memorandum prepared by T. Mule, DSSD 2010 Census coverage measurement memorandum series #2010-G-01, U.S. Government Printing Office, Washington, DC.

Vanneman, R., and A. Dubey. 2013. "Horizontal and Vertical Inequalities in India." In *Income Inequality: Economic Disparities and the Middle Class in Affluent Countries*, edited by J. C. Gornick and M. Jäntti. Stanford, CA: Stanford University Press.

Woolley, F., and Z. Chen. 2001. "A Cournot-Nash Model of Family Decision Making." *Economic Journal* 111: 722–48.

Woolley, F., and J. Marshall. 1994. "Measuring Inequality within the Household." *Review of Income and Wealth* series 40: 415–31.

World Bank. 1978. *World Development Report 1978.* Washington, DC: World Bank. Available at: https://openknowledge.worldbank.org/handle/10986/5961.

———. 1990. *World Development Report 1990: Poverty.* New York: Oxford University Press.

———. 2013. "Getting to Poverty: Lessons from the World Bank's Record on Supporting Poverty Reduction in Country Programs." Approach paper by Independent Evaluation Group, World Bank, Washington, DC.

———. 2014. *Summary of Results and Findings of the 2011 International Comparison Program.* Washington, DC: World Bank.

———. 2015. *A Measured Approach to Ending Poverty and Boosting Shared Prosperity: Concepts, Data, and the Twin Goals.* Policy Research Report. Washington, DC: World Bank.

———. 2016. *Indigenous Latin America in the Twenty-First Century: The First Decade.* Washington, DC: World Bank.

World Bank Group. 2016. *Global Monitoring Report 2015/2016: Development Goals in an Era of Demographic Change.* Washington, DC: World Bank.

Yoshida, N., R. Munoz, A. Skinner, C. Kyung-eun Lee, M. Brataj, W. Durbin, and D. Sharma. 2015. *SWIFT Data Collection Guidelines.* Version 2. Washington, DC: World Bank.

Zhu, L. 2015. "Poverty Measures Taken in China." Submission to the Global Poverty Commission.

Beyond Goal 1.1: Complementary Indicators and Multidimensionality

Chapter 1 of this Report has addressed the first of the two remits of the Commission on Global Poverty. It has examined how best to implement the measurement of progress toward eliminating extreme poverty as defined by the World Bank in setting its future goals and by the United Nations (UN) in the agreement in September 2015 on the Sustainable Goals. Chapter 2 has a wider remit. The question is, now, what alternative indicators should be monitored, and how, more fundamentally, one should seek to measure global poverty. Both of these underlie the Report's proposals for a portfolio of *Complementary Indicators*, to be published by the World Bank alongside the extreme poverty estimates. The architecture of such a portfolio is the subject of the first section in this chapter, which discusses its role and the principles that should underlie its construction. The following sections of chapter 2 are concerned with the possible content, where a number of candidates for indicators are considered. Among them are, in "Enriching the Analysis of Those in Economic Poverty," amplifications of the existing standard, including the depth, composition, and persistence of poverty. This deals with topics that are much debated, such as what fraction of the world's poor are women. The next section moves beyond the existing poverty standard to consider alternative approaches to setting the poverty line. As part of the Commission's work, we have sought views on the formulation of the poverty objective, and many of the replies have been along the lines of "I would not start from here." As a response to such views, this Report considers alternative starting points: subjective assessments, basic needs, capabilities, and minimum rights. These alternative approaches provide a natural bridge to the Twin World Bank goal concerned with shared prosperity, and this is the subject of "Relative Poverty, Income Shares, and Shared Prosperity," which discusses both a new societal-based poverty indicator and the implementation of the Twin World Bank objective.

To this juncture, the Report has been largely concerned with poverty defined in terms of economic resources. As, however, has been stressed in submissions to the Commission, there are many essential dimensions to poverty in addition to money. The arguments for monitoring multiple dimensions have been made in a succession of World Bank documents, dating back at least to the first World Development Report in 1978. Multidimensionality is embodied in the Sustainable Development Goal (SDG) Goal 1.2, which "addresses poverty in all its dimensions." The measurement of multidimensional poverty is taken up in the final section, "Nonmonetary Poverty," where a dashboard approach is proposed as part of the Complementary Indicators, together with a measure of the extent of overlapping deprivation. It should be stressed that, in making it a finale, rather than an overture, the Report is in no way seeking to downplay the key role of the multidimensional approach. Some readers of the draft of the Report have taken issue with the fact that the treatment of multidimensional poverty comes at the end of chapter 2, arguing that it should rather be the point of departure. Although this position has an evident logic, the Report has retained the present structure, progressively widening the analysis from $1.90 a day, to alternative resource-based poverty lines, and ending with a portfolio that covers a number of dimensions of poverty. One reason for adopting this order is that, while the World Bank serves as the leading international institution in monitoring monetary poverty, the extension to nonmonetary dimensions takes the Report into fields where other UN agencies may be expected to take the lead, such as health, education, housing, and nutrition. The recommendations made here concerning the dashboard of nonmonetary indicators depend on cooperation with other UN institutions.

Finally, it should be noted that in what follows the Report draws on the large and long-standing literature on the measurement of poverty, but no attempt is made to provide a comprehensive summary.[1]

The Design of the Complementary Indicator Portfolio

The analysis of chapter 2 leads to proposals for a parsimonious portfolio of indicators that are complementary to the extreme poverty goal, and it is necessary first to explain their role within an annual output from the World Bank that is envisaged as having three key constituents:

1. Report on Goal 1.1 (extreme poverty)
2. Report on the portfolio of Complementary Indicators (CI), which includes the Twin Goal of the World Bank of boosting shared prosperity and nonmonetary indicators of poverty
3. National Poverty Statistics Reports (NPSR) for each country, encompassing the extreme poverty measure and the Complementary Indicators for that country.

Purpose of Complementary Indicators

The purpose of the Complementary Indicators is threefold. The first role is to provide context for the interpretation of the findings with regard to the Global Poverty figure. There is not a complete divorce between chapter 1 and chapter 2. The purpose of the portfolio of indicators proposed in chapter 2 is to *complement* the headline goal. The Complementary Indicators will enter the text accompanying the publication of the results on the $1.90 indicator, and thus enlarge our understanding of the evolution of poverty. Such a role may be seen as engaging with SDGs beyond Goal 1.1. Hunger (Goal 2), health (Goal 3), and education (Goal 4) are among the nonmonetary dimensions discussed in the section on "Nonmonetary Poverty." In this way, the third role is to make a reality of multidimensionality. The SDGs raise issues of gender (Goal 5), considered in the second section, "Enriching the Analysis of Those in Economic Poverty." Goal 10 is concerned with inequality, relevant to the discussion in the fourth section, "Relative Poverty, Income Shares, and Shared Prosperity."

The second role of the portfolio of Complementary Indicators is to provide space for alternative approaches to the definition of the International Poverty Line. The third section in this chapter, "Alternative Approaches to Measuring Poverty," considers a range of indicators that start further back, seeking to ground the measurement in definitions of poverty that are founded not on national poverty lines but on perspectives based on subjective assessments, basic needs, capabilities, and rights. For those who are critical of the $1.90 indicator, the Complementary Indicators can provide an alternative perspective. Moreover, the function of the Complementary Indicators is taken to encompass the Twin Goal of the World Bank of boosting shared prosperity, and to relate the measures of poverty to those of economic inequality. The provision of Complementary Indicators is particularly important in the light of country heterogeneity of performance. Some countries performing less well in terms of Goal 1.1 may be doing much better on other dimensions. There may indeed be tensions between them.

In seeking to meet these varied purposes, it would be tempting to propose a long list of Complementary Indicators. However, a long list would be counterproductive. The length of the list of SDGs and associated targets has led to their being dismissed by some commentators. In order to be effective, the list of indicators included in the World Bank CI portfolio has to be sufficiently short that the new indicators get attention from the outside public and from policy makers. The number proposed here for the portfolio of Complementary Indicators is seven—see box 2.3 at the end of this chapter—although the method of counting adopted here is a little deceptive. In particular, an important element is the dashboard of nonmonetary indicators, which contains several dials. But even here parsimony is advocated. This should not be taken to imply that the many other possible indicators are without value; rather those selected are ones to which it is suggested that priority should be attached. There is a difference in this respect between the range of indicators made available via PovcalNet[2] (where no limits need apply) and the Complementary Indicators to which the World Bank gives prominence. The focus here is on the latter, while encouraging the further development of PovcalNet as a most valuable service.

Recommendation 11: The Bank should publish, alongside the global poverty count, a portfolio of Complementary Indicators (CI), including a multidimensional dashboard of outcome indicators, where the number of such indicators should be sufficiently small that they can receive prominence in public debate and in policy making; the selection of the Complementary Indicators should be based on an explicit set of principles, and the implementation of these principles should follow external consultation, including with the proposed external audit body.

The principles on which the Complementary Indicators should be based are the subject of the next subsection.

Principles for the Design of Indicators

In what follows, proposals are made for the Complementary Indicators, but it is fully recognized that those proposed here will simply enter together with others into the final decision process. There will be many inputs. The Report can, however, offer a further contribution: a synthesis of the principles that should be followed in drawing up a portfolio of indicators. The principles are not novel and underlie much of best practice in the field. (Indeed, a number underlie chapter 1 of this Report.) They are not, however, typically made explicit. Making them explicit—and open to debate—may serve to cement their role in the decision-making process.

The first principle for inclusion in the portfolio was enunciated clearly in the formulation of the SDGs, which are described as "global in nature and universally applicable" (United Nations 2015, para 55):

Principle 1: The coverage of the indicator should be truly global, covering the whole of the world population.

One immediate implication is that the calculations should, in principle, be susceptible of being implemented for all countries, developed as well as developing. It cannot be decreed by assumption that there is no poverty or deprivation in rich countries. This is likely to be particularly significant in the case of nonmonetary dimensions, where the thresholds may need to be set in a way that takes account of the level of development.

The second principle governing inclusion in the portfolio is one of transparency: that the indicator should have a clear purpose and be readily understood:

Principle 2: The indicator should be transparent and identify the essence of the problem.

The indicator must have intuitive validity and be meaningful to the user. This implies that the indicator itself should be easily explained and that the methods used to construct the indicator must be transparent and understandable.

The third principle governing inclusion in the portfolio is one of acceptability and normative interpretation:

Principle 3: The definition of the indicator should be generally accepted as valid and have a clear normative interpretation.

There has to be agreement both about the way the indicator is defined and about the direction of change that represents an improvement. For example, the gender composition of those below the poverty line is an issue discussed below. Examination of this dimension reflects the widespread concern about gender inequality, which features in the SDGs, and a belief that women are at present overrepresented among the deprived. In terms of acceptance, this principle underlines the need for widespread consultation, including listening to the "voices of the poor" via participatory activities (see Narayan et al. 2000).

The fourth principle for inclusion is that an indicator should be measurable in a way that commands general support:

Principle 4: The indicator should be sufficiently robust and statistically validated; there should be a clear structure of accountability for its definition and construction.

This requirement is evident from the discussion in chapter 1. Here two obvious considerations are underlined. The first is that the construction of new Complementary Indicators may take the World Bank into uncharted areas, raising potential new statistical problems. The second is that the circumstances of those suffering poverty or social exclusion (for example, those at the bottom of the income distribution, or the unemployed, or those living in institutions and the homeless) are among the most difficult to measure statistically. (The same may also be true of those at the very top of the distribution, such as the rich living in gated communities or with offshore assets.)

In chapter 1, stress was placed on the need to reconcile the global estimates of extreme poverty with the national estimates of the extent of poverty (measured possibly according to a different standard). The same issue of reconciliation applies to the Complementary Indicators:

> Principle 5: Indicators constructed with global coverage of countries should be cross-checked against information available at the level of individual countries.

This principle is embodied in concrete shape via the proposed publication by the World Bank of National Poverty Statistics Reports, but it also underlines the need for external audit, and for the active engagement with the wider statistical community.

The introduction of multidimensional indicators raises new issues:

> Principle 6: Where indicators are either combined as in a multi-dimensional measure, or presented in conjunction as in a dashboard, the portfolio of indicators should be balanced across different dimensions.

In seeking to secure such balance, it is necessary to consider the theoretical and ethical underpinnings for the inclusion of different indicators and the way in which they interact. These issues are discussed further in the section in this chapter on "Nonmonetary Poverty." It should be noted that this principle is *not* assumed to apply across the different components of the portfolio of Complementary Indicators. There is no suggestion, for instance, that indicator (1) (the poverty gap) has equal importance with the dashboard of nonmonetary measures. The relative significance of the different CI components is a matter on which users and policy makers will have different views.

The final principle is that the measurement of an indicator should not impose too large a burden on countries, nor on enterprises, nor on citizens:

> Principle 7: The design of social indicators should, wherever possible, make use of information already available. Where new information is needed, then it should be obtained, as far as feasible, using existing instruments or by making use of administrative data.

The cost of the assembly of the proposed statistics does not simply consist of the salaries of those in central or regional offices; it is not limited to the state budget. The cost arises in the diversion of clerks from drawing up payrolls and from the diversion of the time of farmers in a busy harvest season. The costs may not only be time and money. The survey process may have unseen costs via the generation of fear and suspicion about the use to which the information could be put. New sources of data, such as via the suppliers of Internet services, may initially mask the collection of data but later give rise to widespread concern.

What Are We Looking For?

In each case, as one considers complements to the SDG Global Poverty goal, it has to be asked how the new indicator would affect our understanding of concrete aspects of extreme poverty measurement. First, does the indicator affect appreciation of the scale of the problem and how it is changing over time? In its estimate of 896.7 million is the World Bank understating, as some critics say, or is it overstating, as others assert? How would alternative approaches lead us to take a different view of the changes over time? Again there are divisions of view between those who believe that the rate of progress has been more rapid than recorded by the $1.90 a day-based statistics (for example, Sala-i-Martin and Pinkovskiy 2010) and those who argue that alternative approaches lead to a sense of even greater urgency. Second, by focusing on consumption, are other important dimensions of material deprivation being missed (including those covered by other SDGs)? How important is the omission of nonmarket goods, such as access to education or health care? What happens when the problem is viewed in terms of multidimensional deprivation, and how can the overlap of deprivations best be taken into consideration? Third, how do different concepts and measures lead us to take a different view about the composition of poverty? Does it have a different geographic distribution? Is it more rural or more urban? How does it differ by gender? Are there important ethnic or cultural dimensions? An important instance has already been signaled: Complementary Indicators may be available on an individual basis, casting light on within-household inequality.

In each case, one has to look ahead to the uses to which the indicators—both monetary and nonmonetary—may be put in policy design. In the United States, the official poverty line has come to play a central role in government policy; it is the basis for determining eligibility for many federal and state government programs (Office of the Federal Register 2015, 3237). In China, the government of China "has launched the 'Accurate Development-oriented Poverty Alleviation Project' that uses multidimensional poverty indicators to identify and register every poor household and poor village into the information system. This will provide the data for a more effective way to target, to monitor poor households and villages, and to improve the effectiveness of the development-oriented poverty policies and programs."[3]

Enriching the Analysis of Those in Economic Poverty

This section maintains the basic measuring rod of consumption per head, and the application of a poverty line based in origin on national poverty standards, but considers alternative analyses of the results designed to enrich our understanding of poverty and to guide policy making.

Poverty Gaps and the Depth of Poverty

The depth, as well as the extent, of poverty is an important consideration. People living on less than half of $1.90 a day are indeed extremely poor. Depth is not captured by the simple head count (or head count ratio), and there is strong support for measuring the poverty gaps (see, for example, Cruz et al. 2015). There are concerns that, although the extent of poverty may have declined, the very poorest may have fallen further behind (see, in the case of the United States, Jencks 2016).

The limitations of the head count as a summary measure of the extent of poverty have been well known since the article by Sen (1976) on the theory of poverty measurement. The head count pays no attention to how far people fall below the poverty line. In one country, everyone may be close to reaching the poverty standard; in another, many people may be far below. Using the head count as the criterion may lead to apparently perverse conclusions. Suppose that 5 rupees are given to a person who is 2 rupees below the poverty line, raising the recipient out of poverty, but that the 5 rupees are found by taking them away from another person who is 2 rupees below the poverty line. Poverty measured by the head count falls, but it is not evident that this should be chalked up as a policy success, since the second person has been left in more serious poverty. This is not just a theoretical concern. It may be tempting for policy makers to concentrate help on those most easily raised above the poverty line. In the design of social security transfers there is often a choice between raising universal benefits and targeting transfers to those with the lowest incomes. Income-tested transfers, however, commonly reach only a proportion of those entitled on grounds of incomplete take-up or lack of information (Atkinson 2015, 210–11). This means that, while the targeted transfers may raise the recipients above the poverty line, they do not help the worst-off at the very bottom (those not reached). The poverty head count ratio in this way can overstate the relative effectiveness of targeting. (For a concrete example of the impact of different policies in reducing child poverty in the United Kingdom, see Sutherland and Piachaud 2001.)

The poverty gap, in contrast, is defined as the mean shortfall in consumption from the poverty line, where the mean is measured over the whole population, counting the nonpoor as having zero shortfall, and where the mean is expressed as a percentage of the poverty line. If all those below the poverty line were to have no consumption, then the shortfall in every case would be equal to the poverty line, and the poverty gap would be equal to the head count ratio.[4] In reality, the extreme poor have some positive consumption, so that the shortfall is less than complete, and the poverty gap as a percentage is less than the head count ratio. In 2012, the PovcalNet estimates, with the 2011 PPP\$1.90[5] a day per person poverty line, show the poverty gap as 3.72 percent and the head count ratio as 12.73 percent. In aggregate terms, the 896.7 million in extreme poverty had a total annual poverty gap of 182 billion international dollars (3.72 percent of 7.04 billion times \$1.90 times 365). An alternative is to divide the poverty gap by the head count ratio, yielding what is called the "income gap ratio" (3.72 divided by 12.73 gives 29.2 percent) (Sen and Foster 1997, 169). The income gap ratio is the gap averaged over those in poverty, not over the whole population. In 2012, the extreme poor on average were about 55 cents a day (29.2 percent of \$1.90) below the poverty line.

At an aggregate level, the poverty gap provides a valuable gauge of the scale of the problem—3.72 percent seems more manageable than 12.73 percent, and corresponds to the reality that most of the extreme poor are not totally without resources. At the individual level, it avoids the perverse outcome of the rupee example given above: the total gap falls by 3 (and hence the mean is reduced). At the same time, Sen (1976) also criticized the poverty gap on the grounds that it attached the same weight to all shortfalls of income below the poverty line. This led him to propose, but not christen, the Sen poverty index, which weights the poverty gaps according to the rank of the household in the distribution of people below the poverty line, so that the very poorest gets the highest rank, and the household nearest the poverty line gets zero weight. In its use of rank as a weight, the Sen poverty index is the counterpart of the Gini coefficient of inequality.[6]

There have subsequently been proposals for a variety of different poverty indexes, of which the most widely used is that proposed by Foster, Greer, and Thorbecke (1984).[7] The FGT index, as it is known, weights the poverty gaps according to the distance from the poverty line, relative to the poverty line. The weight is the relative distance to a power, so that, when combined with the poverty gap itself, the relevant expression is the relative distance to an exponent equal to the power of the weight *plus one*. For the poverty gap itself, the power is zero, and the measure is referred to as FGT1. Where the power is greater than 0, more weight is given to larger gaps. PovcalNet gives routinely "the squared poverty gap," FGT2, which corresponds to taking weights with a power of 1, giving an exponent of 2. These weighting systems can be quite different.[8]

Use of the poverty gap as a representation of the depth of poverty is attractive, but there are several qualifications. The first is that—despite the excellent expositions that exist—it remains the case that these more complex measures are not easily explained to a wider audience. This applies to the indexes: What "can a squared-poverty-gap index actually signify? And how to explain it to a government Minister" (Duclos and Araar 2006, 84). Of poverty depth measures in general, Castleman, Foster, and Smith (2015, 2) say that, while they capture "the intensity as well as the prevalence of poverty, they are often not central to policy discourse because they are perceived to be too 'unintuitive' to have traction."

Greater efforts in exposition are needed to overcome these obstacles to transparency and to satisfy Principle 2.

The second concern is practical (Principle 4). The sensitivity of the poverty gap, and of the poverty indexes, to differences in the depth of poverty implies—by the same token—that the measure is more sensitive to errors of measurement. Put simply, the statisticians may be confident that a household is below the poverty line of 30 rupees but less confident as to whether the shortfall is 10 or 15 rupees, a difference that would change the weight with the FGT2 measure from one-third to one-half. In the case of the poverty gap, there are reasons to expect the poverty gap to be proportionately more affected by nonsampling error, particularly those arising from recording errors of low incomes. Zero is quite frequently recorded for income, and indeed recorded income may be negative, almost certainly mismeasuring consumption.[9] Grounds for believing that this is the case are provided by the countries in PovcalNet where results on both bases are quoted: in Mexico in 2012, the income-based survey reported a head count ratio that is 2.2 times that in the consumption survey, but the poverty gap is 3.3 times that in the consumption survey. When using measures of the depth of poverty, such as the poverty gap, it becomes even more problematic to amalgamate income and consumption measures.

The third reason arises from consideration of the underlying judgments. Concern with the depth of poverty has been represented by the weighting of the poverty shortfall. The weights can, however, vary considerably across the households below the poverty line, and it is not evident that this degree of variation is appropriate. In the case of the rank order version of Sen (1976), there are good reasons, as shown by Shorrocks (1995), for taking the ranks, not just within the poor population but also over the whole population in the country. Probing further shows that the rank order weights, modified as above, have, when viewed over the whole distribution of consumption, a slow/quick/slow property: initially, the weights fall slowly with the level of consumption, but then the decline accelerates up to the mode (assuming a single mode), after which the fall slows down again as the top is reached (Atkinson and Brandolini 2010, 17). Seen this way, the rank order weights appear to be steering us back toward the simple head count ratio. In the limit, the extreme poverty line is drawn so low that sharp distinctions are not drawn between people living below. Such an "either/ or" view is, moreover, the natural result of adopting the alternative "rights" view of poverty, under which a minimum standard of living is seen as a basic right (Atkinson 1987). For assessing SDG 1.4 ("equal right to economic resources"), the head count ratio may be sufficient.

These reservations about the poverty gap lead to the conclusion that the poverty gap is unlikely to replace the head count as the headline indicator, but its evident advantage in highlighting the severity of poverty means that, when properly conveyed, it can play a valuable role in the portfolio of Complementary Indicators.

> Recommendation 12: The portfolio of Complementary Indicators should include the mean poverty gap, relative to the International Poverty Line, measured over the whole population and expressed as a percentage of the poverty line.

This could be supplemented by the total poverty gap in currency terms (multiplying by the total population and by the poverty line). This currency total, seen as the minimum of the amount required to deal with extreme poverty, provides a graphic guide to the scale of the resources necessary to tackle global poverty.

Alternative Poverty Lines

For many years the World Bank has recognized multiple poverty lines. The 1990 World Development Report (WDR) applied a line of $275 a year for the "extremely poor" and $370 a year for the "poor" (World Bank 1990, table 2.1). The 2000/2001 WDR, in addition to the $1 a day (strictly $1.08 a day), showed the results of an upper poverty line of $2 a day, "reflecting poverty lines more commonly used in lower-middle-income countries" (World Bank 2001, 17).

Employment of multiple poverty lines provides one test of the sensitivity of the estimates, and it can form a valuable part of a battery of such tests. There can be greater confidence in the monitoring exercise if a range of poverty lines around the International Poverty Line all show a decline in the head count ratio: there is then "dominance" (Atkinson 1987). However, it is not clear that multiple poverty lines should be elevated to the status of an indicator. Use of a different— higher—poverty line is one way of allowing for the possibility that

Table 2.1 Characteristics of Different Approaches to Poverty Measurement

	International Poverty Line as set by World Bank	Basic needs–based indicator	Capability approach	Minimum rights
Focus	Standard of living	Satisfaction of basic needs	Capabilities	Enjoyment of minimum rights
Dimension of poverty line	Single	Single	Single or multiple	Single or multiple
Unit of analysis	Household	Household	Individual	Individual
Allows for diversified characteristics of household or individuals	No	Equivalence scale	Wider class of differences	Wider class: for example, rights of child
Context in which poverty status assessed	Isolated	Isolated	Societal	Societal
Empirical feasibility	Yes	Yes	Probable	Probable

people above the International Poverty Line are in fact close to poverty, and are at risk of falling below, but simply taking a mechanical multiple does not seem to be the right course. It would fall foul of Principle 3 in that there is no evident justification for taking a particular multiple. It would not satisfy those who are critical of the existing $1.90 line. It would adjust all country lines by the same percentage, whereas the relativities are open to question. As put to us by the International Movement ATD Fourth World (2015, 5), "tracking poverty on other lines, such as $4 or $10, would just replicate the same problems and weaknesses." Rather, the later sections of the Report explore alternative starting points that generate alternative poverty lines.

Women and Children in Poverty

There is widespread concern that both women and children are disproportionately represented among the global poor. The *Millennium Development Goals Report 2015* states that "women face a greater risk of living in poverty" (United Nations 2015a, 16). According to the Global Coalition of Partners to End Child Poverty (2015, para 1.5), "the most recent data tell us that nearly half of the world's extreme poor are 18 years old and under, whilst they constitute one third of the world's population. In nearly every country with available data, children are more likely to live in poverty than other groups (even in the world's most developed countries)." Moreover, as expressed powerfully by Peter Saunders, a member of the Advisory Board, "child poverty differs fundamentally from adult poverty not only in how it is experienced and the extent to which those affected can be regarded as being responsible for their plight, but also in terms of its longer-term effects" (Saunders 2015, 9).

Concern with the position of women and children permeates the SDGs. Right from the first goal, Goal 1.1 refers explicitly to "men, women, and children." SDG Goal 4 on education refers to girls and boys, men and women, and Goal 4.5 refers to the elimination of gender disparities in education. SDG Goal 5 is specifically concerned with "Gender equality and empowering all women and girls." Goal 8 on "Decent work" refers to this as an objective for "all women and men," as well as introducing the subject of child labor. Goal 10 is directed at ensuring social inclusion for all, irrespective of age and sex. Goal 11 on sustainable cities and communities treats the "needs of those in vulnerable situations" and the need for "safe places," where those identified include women and children. The SDGs also refer in Goal 8 to the position of "youth," seeking to "reduce the proportion of youth not in employment, education or training" and referring to a "strategy for youth employment." Many countries, including high-income countries, have policies directed at this age group. The Arab Republic of Egypt devoted its 2010 Human Development Report to youth in Egypt, noting that those aged 18–29 accounted for a quarter of the population (UNDP and Institute of National Planning 2010).

These groups have to be defined if they are to be the basis for social indicators. There is wide agreement that "children" should be defined according to the internationally agreed age definition 0–17 under the Convention of the Rights of The Child. The definition of "young adults" requires consideration. The United Nations, for statistical purposes, defines "youth" as "those persons between the ages of 15 and 24 years, without prejudice to other definitions by Member States" (UNDESA 2016), but this would overlap with the definition of children at ages 16 and 17. Here it is proposed that "young adults" covers those aged between 18 and 24 years.

Gender and childhood/youth are, of course, two different dimensions. The disadvantaged position of women is a matter of concern independently of issues of child poverty. Conversely, child poverty is related to the poverty of women but is a distinct issue. They are discussed together here, not to conflate them, but because they are the two dimensions where priority is given to disaggregation of the global poverty figure. On account of the (separate) intrinsic concerns and of the evident interconnections in both directions with the other SDGs, it is recommended that:[10]

> Recommendation 13: The global poverty figure, and the counterpart national figures, should be accompanied by the numbers of women, children, and young adults living in households with consumption below the International Poverty Line, as well as the number of female-headed households below the International Poverty Line.

The recommended disaggregation by gender and age would meet the request by bodies such as the U.S. Agency for International Development (USAID), which in its section on "applying rigorous analysis" refers to the need "for sex-disaggregated, gender-sensitive poverty statistics in a gender analysis" (USAID 2015, 37). It would respond to the call in the World Bank Group Gender Strategy for "a stronger monitoring system to capture results . . . whether gaps between males and females are being closed" (World Bank 2015a, 29). At the same time, the disaggregation should be accompanied by a clear health warning, particularly with respect to that by gender. As explained in chapter 1, the global total refers not to individual poverty but to people living in households that as a whole are poor. The proposed figures for women would equally refer only to those living in poor households. This highlights the need for a clear distinction between

> Question 1: How many women live in households that have consumption below the poverty line?

and

> Question 2: How many women have individual consumption below the poverty line?

The recommended statistic provides an answer only to Question 1. As such, it may not satisfy Principle 2, because it does not necessarily identify the essence of the problem. It would not provide support, or otherwise, to the often-quoted, but rarely footnoted, statement that "70 percent of the world's poor are women" (see Marcoux 1998; Greenberg 2014; and Ravallion 2016a, box 7.4)—a statement that presumably, although not made clear, refers to Question 2. This is indeed important, because the 70 percent statement has typically been challenged by studies that answer Question 1, and that cast doubts on the 70 percent figure based on demographic implausibility. For example, Marcoux (1998) refers to within-household inequality, but his approach, based on the greater poverty rate of female-headed households, does not allow for greater poverty of women in male-headed households. This does not involve "excess" women in the poorest households, because the men are still there—just better off.

Recommendation 13 is therefore accompanied by strong support for the initiatives already in train in the World Bank to develop estimates of individual poverty status, such as the work of the Gender Cross-Cutting Solutions Area (World Bank 2016a). These individual measures may be obtained indirectly via inferences from household consumption, as discussed in chapter 1, or may be direct measures based on nonmonetary indicators that can be recorded directly on an individual basis, as discussed later in this chapter.[11] Investment in this research is essential if we are to provide a satisfactory answer to the question that everyone seems to skirt, but to which they would like to know the answer: How many women are poor?

For children, the same issue arises. The proposed statistics would tell us the number of children living in households with consumption below the poverty line, but not the number of children whose individual consumption is below the poverty line. But there is also a further issue, on which the recommended statistics throw no light, but which should enter into their interpretation: child labor. Child labor is extensive. The estimates by the International Labour Organization (ILO) show that, according to their definition, worldwide 120 million children aged 5 to 14 were engaged in child labor in 2012 (ILO 2013, figure 5l see also ILO 2015),[12] boys and girls being almost equally represented. The policy implications are complex (Basu 1999) and are likely to vary from country to country, but there are evident potential conflicts with achievement of other SDGs. This is an issue that should qualify the statistics under discussion. The potential consequences of a scaling back of child labor, as educational objectives are achieved, could be tracked in "counterfactual" poverty rate calculations showing the impact on total measured poverty if child labor were to be discounted from household resources in monetary poverty measurement.

Within-Country Disaggregation

In chapter 1, the issue of rural/urban disaggregation was investigated, and the breakdown by gender and age has just been considered. There are, however, a number of reasons why there is interest in subnational poverty measurement. In part, these are geographical—provinces, states, and districts—and in part they involve disaggregation across socioeconomic groupings such as formal or informal sector, ethnicity, religion, and caste. For instance, SDG Goal 10.2 refers to "the social, economic and political inclusion of all, irrespective of age, sex, disability, race, ethnicity, origin, religion or economic or other status." (It should be noted that this does not refer here to the issue of group-specific poverty lines developed because of price differences—for example, rural-urban—or needs differences—for example, gender.)

What, then, is the "right" level of (dis)aggregation for poverty measurement? The answer depends in turn on the reason for the disaggregation. There are two reasons why one might wish to disaggregate an index of poverty; one is instrumental, the other intrinsic. These are considered in turn.

The instrumental reason is related to the design of policy, where the objective is taken to be that of national poverty minimization. But suppose that policy instruments to achieve this goal are limited in number and scope, for example, if constitutional constraints prevent the central federal government from dictating distributional policy within its constituent provinces or states, but that it can allocate central funds differentially across these provinces. Then it should be clear that provincial poverty may well appear in the formula for national poverty-minimizing allocation. This is shown, for example, in Kanbur (1987) in a model of indicator-based targeting. More generally, the availability of any form of "tagging" information allows policy makers to target expenditures more efficiently for national poverty minimization, but the rules for tagging will depend on the statistical properties of the groups being tagged, including their poverty index, or some transformation of their poverty index. This rationalizes disaggregated presentation of poverty data.

Could there be an intrinsic rationale for considering group-specific poverty above and beyond its contribution to national poverty? Consider the case of two provinces in a nation, one of which has a low incidence of poverty but a large population, whereas the other has a high incidence of poverty but a much smaller population, so much so that it accounts for a lower share of the nation's poor. It could therefore be seen as a lower policy priority. However, the argument could be made that poverty is such a fundamental characteristic of a province as an entity that population weights should not be applied in calculating contribution to national poverty. Rather, each province's poverty should be given equal weight in national deliberations. An analogous argument on political representation establishes that in many federations one of the houses of parliament has equal representation from the constituent provinces or states (as in the U.S. Senate) rather than representation in proportion to population.

A case can, moreover, be made for a range of sociodemographic groupings relevant to assessing the degree of inequality of opportunity. The arguments put forward by, among others, Roemer (1998), suggest that distributional differences across groupings that capture features exogenous to individual effort (ethnicity, for example) have special normative significance. Thus, among other indicators, poverty differences across such groupings capture structural unfairness of economic processes in a society. In this sense, presentation of poverty at this disaggregated level conveys normative content that would be obscured in the overall poverty measure.

Particular reference should be made here to the position of indigenous peoples. According to the United Nations Permanent Forum on Indigenous Issues (UNPFII) (2016), there are some 370 million indigenous peoples living in 70 countries across the world. There is evidence that they face much higher rates of poverty. The World Bank (2016) study in Latin America, where there are estimated to be some 42 million indigenous people, found that they face poverty rates that are on average twice as high as for the rest of Latin Americans. Measured in terms of the percentage of people living on less than the International Poverty Line ($1.25 PPP in the late 2000s), 9 percent were below compared with only 3 percent for nonindigenous people, based on a weighted average for Bolivia, Brazil, Ecuador, Guatemala, Mexico, and Peru (World Bank 2016, figure 10). Nor can the difference be fully explained by demographic and economic differences between indigenous peoples and the rest of the population. In Bolivia, Ecuador, Guatemala, Mexico, and Peru, only about half the gap in poverty rates between indigenous and nonindigenous peoples can be accounted for in this way (Calvo-González 2016).

No recommendation is made here regarding further disaggregation, but the considerations set out above, and the principles set out in the previous section, provide a basis for assessing any future case.

Persistence of Poverty

Poverty measures calculated from household survey data typically provide "snapshots" of the extent of poverty at the time of the survey, because they are cross-section surveys. This means that when a new survey is mounted in a given country it comprises an entirely new sample of households. One is unable to track the circumstances of individual households over time, and one cannot, therefore, say anything about the duration, or persistence, of poverty. Thus a comparison of the incidence of poverty in India between 2004 and 2009 is able to tell us how much overall poverty increased, or decreased, during this interval. What the comparison is unable to tell us is what proportion of the poor in 2004 remained in poverty in 2009, or how many of the poor in 2009 were not in poverty five years earlier.

There are multiple reasons as to why information about the persistence of poverty might be of interest. There may be normative grounds to worry more about poverty if it is a "chronic" condition than if there is a high rate of turnover among the poor. Certainly, the nature and form of policy interventions is likely to be different when addressing "transient" versus "chronic" poverty. In the case of the former, policy makers might focus on introducing or strengthening a safety net that aims to prevent households from falling into poverty as a result of some unforeseen event.[13] In the case of chronic poverty, policy makers will be generally more focused on enhancing human and physical assets of the poor—in an effort to lift them, in a sustained way, out of poverty.

To produce estimates of the persistence of poverty, cross-section surveys are not enough. Panel data are needed. Panel surveys follow the same households over time, and are therefore able to observe directly whether households drop in or out of poverty, or remain in poverty over extended periods of time. But panel data remain scarce in practice, particularly in the developing world. There are currently too few proper panel data sets to allow for a reliable estimate of the persistence of poverty at the global level. Such surveys are typically expensive, are administratively and logistically complex, and are associated with a variety of analytical challenges linked to measurement error and attrition. It is unlikely, therefore, that there will be a dramatic expansion of panel surveys in the near future.

It is therefore necessary to consider alternatives. One potentially promising direction concerns recent efforts to apply statistical imputation methods to convert multiple rounds of cross-section surveys into "synthetic panels." Such synthetic panels offer an ability to decompose national poverty estimates into a chronic and transient component without having to draw on true panel data. A growing number of studies compare estimates of poverty dynamics from such synthetic panels to those that derive from true panel data, with encouraging results (Bourguignon and Moreno 2015; Cruces et al. 2011; Dang et al. 2014; Dang and Lanjouw 2013, 2014, and 2015; Martinez et al. 2013). It remains, however, that this is a recent field of analysis; and it cannot be judged, at present, to be ready for the scaling-up effort needed to produce estimates across the globe. Indeed, with respect to the Principles governing inclusion in the portfolio of Complementary Indicators, one would currently still worry about the transparency (Principle 2) and robustness (Principle 4) of the estimates of poverty persistence derived from these synthetic panel methods.

Alternative Approaches to Measuring Poverty

This section considers four different points of departure: subjective views ("asking people"), basic needs, capabilities, and minimum rights. In each case, these can lead to a different view *either* about the assessment of individual/household status *or* about the poverty standard to be applied (as with the alternative poverty lines referred to earlier), *or* about both. The four starting points are different from that adopted in the World Bank estimates, but they may have entered indirectly via the national poverty lines that lay at the origin of the $1.90 standard. Quite a number of the national poverty lines are, for example, derived on a basic needs approach. Moreover, in many cases, the poverty lines applied in the World Bank country Poverty Assessments are constructed using some version of the basic needs method.

Asking People

A criticism commonly expressed in submissions to the Commission is that more should be done to solicit the views of the people living in extreme poverty. Such a participatory approach should learn from the experience of the poor in the countries where most of them are to be found. Why, it is asked, is the measurement of poverty designed in an institution based in a country where extreme poverty is assumed to be nonexistent? Why does the discussion seem to be dominated by the research of those who—like the Chair of this Commission—live in high-income countries?

This criticism overlooks the fact that the World Bank has based its poverty line on the national lines found in the poorest countries for which such lines exist (see the first section in chapter 1). From the outset, the World Bank was drawing on conceptions of poverty in poor countries. At the same time, there is a case for wider participation, and for engaging the poor in poor countries. The World Bank has indeed been alive to this criticism. A major feature of the *World Development Report 2000/2001* was the "Voices of the Poor" background study. This was based on a review of participatory studies involving some 40,000 poor people in 50 countries, and on a comparative study in 1999 in 23 countries engaging about 20,000 poor people (World Bank 2001, 3, box 1). There were a series of books (Narayan et al. 2000 and 2000a, and Narayan and Petesch 2002), the first of these stating that "the development discourse about poverty has been dominated by the perspectives and expertise of those who are not poor" (Narayan et al. 2000, 2). More recent research has demonstrated the potential. Just to give one example, using household survey microdata from Benin (low income), Mexico (upper-middle income), and the United Kingdom (high income), Nandy and Gordon (2015, abstract) "show how, in each of the countries selected, there is a high degree of consensus about the necessaries of life, and that such consensus allows for the identification and establishment of social norms and those individuals/groups unable to meet such norms due to a lack of resources to be identified."

At the same time, there are limits to what can be learned from "asking people," and not all views are equally valid.[14] In particular, we may wish to ignore completely expressions of negative feelings toward others, such as the denial of the existence of poverty and hardship. Many years ago, in a more vigorous treatment of welfare economics than typically takes place today, Sir Dennis Robertson (1954, 678) dismissed such elements, saying that our judgments should not "be eroded by the gnawings of the green-eyed monster." He was referring to jealousy, but his warning would apply today to views based on religious bigotry and xenophobia.

With this qualification, much can be learned from a participatory approach. As put by the Global Coalition of Partners to End Child Poverty (2015, para 1.4), it is "only through a better representation and understanding of poverty—including who is poor . . . and how they experience poverty—[that] we can meet the urgent challenges of ending poverty in all its dimensions and reducing inequalities, leaving no one behind." The reference to "all its dimensions" is important. The findings of the "Voices of the Poor" study suggested that poverty was seen as consisting of many interlocking dimensions, where lack of food, poor health, and illness; lack of access to public goods; and powerlessness were judged to be more important than monetary poverty. This underlines the significance of multidimensional indicators, discussed below in "Nonmonetary Poverty," and the potential role of the participatory approach in identifying the relevant domains.

It remains nonetheless the case that the participation approach can inform the measurement of monetary poverty. What can be learned? Subjective questions directed at estimating the extent of poverty can involve four types of approach:

1. The first is to ask people to assess their own poverty status without any reference to a poverty line, and the total in poverty is then those who classify themselves as "living in extreme poverty" (where the exact formulation of the question is clearly crucial).

2. The second asks people about the minimum consumption they consider necessary to avoid extreme poverty, and then asks whether or not their own consumption meets that standard.
3. The third asks people about the minimum consumption they consider necessary to avoid extreme poverty, and then obtains information about the household's consumption to determine whether or not their own consumption meets that standard.
4. The fourth asks people where the extreme poverty line, defined in terms of consumption, should be set, where this enters into the determination of the poverty line for the whole population (and no assessment is made of the status of the household interviewed).

These are obviously different. The fourth is closest to the World Bank procedure, in that it leads to a population-wide poverty line. It has indeed been extensively used. In the United Kingdom, the 1983 Breadline Britain study (Mack and Lansley 1985) identified the poor as those suffering from an enforced lack of socially perceived necessities. These necessities were identified by public opinion as possessions and "activities" that every family should be able to afford and that nobody should have to live without (only items considered a necessity by at least 50 percent of the population were retained). The other three approaches lead to an assessment at the level of the responding household. The first makes no explicit reference to consumption; the others are mediated through consumption per head. Approaches (1) and (2) are based on *subjective* assessments of poverty status, where subjective is contrasted with *objective* measurement from survey information recorded by external observers, as in approach (3). But in all of the first three approaches, the poverty line being applied varies from one household to another. Any reported poverty line would be an average over respondents. It should equally be noted that both approaches (1) and (2) can be applied to individuals within the household, and may provide a source of evidence about within-household inequality.

In interpreting the information obtained from participatory studies, the differences are important. As is well known (for example from the literature on the use of reported happiness), the responses may reflect both adaptation and aspiration. Where people have adjusted to low levels of living, they may have adapted to these levels and regard mere survival as escaping poverty. In the opposite direction, responses may be influenced by rising aspirations, where people above the objective poverty line see themselves falling behind rising living standards elsewhere. In both cases, there is a potential bias, in the first case downward and in the second case upward. Moreover, the bias may differentially affect different groups. Remote rural communities, for instance, may be more likely to be affected by adaptation and for their extreme poverty to be understated.

In terms of concrete implementation, three possible roles may be envisaged for the collection of information by participatory input. The first is the inclusion of questions on subjective poverty assessment (approach (1)) in the quick surveys carried out to provide more frequent information. Inclusion would provide both more up-to-date measures of progress and a useful triangulation with the Global Poverty statistics. If subjective assessments indicated a different direction of movement, then this would warrant investigation. One situation where the input may be especially valuable is in covering countries that are in conflict, where no regular statistics are available.

The second application is to the choice of alternative poverty lines. As argued above, the alternative lines should not be simple multiples of the International Poverty Line, but based on a reasoned argument. One (although not the only) input into this choice of alternative lines should be information obtained by approach (4). Do those living around the extreme poverty level consider that it is realistic? What is the view of those living in countries where there are many people in extreme poverty? The World Bank has already shown itself open to making use of this kind of evidence, and it is recommended that there be a more systematic employment of the findings, which could be a useful adjunct to the proposal made below for an alternative needs-based poverty line.

The third application is to learn more generally from participatory studies about the design of the portfolio of Complementary Indicators. One aim of the Complementary Indicators is to give voice to those individual circumstances that are not brought out by household-based measures, particularly the position of women and children. The Global Coalition of Partners to End Child Poverty (2015) has stressed how "participatory methods allow us to capture the views and perspectives of children, young people and other vulnerable groups providing valuable insight to better understand and contextualize poverty, vulnerability and exclusion." Referring to the need for greater effort "to ensure that all children are counted as part of poverty assessments, including children living outside of households and/or without parental care," they say that "nothing reveals this more clearly than listening to children themselves, about what they need and what they want" (Global Coalition of Partners to End Child Poverty 2105, para 1.1). Or as Jolly (2012, xxxi) puts it, "child poverty is . . . very different from adult poverty defined in terms of living below \$1.25 a day. . . . For a child, . . . adequacy must be assessed not just in terms of a child's immediate needs but in terms of what the child needs to grow in strength and capabilities so as to reach adulthood, with the basic capabilities needed for being a good citizen, within the community and beyond."

> Recommendation 14: The World Bank should explore the use of subjective assessments of personal poverty status (in "quick" surveys of poverty), and of the minimum consumption considered necessary to avoid extreme poverty, as an aid to interpreting the conclusions drawn from the global poverty estimates.

In implementing this recommendation, a significant role may be played by nonmonetary indicators.

Basic Needs

If the participatory approach to poverty is a relatively recently adopted approach, the foundation of poverty measurement on a concept of *basic needs* has long roots. Each country has its own history in this regard. In the United Kingdom, the chocolate manufacturer Seebohm Rowntree (1901) drew on the work of early nutritionists to determine minimum food requirements for a household to which were added other "necessaries," consisting of clothing, fuel, and sundries, and an addition covering the rent paid. In the United States, an early application of linear programming was to the derivation of minimum cost diets that met specified nutritional requirements (see Dorfman, Samuelson, and Solow 1958, 9n).[15] The official U.S. poverty line developed from work of Orshansky (1965), who took as her starting point the estimates of minimum food expenditure by the U.S. Department of Agriculture, examined the proportion of income spent on food in households of different types, and then multiplied up the food spending by the reciprocal of this proportion. In India, in 1962 the Planning Commission set a minimum consumption level as a target for the fifth Five Year Plan. According to Allen (2013, 8), this is probably based on the "minimal level" diet published by Sukhatme (1961), multiplied up to allow for nonfood spending.

Today, a basic needs approach is widely employed in the derivation of national poverty lines. For example, in Jamaica, starting in 1998, the poverty line has been defined in terms of a food basket designed to provide a minimum nutritional requirement for a family of five. An addition is made for nonfood items to cover the cost of clothing, footwear, transport, health and educational services, and other personal expenses (Planning Institute of Jamaica 2007). Similar procedures are followed in many developing countries. In the European Union, there has been extensive research on consensual budget standards (see, for example, Bradshaw and Mayhew 2011, which contains a synthesis report covering 32 European countries). A major project, the EU Reference Budgets Network (see Goedemé et al. 2015 and, also, Storms et al. 2013), has led to the European Commission publishing for each Member State "the monthly budget requirements for an adequate food intake for three reference households" (for example, in the case of the Netherlands, European Commission 2016).

In considering the role of the basic needs approach in the design of the Complementary Indicators, it is useful to identify the three key steps:

1. Determination of nutritional requirements, here discussed in terms of individual food calorie requirements, which may vary with age and gender
2. Conversion of these requirements into a food budget, which involves the nutrition content of individual foods and their unit cost (taking account of the possible variation in prices)
3. Allowance for nonfood items

Each of these steps requires discussion. The first step may appear to involve no more than a reference to the scientific work of other international bodies, such as the World Health Organization (WHO) and the Food and Agriculture Organization (FAO). However, the specification of nutritional requirements is not straightforward. The calorie levels required depend on the level of physical activity assumed. The FAO (2001, 36) provides estimates of the energy requirement relative to basal metabolism ("sleep") at 1.0 that range from 1.53 when the main daily activity is "sedentary or light" through 1.76 ("active or moderately active") to 2.15 ("vigorous or vigorously active lifestyle"). In more detail, "sitting on a bus or train" is scored at 1.2 for both males and females, whereas pulling a two-person rickshaw is scored for males at six times greater (FAO 2001, 92). This has led to concern that differences in judgments generate widely different specifications of the calorific requirements in national poverty lines.

How far this objection renders the basic food needs approach infeasible depends on how large is the variation. Here a cross-check can be made against national experience (applying Principle 5). This is a matter on which the World Bank has already much information, and it is recommended that a systematic, and fully documented, analysis be conducted covering a wide range of countries. Figure 2.1 shows a selection

Figure 2.1 Calorie Requirements in Different Countries

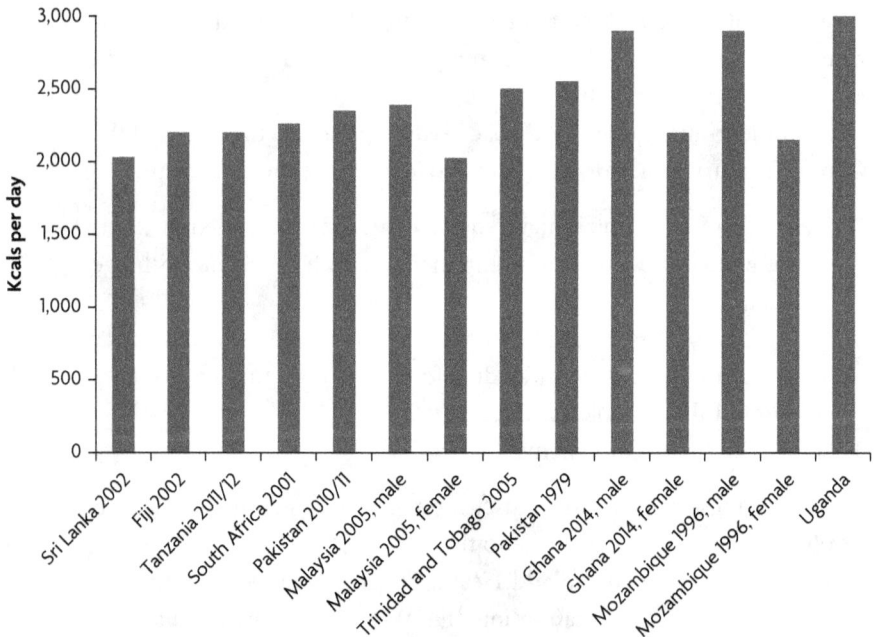

Sources: Sri Lanka Department of Census and Statistics 2004, 2; (Fiji) Narsey 2008, vii; Tanzania National Bureau of Statistics 2014, 92; Statistics South Africa 2008, 16; Pakistan Ministry of Finance 2013, 231; Malaysia Department of Statistics, no date, slides 12 and 13; Trinidad and Tobago Ministry of Social Development 2007, 13; Statistics Ghana 2014, table A8.2; (Mozambique) Datt et al. 2000, table 22; (Uganda) Appleton 1999, 10.
Note: In Sri Lanka, the Calorie requirement in 2002 was 2,030 Cal per day.

of the requirements embodied in national poverty lines, where these relate either to adults or represent a base rate. If the male and female rates are averaged, then all lie in the range from 2,200 to 2,600 Calories per adult per day, apart from Sri Lanka.[16] Such a range does not seem unmanageable. At the same time, the variation underscores the fact that judgment enters at each stage of the process.

The second step is the conversion of the nutritional requirements into food purchases. The diet produced by the early linear programming calculations in the United States led to questions as to whether it was realistic to assume that it would in practice be followed. In the pioneering U.K. study by Rowntree (1901), he drew also on actual dietaries used to feed people in institutions, leading him for example to include tea in the list of goods, even though it has no nutritional value. The minimum food expenditures used by Orshansky (1965) were not based solely on the intake of Calories and other nutrients, but also made judgments regarding an acceptable trade-off between nutritional standards and consumption patterns. These departures may mean that the poverty line is set higher, and that people living below the poverty line may secure the required calories by purchasing less expensive foods. For this reason, it is important to examine the relation between the calculated food budgets and actual food expenditure as it is found in different countries (see below).

The third step involves the addition of nonfood items, where there is considerable room for discretion. These items can be specified directly, in which case the underlying requirements, such as those for shelter, have to be identified. In this case, the overall basic needs poverty line is formed by adding the two parts: food and nonfood. Or the nonfood items can be allowed by multiplying the food part by the reciprocal of the food share. In this latter case, the crucial question is—whose food share? The practice in Ghana is described as follows: the "non-food basket is determined by those whose total food expenditure is about the level of the extreme poverty line (10 percent individuals below and above the line). . . . By selecting the population whose food consumption is around the extreme poverty line, their non-food expenditure is used as the benchmark for estimating the absolute poverty line" (Statistics Ghana 2014, 8). There is a degree of circularity in the calculation, and it may be highly sensitive where the food-spending share varies considerably.[17] If applied globally, there is the issue as to whether or not to apply a common food share across countries. In effect this would limit national variation to the second step. Another option would be the specification of a common procedure to derive the food share, and this should be investigated.

The conclusion is that the claims for the basic needs approach should be stated carefully. It cannot be said to provide a purely physiological foundation for measuring poverty, since at each stage a significant degree of judgment is being exercised. These judgments have to be weighed in the same way as those made elsewhere in global poverty calculations. It is not evident that it could be properly introduced without significant collection of new information (Principle 7). That said, the basic needs approach represents a position on the absolute/relative spectrum that adds to our understanding of poverty, and it is recommended that the World Bank add this to its program of work, in conjunction with other international agencies (box 2.1).

Box 2.1 Two Examples of Studies of Basic Needs at the Global Level

1. The study of food security by Kakwani and Son (2015), who make use of calorie norms that vary with age, gender, and lifestyle: with a range for men aged 31 to 50 from 2,200 Calories a day for a sedentary lifestyle to 3,000 a day for an active lifestyle. Country aggregates are then calculated: for India in 2007–8 they vary from 1,835 Calories sedentary a day; to 2,137 for moderate activity; to 2,420 active (2015, table 2). The authors are unable to measure activity levels within a country and note that "the variation is much larger across activity levels than across countries" (2015, 14). The level taken is 2,100 Calories per day, which is broadly the average for moderate activity across countries. (The National Bureau of Statistics in China has selected 2,100 Calories per day per person as the minimum nutritional intake.) From FAO data on 30 countries, Kakwani and Son estimate a relation between per capita calorie intake and the logarithm of per capita household food expenditure in local currency units that is converted into PPP 2005 dollars. This latter figure is then used, in conjunction with PovcalNet, to estimate for all countries covered the number of people who are living in households with total expenditure per capita below this level.
2. The study by Allen (2016) returns to the linear programming solution of the diet problem and examines the light that it casts on the International

(continued next page)

Box 2.1 (continued)

Poverty Line. He makes use of price data from the International Comparison Program (ICP) and elsewhere to solve for the least-cost diets that satisfy nutritional needs according to a hierarchy of needs, commencing with a 1,700 Calorie model, moving to 2,100 Calories, and then progressively adding to the range of nutrients. He asks two key questions: "the first is whether there is a set of nutritional standards that generates the World Bank's $1.90 poverty line. The second is whether there is a set of nutritional standards that is common across the world and that rationalizes the diets that poor people consume" (Allen 2016, 4). There is an evident parallel with the two roles proposed here, and his work (and that of Moatsos 2015) is a sign of the progress that can be made, as well as indicating the need for further investment in data, particularly with regard to prices.

A Basic Needs Measure of Poverty as a Complementary Indicator

The proposal for a basic needs measure of poverty is motivated by two roles that it can play as a Complementary Indicator.

The first role is that of providing a basis for an alternative poverty line for each country. As suggested earlier in this chapter, the choice of alternative poverty lines should not be based on a simple multiple of $1.90 a day per person. The second role for the basic needs approach is that of "inverting the telescope," as has been proposed in the context of the EU Social Indicators (Marlier et al. 2007). The discussion so far has run from basic needs to the resulting poverty line, but the approach is also illuminating in the reverse direction. The question becomes—what does $1.90 in 2011 PPPs a day per person allow a household to buy? By relating the poverty standard to household budgets, light can be cast on its implications for household living standards. There was a famous occasion in the United Kingdom during an inquiry into dockworkers' pay in the 1920s, when the union leader appeared in court bearing a plate bearing a few scraps of bacon, fish, and bread and asked the statistician (Sir Arthur Bowley) whether this was sufficient breakfast? Today, the basic needs calculations would allow different levels of total consumption to be mapped back to the level of nutritional intakes that they permit. The calculations would allow scrutiny of the allowance for nonfood items. In the case of India,

Drèze and Sen (2013, 189) note that the Indian "reference budget associated with the urban poverty line includes . . . ten rupees per month for 'footwear' and forty rupees per month for health care. The former would just about make it possible to get a sandal strap repaired once a month, and the latter might buy something like the equivalent of an aspirin a day." Subramanian (2009, 68) has similarly commented that in urban Tamil Nadu the official poverty line for a family of four, after allowing for shelter and food, "would have left a good deal less than nothing to spend on education, clothing, and transport." The reverse calculations provide a basis for engaging the wider public in a consultative process: "such an approach would make more meaningful the otherwise arcane statistical procedures on which the risk-of-poverty indicator is based. It would be a good means by which Governments could engage those experiencing poverty and social exclusion" (Marlier et al. 2007, 156).

> Recommendation 15: The World Bank should develop a programme of work, in conjunction with other international agencies, on a basic needs–based estimate of extreme poverty; these estimates would, when developed, form an alternative indicator to be included in the portfolio of Complementary Indicators, and serve to provide an interpretation of what the International Poverty Line would buy.

The construction by the World Bank of a basic-needs measure for these two roles will have to resolve a number of matters. Here two key issues are considered: (i) the structure of the basic needs standard at a point in time, and (ii) the way in which the standard should be adjusted over time.

The construction of the basic needs standard has to make judgments regarding its *structure*. One consequence of the nutritional approach is that the poverty line is usually set at a lower level for women than for men (as used to be the case in the United States). Is this a feature that should be introduced into the World Bank calculations? Given concerns about the gender composition of the poor, such a move would spark definite reactions and is not recommended. The basic needs approach should be implemented with the side constraint that there be no gender differentiation. (There is a parallel with the design of taxation. The labor supply response of women may differ from that of men, and an optimal tax analysis may suggest that they be taxed at different rates, but this may be overruled by a concern for horizontal equity.)

A different issue is raised by the lower calorie requirements for children (see, for example, FAO 2008). This raises the more general issue of "equivalence scales" for households of differing composition. The Global Poverty calculation is made on a per capita basis, and this has not been questioned in chapter 1. Such an assumption differs, however, from that adopted in most estimates of poverty in high-income countries, which typically use an equivalence scale such as the "modified OECD (Organisation for Economic Co-operation and Development) scale" that assigns a value of 1.0 to the first adult in the household, 0.5 to other adults, and 0.3 to children below the age of 14. So that the Jamaican household referred to above would, if it consisted of 2 adults and 3 children, be made up of 2.4 equivalent adults. The implications depend on the absolute level at which the poverty line is then set. If one were to apply the International Poverty Line allowance of 1.90 international dollars as the amount for a single adult, then the total for the household would be reduced to $4.56 from $9.50 a day, and estimated poverty would be substantially reduced (see Batana, Bussolo, and Cockburn 2013 for a calculation of this kind, which also allows for economies of scale). But the International Poverty Line was set with a per capita calculation in mind, and the introduction of equivalence scales would necessitate a reconsideration of the amount for the first adult. With a basic needs foundation for the alternative indicator, it seems impossible to ignore the differing needs of households made up of people of differing age and differing needs. It seems the appropriate point for the World Bank to make use of age-based equivalence scales. This should not, however, be a simple adoption of existing scales. A new indicator should be sensitive to the needs of children as perceived by children themselves, and take account of the investment embodied in current consumption. Equally, the new indicator should explore the way in which the scale can reflect the fact that people with disabilities face higher costs of living (Morciano, Hancock, and Pudney 2012).

The above description of the work program relates to the establishment of the level of the basic needs-based poverty line. The issue of *updating over time* raises serious questions about the approach. A common practice in the case of national poverty lines derived in this way is simply to update by the change in the national consumer price index (CPI)—as advocated for the International Poverty Line in chapter 1. This means that the original calculation would be maintained; there would be no change at any of the three steps. In the case of the food share method, no account would be taken of changing relative prices, or of changes in the mix of foods purchased, or in the share of food spending.

For relatively short periods of time, such as up to 2030, such a national CPI adjustment may be satisfactory, particularly if accompanied by improvements in the construction of the CPI, and this is assumed here to be the practice followed.[18] But over the longer term major doubts arise, and this is why in many developed countries the approach to poverty measurement has tended to depart from a straightforward basic needs indicator. In the studies of poverty in the United Kingdom by Rowntree (1901), his later poverty lines applied in 1936 and 1950 allowed for additional nonfood items, such as a radio, that had not been included—or indeed contemplated—in his first study. The revised standards reflected changes in contemporary living conditions, but lacked any firm point of reference (see Atkinson 1969). There was no underlying conceptual clarity. This led in the United Kingdom to the work of Townsend, who defined poverty in terms of ability to participate in society: "individuals, families and groups in the population can be said to be in poverty when they lack the resources to obtain the types of diet, participate in the activities and have the living conditions and amenities which are customary, or at least widely encouraged or approved, in the societies to which they belong" (Townsend 1979, 31). This is discussed further below, in conjunction with the capability approach.

Adjustments to the basic needs standard may be expected to be upward in the case of nonfood items, as in the example just cited, but the reverse may be true for the food component. The fact that energy requirements are greater for those undertaking heavy work means that the food requirements should vary with the level of activity. A country where most workers are sitting looking at screens should have a lower nutrition requirement than one in which many people are pulling rickshaws. Allen (2013, table 2) shows a time budget for a laborer in mid-eighteenth century London, whose activities required 2.16 times the intake of the basic (sleeping) requirement. If the worker had instead been seated at a desk, the requirement would have fallen to 1.41.

The lower needs may be offset by a smaller food share, and nutritional requirements rise with the greater height and body mass in rich countries, but the possibility should be contemplated that a basic needs–based poverty line should fall with the level of development.

Any continuation of the basic needs approach beyond 2030 (assuming price uprating to that time), has therefore to confront serious issues. The next section addresses the concerns that a fixed set of needs understates poverty in increasingly affluent societies. In the opposite direction is the possibility of overstatement, on account of declining calorie requirements. The latter is well illustrated by the case of India. The pattern of calorie intake in India has been examined in depth by Deaton and Drèze (2009, 62), who find that "average calorie consumption in rural areas was about 10% lower in 2004–05 than in 1983. The proportionate decline was larger among better-off sections of the population, and close to zero for the bottom quartile of the per capita expenditure scale." On the face of it, this evidence points to a lower level of basic needs associated with less demanding activity levels. However, they conclude that "this hypothesis remains somewhat speculative" (Deaton and Drèze 2009, 62). Even more important, they argue that "average calorie intake has serious limitations as a nutrition indicator [and] close attention needs to be paid to other aspects of food deprivation, such as the intake of vitamins and minerals, fat consumption, the diversity of diet, and breastfeeding practices" (Deaton and Drèze 2009, 62). (These considerations are relevant to the nonmonetary indicator for nutrition considered in "Nonmonetary Poverty," below).

Moreover, the issues raised under uprating are relevant not only to what happens after 2030; they also affect the interpretation of the developments in the poverty estimates in the years up to that date. If, as is possible, nutritional requirements decline over time with the changing nature of work and other circumstances, then application of a fixed set of basic needs (adjusted by the CPI) may increasingly overstate the extent of poverty. People whose diet may be inadequate if they are spending all day in the fields may be adequately nourished if they are now working in information technology (IT). This may be salient when seeking to "triangulate" the $1.90 PPP line, and underlines the importance of the textual information that accompanies the estimates in the National Poverty Statistics Reports. One cannot simply take the numbers out of context.

Capabilities

If the basic needs approach is long-standing, the third approach—capabilities—dates from recent decades. In a series of contributions, Amartya Sen (1985, 1992, and 2009), has argued that well-being should be judged in terms of the *functionings* and *capabilities* open to a person.[19] Martha Nussbaum (in, for example, Nussbaum and Glover 1995 and Nussbaum 2000 and 2000a) has proposed functional freedoms, or central human capabilities, as a rubric of social justice, paying special attention to the unequal opportunities of women in different cultural settings. Functionings are the activities and states that are valued by a person, and capabilities are the various combinations of functionings that he or she can achieve: "the actual opportunities of living" (Sen 2009, 233). In the context of measuring poverty, Sen (1993, 41) has argued that this should be seen as the deprivation of capabilities, where that deprivation limits the freedom of a person to pursue their goals in life: "identifying a minimal combination of basic capabilities can be a good way of setting up the problem of diagnosing and measuring poverty."

The capability approach has been embraced by those seeking an alternative to the current World Bank procedure. Reddy and Pogge (2010, 79) state that

> our rejection of the Bank's procedure does not support the skeptical conclusion that the attempt to provide a standard of income poverty comparable across time and space is doomed to fail. There exists a much better procedure which can be easily implemented. This alternative procedure would construct poverty lines in each country that possess a *common* achievement interpretation. Each poverty line would refer to the local cost of achieving a specific set of ends. These ends should be specified at the global level. . . . Each poverty line should reflect the cost of purchasing commodities containing relevant characteristics (for example calorie content) that enable individuals to achieve the desired ends.

The capability approach is rich and offers a different perspective. Table 2.1 shows in stylized form some of the key differences from the International Poverty Line and from the basic needs–based indicator (the minimum rights approach is discussed below). Rather than immediately seek to relate this directly to an alternative indicator, the discussion here of the capability approach seeks to provide a conceptual foundation to the next sections, specifically a societal measure of poverty and multidimensional poverty measurement.

First, capabilities are essentially multidimensional, and the construction of multidimensional indicators, discussed below in "Nonmonetary Poverty," may be viewed as an operalization of the capability approach, where the theoretical foundation provides guidance as to the dimensions to be included. The second feature is that capabilities are individual based, whereas the International Poverty Line and the needs-based indicator are centered on the household. The third feature is that the capability approach, like standard of living measures in general, or basic needs–based measures, is concerned with the diversified characteristics of individuals. But it goes further, as is demonstrated by Sen's lead example of disability: "the relevance of disability in the understanding of deprivation in the world is often underestimated, and this can be one of the most important arguments for paying attention to the capability perspective. People with physical or mental disability are not only among the most deprived human beings in the world, they are also, frequently enough, the most neglected" (Sen 2009, 258). Fourth, assessment of global poverty according to the International Poverty measure or the basic needs–based Complementary Indicator treats each household on its own. The poverty status of each household is evaluated as though it were in isolation, with no neighbors or fellow citizens. With the capability approach, however, there enters an essential interdependence. The capability to function depends on the society in which the person lives: "in a country that is generally rich, more income may be needed to buy enough commodities to achieve the *same social functioning*, such as 'appearing in public without shame.' The same applies to the capability of 'taking part in the life of the community'" (Sen 1992, 115). The last sentence brings out the relation with the concept of social exclusion; the capability approach provides theoretical underpinning for the Townsend (1979) definition of poverty in terms of ability to participate in society.

Minimum Rights

To this juncture, the Report has been largely concerned with a well-being approach to the measurement of poverty. There have been passing references to the fact that a rights-based approach would lead to differences, and attention is now turned to a fuller, but compact, account of a

rights foundation. "Compact" may seem inconsistent with the vast literature on "rights," and indeed a necessary immediate step is to limit
severely the field. First, there is no discussion of the instrumental role of
poverty rights in underpinning a general catalogue of human rights.
Second, there is a return to a governmental view of the definition of
poverty, as in chapter 1 of the Report, taking as given the way that rights
are defined by national—and more especially, international—bodies.
Again, performance is being judged according to stated goals.

How can this be made concrete? Can the objective be formulated in
terms that capture the essence (Principle 2). "Human rights always
come to us in lists," according to Nickel (2014, 219), and he goes on to
say that "international law uses a standard list that mainly comes to us
from the [United Nations 1948] Universal Declaration of Human
Rights. This list consists of seven families of human rights, the first six
of which are found in the Universal Declaration" (2014, page 219), The
sixth on the list is "Social rights that require that people be provided
with education and protected against starvation and severe poverty."
The Universal Declaration itself has a more extensive list. Article 25
includes "everyone has the right to a standard of living adequate for the
health and well-being of himself and of his family, including food,
clothing, housing and medical care and necessary social services" and
Article 26 adds that "everyone has the right to education," with a specific
reference to elementary education (United Nations 1948).

This formulation in the Universal Declaration does not lead us
directly to a poverty line, but it is informative in three respects (see the
final column in table 2.1). The first is that rights are defined on an individual basis. It is true that Article 16 says that "the family is the natural
and fundamental group unit of society and is entitled to protection by
society and the State," but there are no attached rights of families or
households. In this Report, rights are taken as individual (United
Nations 1948). It is, for example, concern with the individual rights of
women that underpins the case being made in the Report for nonmonetary measures that allow gender inequality to be identified. It should,
however, be recognized that, right from the start, the Universal
Declaration was criticized as being too dominated by Western values
with their individual focus. Eleanor Roosevelt, widow of U.S. President
Franklin D. Roosevelt, who was chair of the Declaration of Human

Rights drafting committee in 1947, recalled in her memoirs that some had argued for a more pluralist approach, with one Asian member suggesting that the Secretariat might well study the fundamentals of Confucianism.[20] A starting point of society as a whole, or of distinct population subgroups (defined, for instance, by geography or ethnic composition or religion), may lead to focus on the right to live harmoniously in such a society. As noted below in "Nonmonetary Poverty," this would lead to the extension of the indicator portfolio to include dimensions of a different kind.

The second respect is that the list of rights in the Declaration makes frequent use of the word "everyone" and is explicit as to when they are not neutral between individuals. Otherwise, the rights are universal. To reiterate a point made earlier, this means that there is no justification for the situation when, as in the past was the case, the U.S. official poverty line, derived from a basic needs approach, was lower for women than for men. At the same time, there are exceptions. Article 25 goes on to say that "motherhood and childhood are entitled to special care and assistance. All children, whether born in or out of wedlock, shall enjoy the same social protection." Here particular attention should be paid to the rights of the child (Pemberton et al. 2007), as embodied in the UN Convention on the Rights of the Child, a document which, to quote the former UN High Commissioner for Human Rights, Mary Robinson, "adds value because it provides a normative framework of obligations that has the legal power to render governments accountable" (Robinson 2002).

The third contribution is that the lists identify key dimensions that are relevant when considering a multidimensional approach, as discussed below: education, food, clothing, housing, medical care, and necessary social security. Such a list is similar to that given by rights theorists, although with some interesting differences. For example, Shue (1996, 23) cites "unpolluted air, unpolluted water, adequate food, adequate clothing, adequate shelter, and minimal preventative health care." Here again the focus on the rights of the child is important. "Child mainstreaming" has been stressed in the development of indicators in the European Union. Marlier et al. (2007, 102) stated that the common social indicators were unsatisfactory when viewed from the child perspective: instead, "we need to approach the issue from the opposite direction: to start from

the perspective of children and then consider the selection of indicators."
(For further discussion of child material deprivation, see Guio, Gordon,
and Marlier 2016.) In the present context, the extended listening exercise
proposed for the World Bank in Recommendation 14 should make sure
that the voices heard include those of children.

The implications of the rights approach, and of the capability
approach, for the development of Complementary Indicators are the
subject of the next section.

Relative Poverty, Income Shares, and Shared Prosperity

A contrast has been drawn above between the assessment of global poverty according to the International Poverty Line measure or the basic
needs–based on the one hand, which assess each household's status
independently, and the capability approach or that founded on minimum rights on the other, where there enters an essential interdependence in the evaluation. It is this interdependence that gives a specific
meaning to the term "relative poverty." The capability to function
depends on the society in which the household lives; minimum rights
only have meaning in a societal context. In this section, attention turns
to the way in which absolute concepts of functioning translate into relative concepts of resources. There follows a proposal for a "societal poverty measure." This leads on to an analysis of the relation with the Twin
Goal of the World Bank, which considers the income distribution more
widely and the sharing of growing prosperity.

The Capability Approach and Absolute/Relative Poverty

The measurement of poverty is today seen as a global exercise, and
chapter 1 discussed the extension to high-income countries. This raises
a key conceptual issue. The embracing of both developed and developing countries is often represented as generating an inevitable conflict
between "absolute" and "relative approaches." However, the shift in perspective to a capability approach provides one route to resolve any such
tension (Atkinson and Bourguignon 2000a and 2000b). Not only does
the approach provide an underlying theoretical framework for analyzing deprivation, but also it shifts the standpoint from which ethical considerations are applied.

The application of the capability approach can indeed be seen building on the earlier discussion of the energy requirements of different activities. "Bare survival" may be seen as requiring for an individual a level of food and other inputs, broadly independent of the overall standard of living. On the other hand, "work" does indeed have higher energy requirements (with the caveat about the shift away from heavy labor), but it is an activity where other requirements apart from nutrition are significantly socially determined, and can be expected to rise with the overall standard of living. A linen shirt may have been sufficient at the time of Adam Smith, but today a job seeker requires Internet at home and a mobile phone. Moreover, this dependence can be explained by the effect of rising incomes elsewhere in society on the availability of the supply of goods and services (Atkinson 1995). In order to understand this, it is necessary to look beyond the household sector; a general equilibrium view of the economy is required. The poverty status of households depends on the actions of firms and the state. Potential consumers may be excluded from the market by the decisions of firms regarding which quality of product to supply. As overall living standards rise, shops may no longer offer cheaper cuts of meat, and small-sized packs of food may no longer be available. The cost of food may depend on the location of employment: a worker may have to purchase more expensive meals away from home on account of the increased concentration of production in distant urban locations. A worker dependent on public transport to get to this work may find the service withdrawn as the rest of society gets richer and can afford its own transport. As Sen (1983) has pointed out, if the level of consumption that is required to function within a society varies with the average level of consumption, then a standard that is *constant* in the space of functionings or capabilities would imply a standard in terms of consumption that varies over time and across countries.[21] One immediate implication is that a rise in consumption does not necessarily imply— when the ultimate criterion is ability to function—that the family is less likely to be in poverty (Subramanian 2011a).

This provides a way of understanding the evidence about national poverty lines. Ravallion, Datt, and van de Walle (1991, figure 1) plotted national poverty lines against mean household consumption for 33 countries in 1985. Observing that the national poverty lines tended to rise with mean consumption, they fitted a regression equation with the logarithm of the poverty line as a quadratic function of mean household consumption. The same data, however, suggested to Atkinson and Bourguignon (2000, figure 1) that the national poverty lines were better viewed as the greater of $1 in international dollars a day per person and 37 percent of mean consumption per person. There was a switch, which in the 1985 data took place around the mean consumption of Morocco. They went on to argue that such a switching explanation corresponds to the theory of capability described in the previous paragraph. Below a certain level of mean consumption, the capability associated with basic needs is the binding (fixed in real terms) constraint, but once the specified level is reached, another capability becomes the binding constraint, and this constraint is relative (rising with the overall level of consumption in the country in question).

The different possibilities are illustrated in figure 2.2, where the mean consumption per head in the country is measured along the horizontal axis. To determine whether or not a particular household is in poverty,

Figure 2.2 Absolute and Relative Poverty

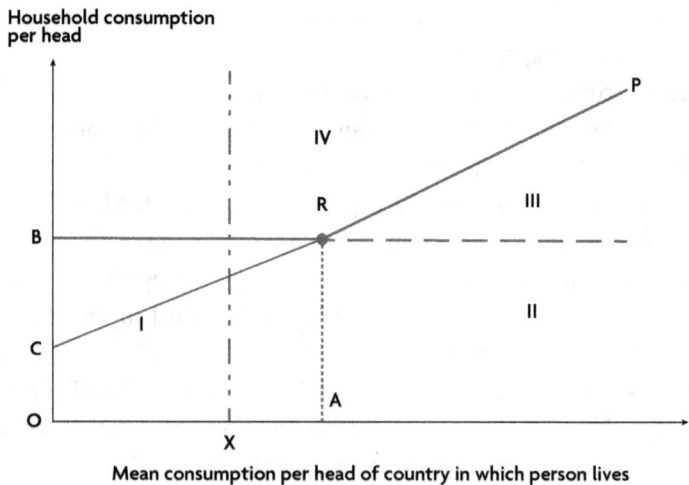

Household consumption per head

IV

R   III

B

II

I

C

A

O

X

Mean consumption per head of country in which person lives

Note: To determine whether a household is below the poverty line, first locate the country in which the household lives according to its mean consumption per head. Then, from point X for example, read off its poverty status from the vertical line. If, in the case of X, consumption per head is below OB, then the household is in absolute poverty. Where the country is to the right of A, then there is also a relative poverty line RP, and a household may be in relative but not absolute poverty (area III).

it is necessary first to identify where their country is located along the horizontal axis—say the point X. Their poverty status is then governed by their individual consumption per head, that is, where the household is located on the vertical line going up from X. For a country with mean consumption to the left of point A, as is the case with X, the applicable poverty line is the absolute horizontal line at distance OB. For countries to the right of A, the relative poverty line is applicable, but, as in chapter 1, there is also concern as to whether or not people are living below the absolute poverty line. From figure 2.2, it may be seen that the world population may be divided into four nonoverlapping groups: (I) those living in countries to the left of A who are below the absolute poverty line, (II) those living in countries to the right of A who are below both absolute and relative poverty lines, (III) those living in countries to the right of A who are above the absolute line but below the relative poverty line applicable in their country, and (IV) those in none of the categories I to III.

How can this more complex approach be best explained? Is it consistent with the requirement of transparency (Principle 2)? There are three parameters. The first is the familiar poverty line, taken here for the purposes of discussion to be the International Poverty Line. The second is the slope of the relative poverty line. Here too there is a degree of familiarity, in that relative poverty measures in high-income countries are typically expressed as percentages of the mean or median income. So, in 2001, the European Union adopted as its official definition of relative poverty, as one of the Commonly Agreed Social Indicators referred to as "poverty risk" (Atkinson et al. 2002), 60 percent of the median equivalized disposable income. This is broadly the counterpart of 50 percent of mean income. In other countries, the figure taken is 50 percent of the median (Morelli, Smeeding, and Thompson 2015, 609), or closer to 40 percent of the mean. The third is the intercept of the relative poverty line: OC in figure 2.2. This appears more mysterious, but its significance may be seen from the fact that the income level determining the point A, where the switch takes place, is given by the reciprocal of the slope multiplying (1 − ratio of OC to OB) times the poverty line. (OB is the absolute poverty line.) If there is no intercept (the Atkinson-Bourguignon case), then the point A is equal to the reciprocal of the slope times the poverty line, so that with a slope of one-half, the poverty line starts moving upward when a country reaches a mean consumption of twice the poverty line. In 2011 PPP terms, this is a mean consumption level equal to $3.80 in international dollars a day per person, which is close to the level in rural China. In contrast, if the intercept were set halfway along OB, then the relative component would set in much earlier: with a slope of one-half, it begins when mean consumption is at the poverty line level. The country must therefore be extremely poor as a whole. In PovcalNet 2011, there are only five countries where the most recent survey has mean consumption below this level ($57.8 PPP 2011 per month per person): Burundi, the Democratic Republic of Congo, Liberia, Madagascar, and Uzbekistan, with Malawi and Mozambique just above. The three key elements do therefore have an intuitive explanation.

A Societal Poverty Measure

The approach described above has been put into effect in a number of recent studies, including the proposal by Ravallion and Chen (2013, 258) for a new class of "truly global poverty measures" (see also Ravallion and Chen 2011 and Chen and Ravallion 2013). Building on their earlier work, they base the selection of the relative component on observed national poverty lines. With an absolute poverty line at $1.25 a day at 2005 prices, they set the relative poverty line at $1.25 for countries whose mean consumption is at or below this level. As just shown, this applies to only a small number of countries. Where the country mean consumption exceeds $1.25 a day, the poverty line is set equal to $1.25 plus 50 percent of the excess of mean consumption over $1.25. On this basis, they make estimates of poverty measures for the world as a whole covering the period 1990 to 2008. In 2008, the global total poverty rate is estimated at 43.6 percent, or 2,912 million people (Ravallion and Chen 2013, table 2). The constitution of this group is shown schematically in figure 2.3, where a distinction is introduced between the developing world and high-income countries. The estimated number of absolutely poor in the developing world is 1,289 million (corresponding to those located in the area 1),[22] with the maintained assumption that there is zero absolute poverty in high-income countries. To these are added the 219 million relatively poor in high-income countries (corresponding to area 3) and the 1,404 million relatively poor in the developing world (corresponding to area 2). Over the period from 1990, the latter figure has more than doubled.

Figure 2.3 Global Poverty and the Developing World

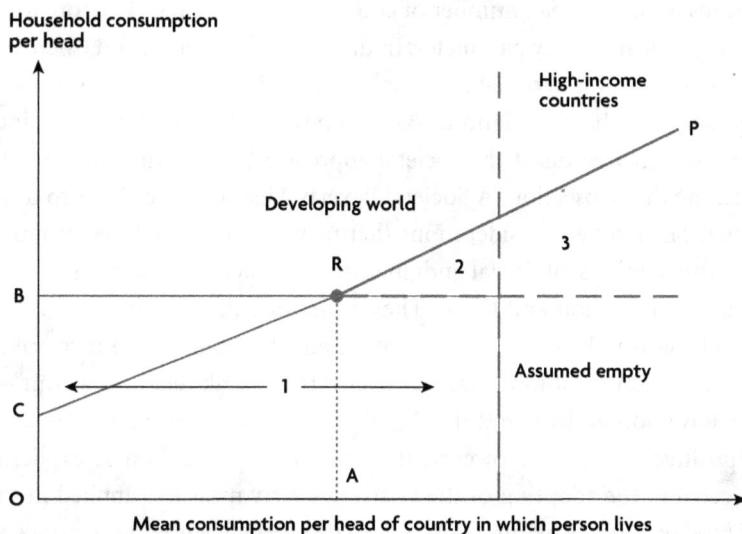

Note: The absolute poor are those in area 1; the relative poor are those in areas 2 and 3.

The approach proposed here differs from that embodied in the pro-visional SDG indicator 10.2.1, for which the World Bank has been iden-tified as custodian (United Nations Department of Economic and Social Affairs 2016, 36). This indicator, representing "social inclusion," differs first in being defined in terms of median income, rather than mean con-sumption per head. Second, the indicator is defined as identifying those with income below 50 percent of the median; in other words, it is a purely relative measure. This means that there would be people living in households with income below the International Poverty Line who would not be counted (as could happen in countries where the median is less than twice the International Poverty Line). It is not evident what justification can be given for this as an index of social exclusion—in contrast to the foundation for the societal indicator proposed here on the basis of the capability approach.

In implementing the societal approach, it is apparent from the earlier discussion that the conclusions can depend sensitively on the third parameter of the relative poverty line. The choice of a ratio of OC to OB of a half, coupled with the reciprocal of the slope being 2, means that the strictly absolute calculation applies in the Ravallion and Chen calculations to only a small number of countries. A choice has therefore to be made regarding a key parameter. In the work of Ravallion and Chen, the value is based on national poverty lines for 75 countries, but this is not the only possible foundation. National poverty lines are one input into the implementation of the societal approach, but not the only one. In heading this subsection "A Societal Poverty Measure," the aim is to draw attention to other considerations that may be introduced, reexamining the implications of social judgments. One such judgment is indeed made by Ravallion and Chen. They argue that the measure of poverty should satisfy the requirement that an equal proportionate increase in consumption must lower world poverty (the "weak relativity axiom"— see Ravallion and Chen 2011, 1252). This is taken by them to require a positive intercept. However, the weak relativity axiom is explicitly rejected in the adoption of the relative poverty measures applied in the EU today. And the axiom continues to be satisfied, with a zero intercept, in the developing world as long as there is positive absolute poverty.

It should indeed be reiterated that the capability approach, even in the one-dimensional form adopted here, involves a shift in perspective. It is for instance possible that a rise in the income of a person below the poverty line leads to an increase in measured poverty. Seen in terms of income, this makes no sense (see Decerf 2015), but seen from the standpoint of capabilities, the consequent rise in mean income may have the consequence that people above but close to the poverty line are more challenged when they seek to participate in that society. A second observation is that the choice of poverty index, to measure the extent of poverty, should be conceived in terms of capabilities, not income. As has been shown by Decerf (2015), use of a measure such as the Foster, Greer, and Thorbecke (FGT) index runs into problems if defined in income space. To avoid such issues, and for the reasons given earlier when discussing the poverty gap, the societal measure is defined purely as a head count ratio:

Recommendation 16: The World Bank should introduce a "societal" head count ratio measure of global consumption poverty that takes account, above an appropriate level, of the standard of living in the country in question, thus combining fixed and relative elements of poverty.

The Twin World Bank Goal

The Twin Goal of the World Bank is that of boosting shared prosperity, defined as promoting the growth of per capita real income of the poorest 40 percent of the population in each country. This is embodied in the SDG Goal 10.1: "By 2030, progressively achieve and sustain income growth of the bottom 40 percent of the population at a rate higher than the national average." The rationale for the Twin Goal has been described in the *Global Monitoring Report 2015/2016* as follows:

> The goal reflects a practical compromise between the single-minded pursuit of prosperity in the aggregate and an equity concern about the ability of the less well-off in society to improve their well-being by participating in a country's prosperity. The goal thus gives more explicit attention to inclusive development and growth than has been the case in the past and paves the way for a focus on inequality. (World Bank Group 2016, 46)

The World Bank President had earlier set the scene:

> A second crucial challenge for the medium term is the problem of inequality. Often, the mention of inequality causes embarrassed silence. We have to break the taboo of silence on this difficult but critically important issue. Even if rapid economic expansion in the developing world continues, this doesn't mean that everyone will automatically benefit from the development process. Assuring that growth is inclusive is both a moral imperative and a crucial condition for sustained economic development.[23]

The focus on inequality is today represented by SDG Goal 10, but, as the *Global Monitoring Report* noted, it is remarkable that the Twin Goal dates back to the speech of World Bank President Robert S. McNamara to the Annual Meeting in 1972:

> The first step should be to establish specific targets, within the development plans of individual countries, for income growth among the poorest 40 percent of the population. I suggest that our goal should be to increase the income of the poorest sections of society in the short run—in five years—at least as fast as the national average. In the longer run—ten years—the goal should be to increase this growth significantly faster than the national average." (World Bank Group 2016, 47)

The World Bank has been clear in its statement of the Twin Goal: to raise the living standard of the bottom 40 percent, referred to by the

World Bank as the "B40." As stated in the *Global Monitoring Report 2015/2016*, "the average income growth among the B40 has become the agreed-upon indicator of shared prosperity" (World Bank Group 2016, 47), where growth is understood to mean growth of the group per capita. But the placing of this goal in the context of "inequality" leads to potential confusion. Raising B40 is not the same as reducing inequality. Indeed, McNamara, in his speech, confounded two related, but distinct, goals. They have different implications. The World Bank B40 approach would favor an outcome (A) where growth for the bottom 40 percent was at the rate of 4 percent, and the national average 5 percent, over an outcome (B) where growth for the bottom 40 percent was at the rate of 3 percent, and the national average 2 percent. Yet in the former case relative inequality rises and in the latter case relative inequality falls—and would meet the goal set in McNamara's final sentence. Coming to the present day, there is the same confounding in the statement of the SDG Goal 10.1. Outcome (A) would not meet the Goal as currently formulated.

The formulation in terms of inequality judges performance by whether the point on the Lorenz curve corresponding to the bottom 40 percent indicates a higher share: the Lorenz curve has shifted upward at this point.[24] The satisfaction of such a test does not imply that overall inequality has been reduced because it does not capture what is happening elsewhere along the Lorenz curve (Basu 2013): at other points the share may have fallen. But it represents a simple and easily explained criterion. Adoption of a share approach would indeed be simpler. The necessary statistics have long been produced by the World Bank as part of the World Development Indicators. There are a number of questions that can be asked about these income distribution statistics, but they have been well rehearsed elsewhere. Moreover, in terms of the discussion earlier in this section, the share of income formulation is relative in conception.

In contrast, the formulation in terms of rising living standards is concerned with purchasing power, and encounters similar issues to those involved in measuring poverty according to a standard such as the International Poverty Line. Because this is clearly the formulation intended by the World Bank, endorsed in this Report, attention is concentrated here on the issues of particular relevance to the B40 interpretation, referring back to earlier sections.

Raising the Living Standards of the Bottom 40 Percent

The *Global Monitoring Report 2015/2016* contains a wheel diagram showing the growth over the period 2007 to 2012 (World Bank Group 2016, figure 1.9), although it also includes the growth for the total population and hence visually tends to confound the two different interpretations. Figure 2.4 shows a simpler version, just covering the B40 income growth indicator, for the developing counties covered by the Global Database of Shared Prosperity. The majority of developing countries showed positive per capita income growth for the B40. It should be noted that the goal applies to all countries, middle income and high income included. For high-income countries, not shown in figure 2.4, the picture over this period was much less satisfactory, with many recording negative growth.

The B40 income growth indicator makes use of the ingredients discussed in chapter 1: household survey data to give the consumption share of the bottom 40 percent and mean consumption per capita in local currency from the same source, converted to PPP dollars. So that in the case of Thailand, for example, the share of the bottom 40 percent was 16.5 percent in 2008 and 17.1 percent in 2012, and this combined with the fact that mean consumption per head in 2008 was $378.7 per month at 2011 PPP and $442.2 per month in 2012 yields an overall growth rate in B40 of 4.8 percent at an annual rate (World Bank Group 2016, 265, table C.1).

The fact that the ingredients are similar means that the same questions arise, such as the issue of coverage. The results presented in the *Global Monitoring Report* relate only to countries for which comparable data exist over the relevant period (broadly 2007 to 2012). In Sub-Saharan Africa, only 16 of the 48 countries have shared prosperity numbers even though more survey years exist (World Bank Group 2016, 52, note to figure O2). If "shadow" estimates were to be added, then consideration would have to be given as to how the survey data should be extrapolated. In particular, this indicator based on absolute changes depends on the accuracy of the CPI used to deflate the growth in the money value of consumption. If a price index for the poor were to be employed, as proposed in chapter 1 in Recommendation 9, then this could change the picture.

The indicator described above is purely national in focus: each country is treated in isolation. While the SDGs refer to national

Figure 2.4 Growth in Real Consumption (Income) per Head for Bottom 40 Percent, 2007–12

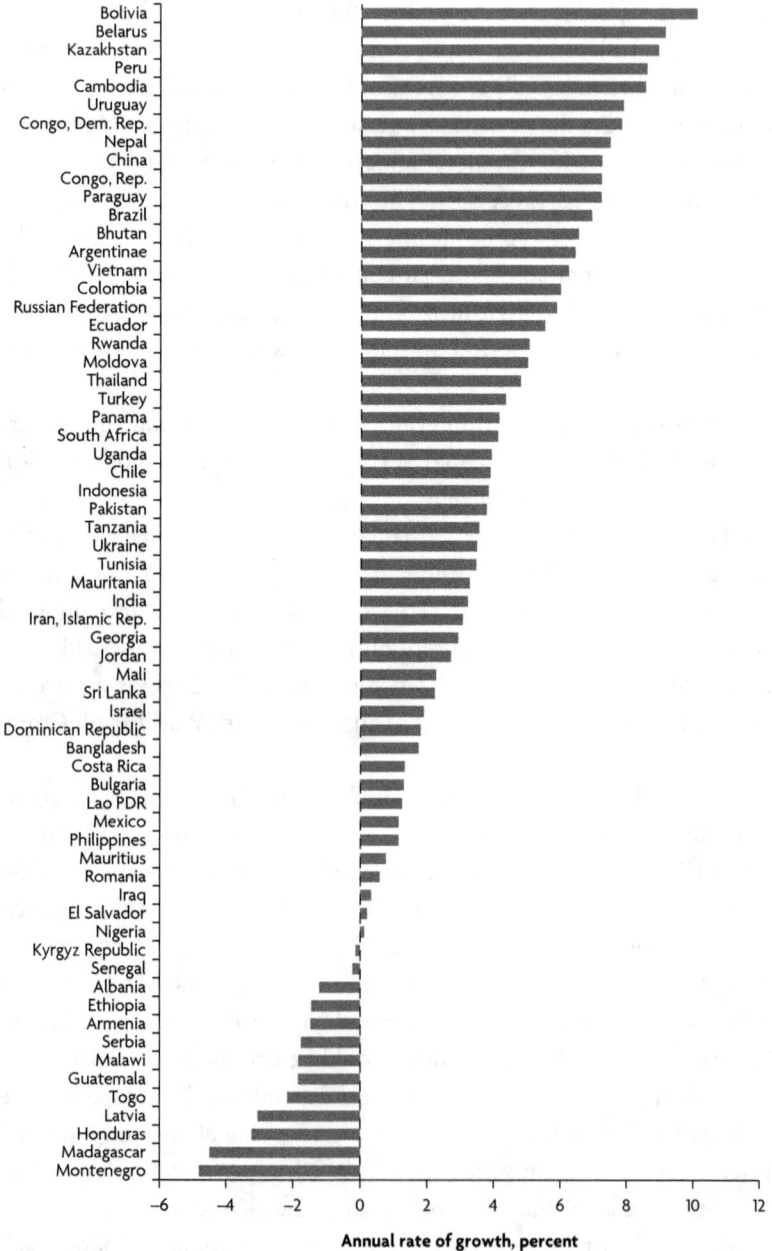

Annual rate of growth, percent

Source: World Bank Global Database of Shared Prosperity.
Note: In Montenegro, the annual rate of growth in real consumption per head was –4.8 percent.

poverty objectives, there are good reasons why the World Bank should also view shared prosperity from a global perspective, where the bottom 40 percent consists of those who are the lowest 40 percent in the world distribution of consumption. "There is no explicit target set at the global level" (World Bank Group 2016, 23), but, having taken a first step, there will no doubt be pressure to monitor progress at the world level. The national level figures already published should be accompanied by an annual statistic showing the rate of growth of consumption per capita among the bottom 40 percent of the world distribution—satisfying Principle 1 of being a truly global measure.

> Recommendation 17: The indicator for the shared prosperity goal should be unambiguously stated as raising the living standards of the bottom 40 percent in each country (not confounded with their relative share), and extended to include an indicator identifying the growth of per capita real consumption of the bottom 40 percent of the world distribution of consumption.

The avoidance of ambiguity regarding the Twin Goal is particularly relevant if there is any prospect of periods when the growth of per capita real consumption is negative. (As noted above, this has been the case in recent years in a number of high-income countries.) In such a less optimistic scenario, it is the absolute living standards that should be the concern of the Twin Goal.

The additional indicator would be based on the world distribution of consumption, the counterpart of the estimates of the world distribution of income prepared by, among others, Bourguignon and Morrison (2002), Bourguignon (2015), and Lakner and Milanovic (2015). Figure 2.5 shows the evolution of the real income of the bottom 40 percent as revealed by the estimates of the latter. Today the world B40 group includes some 2.8 billion people. It also shows the real income of the bottom quintile group (bottom 20 percent), as had earlier been proposed by Basu (2001) and Subramanian (2011). According to these estimates, the real income of the bottom 20 percent has been growing less rapidly. The income of those in the top half of the B40 group was 164 percent of that in the bottom half in 1988, but this figure has risen to 191 percent in 2008. On the other hand, the long-run estimates of

Figure 2.5 **Growth of Real Income of Bottom 40 Percent and Bottom 20 Percent of World Distribution**

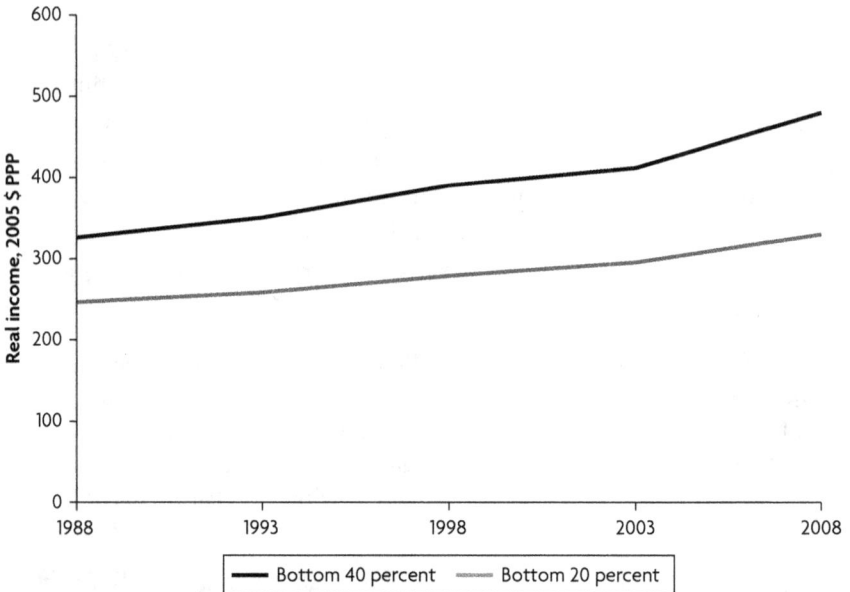

Source: Lakner and Milanovic 2015 and data supplied by C. Lakner.
Note: In 1988 the mean annual real income of the bottom 40 percent was $325 in 2005 PPP and that of the bottom 20 percent was $247.

Bourguignon and Morrisson, dating back to 1820, shown in figure 2.6, indicate that the real incomes of the two groups moved in a broadly similar way up to 1992.

The *Global Monitoring Report 2015/2016* stresses that the income focus of the Twin Goal should not be seen as a reason for neglecting the nonincome dimensions of poverty, and these are the subject of the next section.

Nonmonetary Poverty

Many submissions to the Commission have stressed the need for a multi-dimensional approach, incorporating nonmonetary dimensions.[25] Indeed, the argument for considering dimensions in addition to economic resources follows naturally from the capability and minimum rights approaches considered in the section above on "Alternative Approaches to

Figure 2.6 Long-Run View of Real Income of B40 and B20

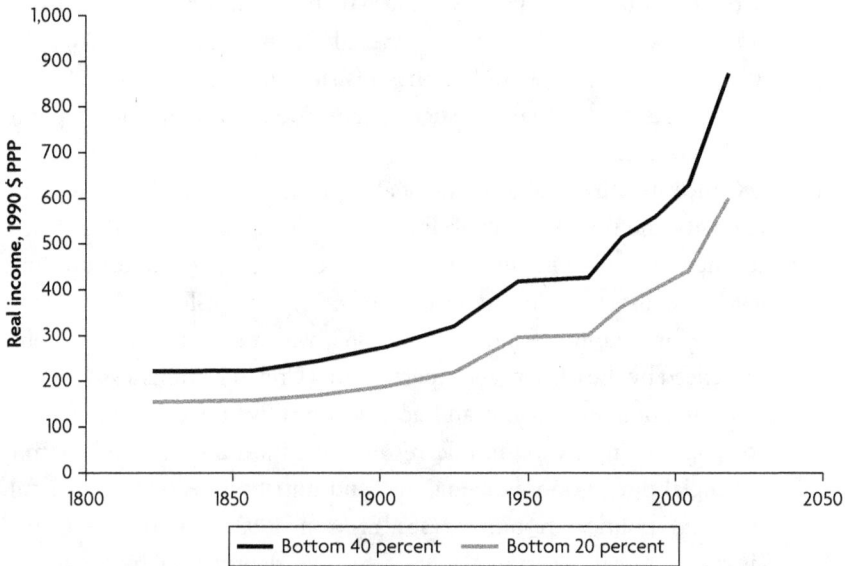

Source: Bourguignon and Morrisson 2002, table 1.
Note: In 1820 the mean annual income of the bottom 40 percent was $222 in 1990 PPP, and the mean for the bottom 20 percent was $155.

Measuring Poverty." Robeyns, in her entry for The *Stanford Encyclopedia of Philosophy* for the capability approach, stresses

> that it is not sufficient to know the resources a person owns or can use in order to be able to assess the well-being that he or she has achieved or could achieve; rather, we need to know much more about the person and the circumstances in which he or she is living. . . . "capability" [does] not . . . refer exclusively to a person's abilities or other internal powers but to refer to an opportunity made feasible, and constrained by, both internal (personal) and external (social and environmental) conversion factors. (Robeyns 2011)

The capability approach "rejects normative evaluations based exclusively on commodities, incomes, or material resources. . . . Resource-based theories do not acknowledge that people differ in their abilities to convert these resources into capabilities" (Robeyns 2003, 63). At the same time, the capability approach does not provide an immediate step to a multidimensional set of indicators. (Nor does the minimum rights approach lead directly to such a set.) While one of the founders of the capability approach, Martha Nussbaum, has drawn up a list of capabilities that can be applied generally (Nussbaum 1988, 176; 2000; 2003), the other, Amartya Sen, has resisted the adoption of a definite list, and has argued that any such specification of dimensions depends on the context.

Concern with a multidimensional approach did not, of course, originate with the theory of capabilities. It has long underpinned the measurement of well-being in Nordic countries, and these applications have developed lists of relevant dimensions. The Swedish Level of Living Survey, for example, conducted in 1968, was multidimensional, being influenced by the earlier UN expert group (United Nations 1954). There were nine domains: health and access to health care, employment and working conditions, economic resources, education and skills, family and social integration, housing, diet and nutrition, recreation and culture, and political resources (see Erikson 1993, 68). In the United Kingdom, the pioneering study of relative deprivation by Townsend (1979) made use of some 60 indicators covering, among other dimensions, diet, clothing, fuel and light, housing, conditions and security of work, recreation, health, and education. A lack of, or nonparticipation in, these dimensions was seen as an indicator of deprivation. Multidimensionality has been at the heart of the European concept of social inclusion, and, when the Member States of the European Union came to agree on an overarching portfolio of indicators, it was multidimensional: in the portfolio revised in 2015, the outcome indicators included income poverty, material deprivation, access to health care, education, employment, housing deprivation, and participation in the labor force (Social Protection Committee Indicators Sub-Group 2015). In the present context, the multidimensionality of poverty is not only widely accepted but is essential to the SDGs. Goal 1.2 refers to the reduction "at least by half the proportion of men, women and children of all ages living in poverty in *all its dimensions* according to national definitions" (italics added). The national definitions of particular relevance are those in countries that have adopted at a national level Multidimensional Poverty Indexes (MPI), developed by the Oxford Poverty and Human Development Initiative (OPHI) and included in the *Human Development Report* of the UN Development Programme

(UNDP) for 2010 and later years.[26] The countries adopting an official national MPI include Bhutan, Chile, Colombia, Costa Rica, Ecuador, Pakistan, and Mexico.[27] In what follows, the Report considers the major implications of a multidimensional approach, although, as explained at the outset, it does stop short of attempting an evaluation of the global Multidimensional Poverty Index.

The implementation of the multidimensional approach raises a number of key issues. Some of these are similar to those already discussed with regard to monetary poverty (see box 2.2). The quality and timeliness of household surveys is an example, as is the availability of reliable population figures. These will not be re-rehearsed. Instead attention is focused on the concrete proposal made here, which is for a multidimensional dashboard showing a set of nonmonetary dimensions, in conjunction with a measure of the extent of overlap between different forms of deprivation.

Box 2.2 Recommendations in Chapter 1 Relevant to Nonmonetary Indicators

Recommendations from chapter 1 (in abbreviated form) relevant to nonmonetary indicators are as follows:

- Recommendation 2: The National Poverty Statistics Reports (NPSR) for each country should include the dashboard of nonmonetary indicators.
- Recommendation 3: Investigate the extent to which people are "missing" from household surveys, and make proposals made for adjustments where appropriate for survey underrepresentation and noncoverage; review the quality of the baseline population data for each country, and the methods used to update from the baseline to the years covered by the estimates.
- Recommendation 5: The estimates should be accompanied by an evaluation of the possible sources of error, including nonsampling error.
- Recommendation 6: There should be explicit criteria for the selection of household survey data, subject to outside scrutiny, and assessment at national level of the availability and quality of the required household survey data, and review of possible alternative sources and methods of ex post harmonization.
- Recommendation 8: Investigate for a small number of countries alternative methods of providing current poverty estimates using scaled-down surveys, or the SWIFT or other surveys.

The Case for a Dashboard

The proposal made here is for a dashboard of outcome indicators, where the term "dashboard" refers to a set of dials, each referring to a specific dimension of deprivation. (The parallel with a car dashboard is not, in fact, exact, as explained below.) What, however, is the case for a multidial dashboard? As is stressed by Aaberge and Brandolini (2015, 142), "acknowledging the multidimensional nature of well-being does not necessarily imply that the social evaluation must also be multidimensional."

In considering the rationale for a dashboard, one has to begin with the fact that broad support for a multidimensional approach, in fact, reflects a diversity of concerns, and that one has to distinguish a number of perspectives, since they can lead in different directions when it comes to implementation. In particular, a contrast may be drawn between the standard of living perspective, on one side, and the capabilities/minimum rights perspectives, on the other side. Moreover, the reasons for adopting a multidimensional approach may be either instrumental or intrinsic.

Where the concern is to deepen understanding of the standard of living, there are many reasons, as discussed in earlier parts of the Report, why household consumption as measured in the World Bank estimates (and in other studies) is less than a fully satisfactory indicator. There is incomplete coverage where consumption is not recorded from home production or the services of assets. There are issues of timing, where the observed consumption depends on the season or is affected by temporary fluctuations. Hence, the distinction drawn between observed "transitory" consumption/income and unobserved "permanent" consumption/income. The survey may not record individual consumption of publicly provided health care or education. Collection of information on other variables in these circumstances can improve the assessment of the standard of living of the household. But it does not follow that, for this purpose, multiple indicators are required. The additional information may be incorporated in an improved measure of "extended consumption." The value of assets, which may well be negative, can be converted into a flow and added to the consumer expenditure. Publicly provided education or health care can be valued in the light of the market prices for these services and, again, added to extended consumption. This generates a richer representation of consumer well-being, but one that remains one-dimensioned. (As emphasized earlier, any extension of the definition of consumption should be accompanied by a reconsideration of the level of the poverty line; one cannot simply add to one side of the analysis.)

The extended consumption formulation offers a route to remaining with a single dimension, but there are several reasons why this may not always be possible or acceptable. The market prices required to value different items may not exist or may be unrepresentative. The fees charged for private education may bear no relation to the value of a poorly maintained village school without a regular teacher. The implications of debt owed to a landlord may not be captured by ruling interest rates. The value of health services depends on the circumstances of the individual and household. To these considerations should be added the intrinsic reasons why, on a standard of living approach, there may be a case for multiple indicators. As argued, for instance, by Tobin (1970), in addition to an overall evaluation in terms of the standard of living, there may be scarce commodities whose distribution is a specific matter of concern. Under the heading of "specific egalitarianism," he argued that there should be an express concern with the basic necessities of life, health, and citizenship. These dimensions should be kept separate in the social evaluation. A more general formulation is provided by Walzer (1983), whose book *Spheres of justice* is subtitled "A Defense of Pluralism and Equality." His approach requires that each dimension be kept distinct, and there can be no reduction to a single index of well-being. There are therefore both instrumental and intrinsic grounds for a standard of living perspective to lead to a dashboard.

The capabilities/minimum rights perspectives, in contrast, are intrinsically multidimensional. For Alkire et al. (2015, 5), defining poverty in the space of capabilities implies, first of all, that the measurement must be multidimensional. They quote Sen: "the capability approach is concerned with a plurality of different features of our lives and concerns" (Sen 2009, 233). The lists relevant to human rights referred to in the section above, "Alternative Approaches to Measuring Poverty," were not inputs into a general index of rights but identified distinct domains where there is no presumption of a possible trade-off.

Choice of Dimensions

There are therefore a variety of perspectives that lead to the adoption of a multiple indicator approach. These perspectives may, however, have different implications for its design. Viewed in terms of a dashboard, the design includes both the specification of the individual dials and the composition of the portfolio of indicators as a whole. Which nonmonetary indicators should be selected, and how should they individually be designed? How can such choices be guided by the principles set out at the beginning of this chapter?

The rationale for the multidimensional approach influences the choice of dimensions. If the aim is, instrumentally, to improve the evaluation of the standard of living, then an indicator highly correlated with observed household consumer expenditure may bring little added value to the measurement of that one dimension. In contrast, such a high correlation may be of considerable significance if there is an intrinsic concern for different functionings. A low score on both dimensions represents the cumulation of deprivations. As is explained by Alkire et al. (2015, 229), "if indicators are very highly associated in a particular dataset, that is not sufficient grounds to mechanically drop either indicator; both may be retained for other reasons. . . . The normative decision may be to retain both indicators . . . but the analysis of redundancy will have clarified their justification."

In considering the process by which the dimensions of the dashboard can be determined, the first issue is that of process. One aim of the Complementary Indicators is to give voice to the concerns of the world's citizens, and earlier it has been recommended that the World Bank should extend its engagement in participatory studies. These should play an influential role in the choice of dimensions to be represented in the multidimensional dashboard. The consultation may be direct, as with the Voices of the Poor approach, or it may operate through institutions, as is illustrated by the case of Mexico. The Mexican Congress established CONEVAL, the National Council for the Evaluation of Social Development Policy, as an independent institution to measure poverty and evaluate social policy. The approach adopted by CONEVAL to the choice of dimensions involved three criteria: (i) legal norms, where they existed; (ii) criteria defined by experts or by specialized public institutions in each field; and (iii) results derived from statistical analysis, with final decisions made by the Executive Committee (see CONEVAL 2010). By whatever route, there should be space within the list of dimensions for the conclusions reached via consultative exercises.

The construction of the dashboard proposed here should therefore be informed by consultative processes, but these cannot be the only input into its design. The World Bank, in embarking on the process of design, has undoubtedly prior views about essential dimensions. Many international organizations either have adopted multidimensional indicators or have expressed views about their composition. A number of the considerations underlying the concern with multidimensional poverty arise from international standards, such as those based on the rights of the child. National governments have embodies their views in multidimensional indicators.

There are indeed strong ex ante views about the domains to be covered, confirmed by the Commission's consultations, and by consideration of earlier multidimensional approaches (as cited at the beginning of this section). There is wide agreement that the dimensions should, like the Human Development Index (HDI), include education and health status (represented in the HDI by life expectancy). The concept of specific egalitarianism advanced by Tobin (1970) would point to the inclusion of nutritional status, and this would follow naturally from the basic needs approach. For adults, nutritional status is commonly measured in terms of the body mass index (BMI), defined as weight in kilograms divided by the square of height in meters. For children, there are measures of "stunting" (low height for age) and "wasting" (low weight relative to height). (For further discussion of such anthropometric measures, see Ravallion 2016a, 356–58.) Further strong candidates for inclusion are variables measuring deprivation in terms of shelter (housing) and personal security. The strength of the case for these two dimensions is underlined by the fact that, in contrast to education and health status, there is a serious risk that outcomes may be worsening for significant fractions of the population. The adequacy of housing is threatened by population movement, on the one hand, and by climate change, on the other hand. Personal security is threatened by internal and external conflict.

The domains identified above find resonance in the domains adopted in the national Multidimensional Poverty Indexes that have recently

Table 2.2 Dimensions in Official Multidimensional Poverty Indexes in Latin America

	Dimensions	Reference
Chile	(1) Education, (2) Health, (3) Work and social security, (4) Basic standard of living	Government of Chile 2015
Costa Rica	(1) Education, (2) Health, (3) Work and social security, (4) Basic standard of living	Government of Costa Rica 2015
Colombia	(1) Education, (2) Childhood and youth, (3) Work, (4) Health care, (5) Housing and public services	CONPES 2012
Ecuador	(1) Education, (2) Health, water and nutrition, (3) Work and social security, (4) Housing and public services	Castillo Añazco and Jácome Pérez 2016
El Salvador	(1) Education and childhood, (2) Health and food security, (3) Work, (4) Housing, (5) Security and environment	Government of El Salvador 2015
Mexico	(1) Education, (2) Access to health care, (3) Access to food, (4) Access to social security, (5) Housing, (6) Basic home services, (7) Income	CONEVAL 2010

been adopted by governments. Table 2.2 summarizes these for six Latin American countries.[28] As may be seen, there are differences. Mexico, for example, includes in its indicator list, with a weight of 50 percent, a basic income indicator. But there is considerable common ground, with education, health, housing, and access to work appearing in all cases.

On the basis of these considerations, the starting point for the dashboard proposed here is the following list of six domains:

1. Nutrition
2. Health status
3. Education
4. Housing conditions
5. Access to work
6. Personal security

Does this choice of domains satisfy the principle of balance (Principle 6)? This is clearly open to debate, but before reaching any conclusion it is necessary to consider how the domains are represented by indicators.

Clarifying Concepts

The first clarification concerns the need to distinguish between outcome variables, on the one hand, and input or contextual variables, on the other hand. While most of the indicators employed in the national MPIs fall in the former category, there are variables that are not strictly out-come variables. For example, the indicators for Mexico include "access to social security," which is better seen as an input variable. Social security transfers may prevent financial poverty, but their impact should be recorded as such.

A second key definitional issue concerns the unit of analysis.[29] One significant concern with the Global Poverty measure is that it is household-based and takes no account of individual circumstances within the household. It was suggested earlier that measures of multiple deprivation could provide an avenue for illuminating within-household inequality and hence the possible gender and generational fault lines. This means that there needs to be clarity about the unit employed. Does the information relate to the whole household (for example, the household has no electricity), to everyone in the household (no one has primary education), to a specified person within the household (the respondent or the head of household), or to any unspecified person in the household? The global MPI has ten dimensions (Alkire et al. 2015, table 5.5), of which six relate to the household and four to any member of the household. As the example of the MPI illustrates, different units may apply to different dimensions. This does, however, raise the question: To whom does the dashboard relate?

A related definitional question concerns the reference population. With the monetary poverty indicator, the reference population is the entire population, but this is not evidently the case with a number of nonmone-tary indicators. While the majority of the indicators in the MPI—such as those for nutrition or access to safe drinking water—apply to the whole population, there are some indicators that only apply to a subset of the population. For example, in the case of the education domain, the second test applies only where there are school-age children in the household.

Then there is the decomposition of indicators by subgroups. As in the discussion of monetary poverty, important dimensions are gender and age. As was noted when discussing the within-household distribution of economic resources, and the difficulty in measuring inequality between male and female members, nonmonetary indicators can provide evi-dence about deprivation at the level of the individual. Nutritional status is an example. It does, however, require that information be collected for all relevant individuals within the household. In terms of age groups, there are good reasons for considering children and young people, as discussed earlier, but the position of the elderly should not be overlooked. In this connection, it should be noted that a number of the statistical sources do not interview individually older persons. For example, the Demographic and Health Surveys are designed to collect data on marriage, fertility, family planning, reproductive health, child health, and HIV/AIDS; and the focus of the surveys is on women of reproductive age (15–49) who are the subject of the individual questionnaires. Breakdown by gender and age is not simply a matter of decomposition; it also should influence the choice of indicators (and the cutoffs, as with nutritional requirements). One example of such an approach is the Youth Well-Being Index proposed in Egypt's 2010 Human Development Report, where it is said that "while education, health and income indicators are included, the greater benefit will come from the ability to measure such qualitative indicators as leisure and satisfaction, the quality of jobs, and even social capital and cohesiveness" (UNDP and Institute of National Planning, Egypt 2010, 12; Handoussa 2010). This builds on earlier work, such as the Youth Well-Being Index constructed for Brazil by Dell'Aglio et al. (2007).

From Domains to Indicators

For each individual domain, there has to be a process of moving from the broad field to a specific indicator or set of indicators. This involves a series of key steps, such as:

1. Identification of the possible set of indicator variables, and consideration of the extent to which they potentially fulfill the desired objectives. In this respect, weight should be attached to Principle 2—that the indicator be transparent and identify the essence of the problem—and Principle 3—that it have a clear normative interpretation.
2. Exploration of the availability of data that allow the establishment of a baseline and the monitoring of changes over time (Principle 7). The exploration involves both multitopic household surveys with global or multiregional coverage and national sources.
3. Choice among the potential candidates that satisfy the desiderata and for which empirical data are available for a sufficient range of countries and years.
4. Determination of the cutoff(s) to be applied.

5. Validation of the robustness of the results for the selected indicator(s) (Principle 4).

This represents a major undertaking for each of the dimensions, and it is one that the World Bank cannot be expected to undertake single-handed. In its use of statistics on nonmonetary poverty from a variety of international sources, the World Bank is not alone. UNDP, in its Human Development Report 2010, which initiated its Multidimensional Poverty Index, raised a number of the key questions (UNDP 2010, technical note 4) that are equally relevant to the single domains presented in the proposed dashboard. Rather, the creation of a portfolio of nonmonetary indicators by the World Bank, as part of the Complementary Indicators, must be seen as part of the wider global assembly of social indicators, and specifically of those designed to monitor the SDGs as a whole. In this data assembly, the World Bank is typically the user of definitions developed by other international agencies. At the same time, as argued earlier, the World Bank should not be a purely passive user, and it should be seeking those statistical developments essential to its own use of non-monetary indicators. In this respect, it is already active in a number of domains, such as the United Nations Children's Fund (UNICEF)/World Health Organization (WHO)/World Bank Joint Child Malnutrition Estimates. In the following recommendation it is proposed that this should be the way forward in constructing the dashboard. The recommendation also looks ahead to the needs of the overlapping poverty measure proposed in Recommendation 19.

> Recommendation 18: The World Bank should establish its own require-
> ments with regard to the measurement of nonmonetary poverty, for
> inclusion in the Complementary Indicators (including the overlapping
> poverty measure) and in other World Bank uses, and ensure that these
> are fully represented in the activities of the international statistical sys-
> tem, particularly with regard to the proposed SDG indicators.

Many of the issues discussed in earlier parts of the Report carry over to the development of nonmonetary indicators. In box 2.2 are summarized some of the main ways in which the earlier analysis may be relevant. Investigation of those missing from survey populations is a necessary accompaniment to measuring the nonmonetary dimensions (Recommendation 3). Consideration of sampling and nonsampling error can take a similar form (Recommendation 5). Nonmonetary variables may be readily collected in scaled-down surveys as envisaged in Recommendation 8 in chapter 1. In some cases, the measurement of the nonmonetary domains may be more straightforward. Issues with regard to seasonality cause fewer difficulties for indicators such as childhood mortality or education (although they can affect indicators of employment opportunities). There is no need for purchasing power comparisons across countries, nor for collection of price data for different geographical areas or for different population groups.

What concretely does this recommended approach entail? In considering the development of the nonmonetary indicator portfolio, it is not possible to examine here the implications for each of the six domains listed earlier, but table 2.3 illustrates the position with regard to SDG Goal 2 Zero hunger, which corresponds to the first domain on the list. The table is based on the Provisional Proposed Tiers for Global SDG

Table 2.3 Nutrition Domain in the SDGs

SDG (and custodian)	Data availability
Line 1 2.1.1 Prevalence of undernourishment (FAO)	Data are available for 116 countries. No data are currently available for developed countries.
Line 2 2.1.2 Prevalence of moderate or severe food insecurity in the population, based on the Food Insecurity Experience Scale (FAO)	Data are available for over 140 countries from 2010 to present and for very few countries from 2000–2009.
Line 3 2.2.1 Prevalence of stunting (height for age < 2 standard deviation from the median of the WHO Child Growth Standards) among children under 5 years of age (UNICEF)	Data are available for 106 countries from 2010 to present and for more countries from 2000–2009.
Line 4 2.2.2 Prevalence of malnutrition (weight for height >+2 or <-2 standard deviation from the median of the WHO Child Growth Standards) among children under 5 years of age, by type (wasting and overweight) (UNICEF)	Data are available for 105 countries from 2010 to present.
Line 5 2.3.2 Average income of small-scale food producers, by sex and indigenous status (FAO)	Data are available for 5 African countries from 2010 to present.

Source: UNDESA 2016.
Note: FAO = Food and Agriculture Organization (UN); SDG = Sustainable Development Goal; UNICEF = United Nations Children's Fund; WHO = World Health Organization.

Indicators, as of March 24, 2016. There have undoubtedly been subsequent revisions, but the table is sufficient to give an indication as to how there may be "read across." Under Goal 2, there are nine proposed indicators in the main section, for seven of which the FAO is the named custodian and for two UNICEF. The first point to note is that, of the nine indicators, four (possibly five) are concerned with inputs rather than nutritional outcomes. For example, indicator 2.4.1 is "the proportion of agricultural area under productive and sustainable agriculture." This tells nothing directly about the achievement of zero hunger. Table 2.3 focuses on the five indicators aimed at outcomes (in the case of the fifth, the link is not close).

The second column in table 2.3 summarizes the information given about data availability. From this, the last indicator—about which doubts have already been expressed—would presumably fall from further consideration. Line 4 refers to the child malnutrition indicator in which the World Bank is actively engaged. The SDG indicators are twofold, but that concerned with overweight (weight for height above two standard deviations from median) does not seem relevant to a goal of zero hunger. This leaves the underweight indicator. The UNICEF Child Nutrition website offers three further indicators: (i) stunting (below two standard deviations in terms of height for age), (ii) wasting (below two standard deviations of weight for height in terms of WHO Child Growth Standards), and (iii) severe wasting (below three standard deviations). There is therefore a choice. In figure 2.7, the individual country data for Bangladesh are plotted. It appears that the use of the stunting indicator would show a similar downward trend—and recall that it is change over time that is our concern here. However, the wasting indicators do not demonstrate a comparable improvement. There may therefore be a question of weighting different indicators even at this elementary level. The primary concern is with the direction of change, but the difference in level raises the question of the cutoffs applied to determine nutritional deficiency. Is stunting much more prevalent than wasting, or is this an artifact of applying a two-standard-deviation criterion in both cases?

The case study just given illustrates the kind of detailed issue that needs to be addressed in creating the portfolio. It also raises the issue of the population coverage. The nutrition indicators relate to children aged under 5.

Figure 2.7 Child Nutrition Indicators in Bangladesh

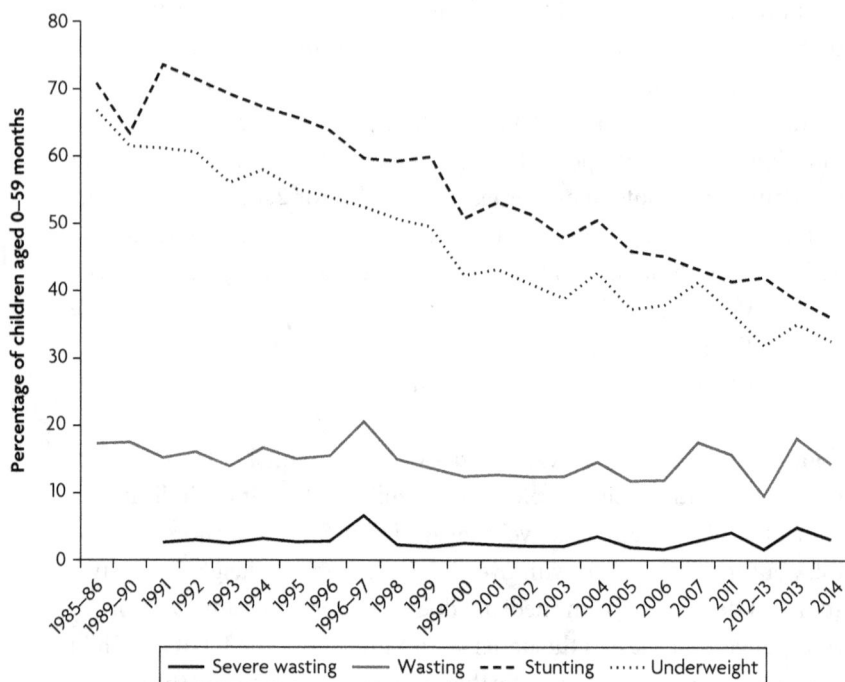

Source: Joint Malnutrition dataset from United Nations Children's Fund, World Health Organization, and World Bank.
Note: In 1985–6 wasting in Bangladesh was 17.3 percent.

Can they be incorporated into a dashboard alongside indicators, such as those for housing, that cover all members of the household? Or, in the case of education indicators, can use be made of school achievement among those currently of school age? There may also be indicators that relate to a larger group than the individual household. The Report does not go as far as it should into the treatment of the definition of personal security (a topic on which information is limited in existing surveys), but this dimension may have a wider scope, covering, for example, all inhabitants in a village exposed to the risk of flooding or located in a conflict zone.

A Global Reach

Principle 1 requires that the dashboard should have global reach, covering all countries of the world.[30] This immediately brings us to the issue, raised earlier in this chapter in relation to the UN Declaration of Human

Rights, as to whether there can be global agreement on a single set of values underlying the choice of indicators. If, across the world as a whole, there is a plurality of values, then this may require a wider set of indicators than considered so far. In making the case for the dashboard, the Report has stressed the importance of individual measures, but these may need to be accompanied by indicators at the level of a society as a whole, such as the degree of peace, harmony, solidarity, cohesion, environmental integrity, or integration (to give just some of the possible alternatives).

At a more detailed level, the translation to specific indicators, and the application of cutoffs, introduces a number of issues, as may be seen from the comparison made in table 2.4 between the indicators underlying the global MPI constructed by Alkire et al. (2015, table 5.5) and some of the indicators that form part of the EU portfolio of Social Indicators (Social Protection Committee Indicators Sub-Group 2015). In this table, not all EU Social Indicators are shown (for example, some relate to inputs or do not address poverty and social exclusion issues), but it encompasses those that are central to the target set in the Europe 2020 Agenda.[31] In 2010, the EU adopted the target for the year 2020 of lowering by at least 20 million the number of people at risk of poverty or social exclusion in the EU (see Frazer et al. 2014 for a discussion of the target). The target indicator of "Risk of poverty or social exclusion" in fact combines three elements: (i) risk of income poverty, (ii) (quasi-) joblessness, and (iii) severe material deprivation.

Comparing the columns in table 2.4, it might appear that the extension of the indicators from a national (or EU) to a global plane is "too big a stretch." The domains may be the same, but the implementation is quite different. There is, however, a parallel with the different cutoffs applied in the societal poverty measure, and the same procedure can be applied. Both education indicators refer to school completion. In one case (MPI), the cutoff refers to primary education; in the EU case it refers to secondary education. Provided that two variables can be employed, a common approach can be adopted, with primary education corresponding to the International Poverty Line and secondary education to the high-income country relative poverty line. As can be rationalized on a capability approach (see the section above on alternative approaches), the hierarchy of functionings leads

Table 2.4 Indicators of Deprivation Contrasted: Global MPI and EU Social Indicators

	Global MPI	EU Social Indicator
1. Education	No household member has completed 5 years of schooling; Any school-age child is not attending school up to class 8.	Early school-leavers who are not in education or training
2. Health	Any child has passed away in household.	Healthy life expectancy Self-reported unmet need for medical care
3. Shelter	Household has no electricity Sanitation facility shared or not improved No access to safe drinking water Dirt, sand, or dung floor Cooks with dung, wood, or charcoal	Overcrowding; housing deprivation (see also material deprivation under 8).
4. Nutrition	Anyone is undernourished according to body mass index	(See material deprivation under 8.)
5. Personal security		
6. Monetary poverty		Risk of poverty (living below 60 percent of median national household equivalized income) Persistent risk of poverty
7. Employment		People living in jobless (quasi-jobless) households Long-term unemployment rate Employment gap of immigrants Employment of older workers
8. Assets (MPI)/ Material deprivation (EU Social Indicators)	Assets: Household owns at most one of the following: radio, telephone, TV, bike, motorbike, refrigerator, and does not own a car or truck.	Material deprivation: aggregate indicator based on enforced lack of 3 or more (severe deprivation = 4 or more): 1 week annual holiday, home adequately warm, meal with protein once a day, no arrears, capacity to face unexpected expenses, having washing machine, color TV, phone, or car.

Sources: Alkire et al. 2015, table 5.5, for the Global MPI; Social Protection Committee Indicators Sub-Group 2015, section 4, for the EU Social Indicators.

Note: The EU indicator is being revised: see Guio, Gordon, and Marlier 2012 and Guio and Marlier 2016. The new indicator will no longer include washing machine, color TV, and phone because these assets have not passed the robustness tests in 2012 (they have become "saturated" in most EU countries). The proposed revised indicator includes six items collected for each adult in the household, which will illuminate within-household inequality. MPI = Multidimensional Poverty Index.

to a staged set of indicators. Lack of "access to safe drinking water" is a clear case of a measure applicable at the first stage, applicable globally. On the other hand, the lack of specified assets (for example, radio, TV, phone, bike, motorcycle, and refrigerator) is a criterion influenced by the prevailing society. Although the former may be identifiable according to physiological needs, the latter may be better approached by a consensual approach, based on the views expressed by the members of the society, including those below the poverty line, about the list of necessities required to have a decent life in the society in which they live.

Multidimensional Poverty Indexes (MPIs)

Reference has been made to the MPI introduced by UNDP in the *Human Development Report 2010* and published regularly since then (UNDP 2015, tables 6 and 7).[32] The desirability of a single summary measure combining the different dimensions is much debated. There are strong supporters, as is well summarized in the submission to the Commission by The Global Coalition of Partners to End Child Poverty (2015, para 2.3): "multidimensional poverty measures that are aggregated into a single composite index can be particularly powerful in summarizing global and national data on poverty in many dimensions. This would allow the dissemination of new figures and findings to broad audiences and mobilize public support to end poverty in all its dimensions." In contrast, Ravallion (2011, 246) is skeptical about the assumptions required to calculate the MPI: "it is one thing to agree that consumption of market commodities is an incomplete metric of welfare—and that for the purpose of assessing poverty one needs to also account for indicators of non-market goods and services—and quite another to say that a single 'poverty' measure should embrace all these things." In the development of social indicators for the European Union, the process stopped short of adopting an aggregate indicator: "even though composite indicators, like the Human Development Index, undoubtedly can play a valuable role in certain contexts, we do not feel that they should be employed as part of the current EU Social Inclusion process" (Marlier et al. 2007, 185).

Views for and against aggregate indicators differ widely and are strongly held. Such is the divergence that Aaberge and Brandolini (2015, 203) end their survey with the statement that "there is little chance that we will ever settle the controversy between the dashboard approach and summary indices." The aim of this Report, however, is not to resolve academic controversy, but to provide advice to the World Bank on the development of its monitoring of global poverty in the face of differing views. To this end, the Report proposes a limited step toward a multidimensional index based on the counting approach, while stopping short of considering the full generality of multidimensional indexes. The theoretical properties of such indexes and their empirical development are subjects that should be on a subsequent agenda.

Overlapping Deprivations and the Counting Approach

The representation of the different dimensions has been described, following custom, as a "dashboard": just as in a car, there is a row of dials recording performance on different dimensions. The parallel is, however, inexact. There can be a dashboard for a single household, telling us how it is faring, but for the society what is recorded is a summary of the performance of all households. It would be as though the speedometer on our car told us how many drivers on all roads in the country are travelling at less than x miles per hour. This distinction is important because the move to a multidimensional concept of poverty involves two key elements: the extension of dimensions and the introduction of correlation between these dimensions across the population. There is interest both in what is shown by each dial and in the relation between what is happening on different dials. It is not just how many people are deprived, but also how many households have a low score on all or several of the dimensions. Do those with low levels of education also suffer from poor health? From the standpoint of evaluating policy, the different dimensions have to be examined in conjunction. In their review of the MDGs at midpoint, Bourguignon et al. (2010, 28) noted that "because MDGs are presented as independent goals, they tend to be evaluated independently," but one needs to know how far—at the level of the individual household—progress is taking place across the board, and how far gains in one dimension are being accompanied by reverses elsewhere. We cannot just look at marginal distributions (Ferreira and Lugo 2013).

For this reason, it is proposed that the dashboard be accompanied by a Complementary Indicator (Number 7) summarizing the interdependence—at an individual level—between different dimensions. There are several possible ways of capturing the correlation.[33] The most widely used procedure, and that recommended here, is based on counting the overlap of deprivations over the population, by means of tabulations or Venn diagrams. Once the threshold along each dimension has been determined, the only decision that has to be made concerns the critical number of overlaps. To be more concrete, the first step is to classify each person's achievement with his or her status with respect to each cutoff for all n dimensions, so that people are identified as being deprived or nondeprived for each dimension, and count the number of dimensions on which the person is deprived. The chosen cutoff, k, determines the number of dimensions in which a person must be deprived in order to be considered multidimensionally poor. The proportion of the population with k or more deprivations is the head count ratio, H, of multidimensional deprivation. The cutoff, k, is likely to lie strictly between 1 and n. A cutoff of 1 would mean that anyone below any threshold is counted: this is the "union" approach. A cutoff of n means that people are counted only if they are below the threshold on all dimensions: this is the "intersection" approach. This is illustrated for a hypothetical case of three dimensions in figure 2.8. With a higher number of dimensions, the graphic device of the Venn diagram becomes unmanageable, but counting remains an easily explained approach: "counting the number

Figure 2.8 The Overlapping of Deprivation

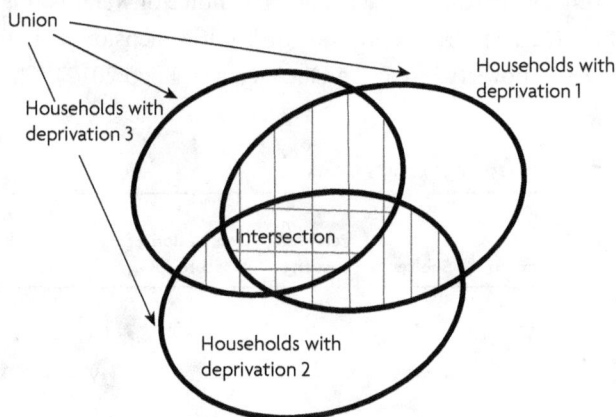

Shaded area = multiple deprivation where k = 2

Note: The ovals show households suffering deprivations 1, 2, or 3. The union includes all households suffering one or more deprivations; the intersection shows households suffering all three deprivations. The striped area, which includes the Intersection, shows all households with 2 or more deprivations.

of observable deprivations in core indicators has an intuitive appeal and simplicity that has attracted not only academics but also policy-makers and practitioners" (Alkire et al. 2015, 143).

> Recommendation 19: the Complementary Indicators should include a multidimensioned poverty indicator based on the counting approach.

It is not proposed that the indicator should include a monetary poverty dimension. In this respect, the Report is following the examples of Chile, Costa Rica, and other countries listed in table 2.2, but not that of Mexico. The aim of Recommendations 18 and 19 is to provide indicators that *complement* the monetary indicator, and not to seek to combine the two different approaches.

The application of this approach is illustrated by an example with $k = 2$ in table 2.5 (based on chapter 5 of Alkire et al. 2015), where the extent of deprivation is represented by a dichotomous (0,1) variable for each of four dimensions. Two of the five households are suffering multiple deprivation (k is 2 or greater) and the head count ratio is therefore 40 percent. The example is simplified in the sense that households are assumed to be the same size, and in that each of the four dimensions is equally weighted. The latter issue of the selection of weights has been highlighted by Aaberge and Brandolini (2015, 153), who say that there is no getting away from the fact that "the choice of weights might have a significant effect on the results of multidimensional analyses of inequality and poverty" (see also Decancq and Lugo 2012). The testing

Table 2.5 Illustration of Overlapping Poverty Index

	Health	Education	Shelter	Personal security	Deprivation score	Poor (with $k = 2$)	Censored deprivation score
Household							
1	1	1	1	0	0.75	Yes	0.75
2	1	1	0	0	0.50	Yes	0.50
3	0	1	0	0	0.25	No	0
4	0	0	1	0	0.25	No	0
5	1	0	0	0	0.25	No	0

Note: 1 = below deprivation threshold; 0 = above threshold. Households are assumed to be equal in size. Dimensions each receive a weight of 0.25, so the score for household 1 is 3 times 0.25. On this basis, 2 out of 5 individuals are suffering multiple deprivation (k is 2 or greater), so that the headcount ratio, H, is 40 percent.

of the robustness of results to the choice of weights has been an important part of the research program underlying the construction of the
Global MPI (see, for example, Alkire and Santos 2014). In considering
robustness to changes in weighting, one needs to distinguish between
"local" and "general" sensitivity. Ideally, the conclusions drawn—for
example about the change over time—should not be materially affected
by modest (local) variations in weights. On the other hand, if the findings are not affected by a major reduction in the weight—a general
change—then this would call into question the pertinence of the component in question.

The example also serves to bring out the limitations of the head count
ratio taken on its own. Alkire and Foster (2011a) have criticized the head
count as failing to satisfy "dimensional monotonicity," by which it is
required that there should be a strict reduction in the index if a person
ceases to be deprived on any dimension. If, in table 2.5, household 1, for
example, ceased to have poor health, then the head count ratio index
would remain unchanged. This is not a surprise, given what is known
about the head count in a single dimension, but this shortcoming of the
head count ratio has to be acknowledged, as should its vulnerability to
manipulation by policy makers. These considerations lead Alkire and
Foster (2011a, 482) to propose the adjusted head count ratio, which mul-
tiplies the head count ratio by the average breadth of deprivation among
the poor. The adjusted head count ratio is used in the global MPI constructed by OPHI, and in a range of national MPIs, with a number of
which the World Bank is already engaged. In the example shown in table
2.5, the average breadth of deprivation is 0.625, which, when multiplied by
the head count ratio, gives a value of 0.25 for the adjusted head count
ratio. This value is sensitive to an improvement in the health status of
household 1: if the censored deprivation score for this household is
reduced to 0.5, the household remains poor but the average breadth of
deprivation is reduced, and the adjusted head count ratio would fall to 0.2.

To sum up, Recommendation 19 envisages the counting approach as
being implemented in terms of the adjusted head count ratio, and its
constituents of the head count and average breadth of deprivation.
In order to apply this, the dimensions are represented in terms of $(0,1)$
deprivation status. As is explained by Alkire et al. (2015, section 5.7) and
Aaberge and Brandolini (2015, section 3.3), it would be possible to

extend the approach to cardinal variables that reflect the degree to which people are below the cutoff, but this is not explored further here. That said, what is recommended here in terms of the counting approach would be a major step.

The Data Required

The creation of the overlapping poverty measure, or of the more general measures of multidimensionality developed by Alkire and Foster (2011a), in one sense raises the stakes with regard to data requirements. In order to ascertain the extent of overlap of deprivation across dimensions, it is necessary to have a data source at the level of the individual or household covering all relevant dimensions. At the same time, the number of questions required per dimension may be considerably less in the case of nonmonetary indicators than is the case with the measurement of consumption for the monetary policy indicator. The multidimensional poverty indicator for Colombia is based on some 38 survey questions, that for Pakistan on 54 survey questions, and for Costa Rica on 77 survey questions.[34] The information required to calculate consumption is typically much more extensive. For example, the 1993–94 survey for Cambodia had a detailed consumption recall list of some 450 items (Gibson 2005, 137). Therefore, it should not be assumed that a non-monetary approach is more data-demanding. Indeed, in the context of Recommendation 14 it is assumed that nonmonetary indicators could form part of the quick surveys.

Following Principle 7, use should be made, wherever possible, of information already available. In the construction of multidimensional indexes, a major role has been played by multitopic household surveys containing data for the measurement of nonmonetary variables: the Demographic and Health Survey (DHS), the Multiple Indicator Cluster Survey (MICS), the Living Standard Measurement Survey (LSMS), and the Core Welfare Indicators Questionnaire (CWIQ).[35] These have global or multiregional coverage as listed in table 2.6. The scope for using these existing surveys has been usefully summarized by Alkire (2014). By their nature, these surveys score relatively well in terms of international comparability. On the other hand, they are only conducted at intervals. The DHS has taken place, on average, every five

Table 2.6 Multitopic Household Surveys with Global or Multiregional Coverage

Survey	Number of countries covered	Brief description
DHS (Demographic and Health Surveys)	More than 90	Collection of national sample surveys of population and maternal/child health, at individual and household level. The sample size is usually between 5,000 and 30,000 households and surveys are typically conducted about every 5 years.
MICS (Multiple Indicator Cluster Surveys)	More than 100	A survey initiative by United Nations Children's Fund, producing data on health, education, and child protection. The first round was conducted in 1995, and the fifth wave ran in 2014. Face-to-face interviews with households. In fifth wave, typical sample size about 11,000 households.
LSMS (Living Standards Measurement Surveys)	About 40	Launched in 1980, the World Bank has been collecting multipurpose household survey data, including poverty measured in terms of consumption. See Grosh and Glewwe 1995 for the early history.
CWIQ (Core Welfare Indicator Questionnaire)	24 listed in International Household Survey Network Catalogue	Developed by the World Bank in the 1990s to provide rapid standardized information on a range of variables, including housing, water and sanitation, education, health care, income, and assets.

Source: Based on Alkire 2014, 8, updated.

years; the MICS had a similar periodicity in the past, but is moving to a three-year cycle. This limits their applicability for annual monitoring.

Investigation of the multitopic surveys should form part of the work envisaged under Recommendation 18. Consideration of the needs for the overlap indicator raises a further question. Where there are missing dimensions—or else the variables are not measured in a satisfactory way or else there is a lack of cross-country comparability—one approach has been to seek to merge data across surveys, the merging of observations being based on assumptions about the degree of correlation. This method has been used in models of policy simulation: for example, imputing consumer expenditure data to a survey of incomes in order to calculate the indirect taxes paid. There is, however, a difference, in that in these cases the interdependence, while affecting the results, is not the central concern. In the case of an indicator of multidimensional poverty, however, it would make little sense to report the extent of overlap when the measure is essentially determined by the researcher's assumptions. It is therefore important that, as with the Global MPI constructed by OPHI, data be drawn from the same survey (in this case, the data in most countries come from DHS or MICS).

Conclusions

The aim of chapter 2 of the Report has been to broaden the consideration of measures of global poverty—to go beyond the monitoring of SDG Goal 1.1 and to confront criticisms that have been made of that poverty indicator. Not all criticisms are valid, but there is wide agreement about the need for alternative starting points, and this is reflected in the proposals made here. There are recommendations both for enriching the existing approach and for new departures. Moreover, the proposals recognize the concerns embodied in the other SDGs and take on board the Twin Goal of the World Bank for shared prosperity. In making the recommendations, the chair has been much helped by the submissions made by all members of the Commission. These, and the responses to the Commission's call for external contributions, have greatly influenced the contents of the Report, enlarging the scope of the Report and leading, directly or indirectly, to significant aspects of the recommendations.

A key element in the recommendations is the adoption of a parsimonious portfolio of Complementary Indicators (CIs), to be published alongside the core Global Poverty estimate and incorporated in the proposed country-level National Poverty Statistics Reports. It is to be hoped that the World Bank will accept this proposal and that it will give it prominence. The selection of a small number of CIs, and their linking to the annual publication of the International Poverty Line numbers, would give a clear profile to the work of the World Bank in measuring global poverty and contribute to building bridges with those who so far have been critics.

Possible constituents of the CI portfolio are summarized in box 2.3. The grounds for the choice of the seven CIs have been given above, and it is to be hoped that the reasoning will be taken seriously. At the same time, if the proposal of CIs is adopted, the Report's arguments will be only one of those entering their determination.

Box 2.3 Possible Portfolio of Complementary Indicators at Country Level

Amplification of the Global Poverty estimate

- The poverty gap, relative to the International Poverty Line, measured over the whole population and expressed as a percentage of the poverty line (for 2 most recent comparable years)
- Number of women, children and young adults in households living below the International Poverty Line (for 2 most recent comparable years)

Alternative global poverty measures

- If available, percentage of people living in households below a new needs-based poverty line set on a global basis and applied at a country level (for most recent year)
- A "societal" head count measure of global consumption poverty, combining fixed and relative elements (for 2 most recent comparable years)

The Twin Goal

- Level of living in real terms of the bottom 40 percent (for 2 most recent comparable years)

Nonmonetary indicators

- Dashboard containing nonmonetary indicators (for 2 most recent comparable years)
- A multidimensional poverty index based on the set of nonmonetary indicators from dashboard (for 2 most comparable recent years)

Notes

1. Among the many references are Sen and Foster 1997, Deaton 1997, Ravallion 1998, Sen 1999, Townsend and Gordon 2002, Duclos and Araar 2006, Alkire et al. 2015, World Bank 2015, and Ravallion 2016.
2. See PovcalNet (database), World Bank, Washington, DC, http://iresearch .worldbank.org/PovcalNet/index.htm?1,0.
3. See the Oxford Poverty & Human Development Initiative Multidimensional Poverty Peer Network (MPPN) website, http://www.mppn.org/participants/china/.
4. The mean shortfall in consumption from the poverty line, measured over the whole population, is in this case zH, where z is the poverty line and H is the head count ratio (the proportion of the population below the poverty line). Expressed as a percentage of the poverty line, this equals H.
5. PPP is purchasing power parity.

6. The Gini coefficient is half the mean absolute deviation divided by the mean.
7. There is a large literature on the measurement of poverty. See, among others, Atkinson 1987, Zheng 1997 and 2000, Duclos and Araar 2006, Chakravarty 2009, and Ravallion 2016a, chapter 5.
8. An interesting new measure has been proposed by Castleman, Foster, and Smith. They introduce a "person equivalent" measure, arguing by analogy "with the notion of a full time equivalent employee, which measures employment using a benchmark workweek to account for variations in the hours worked by different employees" (Castleman, Foster, and Smith 2015, 3–4). The person equivalent measure of poverty is obtained by dividing the total poverty gap by a benchmark figure for the average poverty gap. The choice of benchmark does, however, pose issues, not least regarding differences across countries, a difficulty it shares, in a different context, with the definition of full-time equivalent employees.
9. There may be a case for bottom-coding, replacing negative or zero incomes, or for employing the median rather than the mean poverty gap (see Atkinson et al. 2002, 116–17).
10. Disaggregation of the survey data may lead to concerns about the cell sizes and possible respondent identification. This does not, however, seem likely to be a problem with the disaggregations envisaged in Recommendation 13 with the sample sizes typically available.
11. A strong argument for the use of such measures is made by Case and Deaton (2002), illustrated by the case of self-reported health status.
12. "Child labour is ... a narrower concept than 'children in employment,' excluding all those children who are working only a few hours a week in permitted light work and those above the minimum age whose work is not classified as a worst form of child labour, or as 'hazardous work' in particular" (ILO 2013, 45).
13. For a recent study of vulnerability, see Chakravarty et al. 2015.
14. There are, for example, issues concerned with the comparability of scales across individuals (see Ravallion, Himelein, and Beegle 2016).
15. Stigler (1945) had previously solved the problem by a trial-and-error process and come close to the full linear programming solution.
16. As noted earlier, Cal (with a capital) is used in place of kcal.
17. For further discussion of the food share method, and of the approach based on the food demand function, see Ravallion 2016, 199–203.
18. No back-casting of the estimates is proposed.
19. There are many valuable accounts (see, for example, Basu and Lopez-Calva 2011 and Robeyns 2011). It should be noted that the capability approach has had more impact on normative economics than on positive economics, where the chain Commodities » Characterisitics » Capabilities » Utility (Sen 1982, 30) potentially enriches understanding of household behavior. See, for example, Atkinson 1987, which builds on the relation with the household activity approach of Becker 1965.

20. See the United Nations website on the "History of the Document," http://www .un.org/en/sections/universal-declaration/history-document/.

21. Although in the short term the required set of goods and services may remain largely unchanged. Research in Australia on the identification of "essential" items shows that the list of items attracting at least 50 percent support for being essential was unchanged between 2006 and 2010 (Saunders, Naidoo, and Griffiths 2008; Saunders and Wong 2012).

22. The diagram may be viewed as the horizontal plane in a three-dimensional graph where the vertical dimension, not shown, is the density function, so that the total in that area would be found by integrating the density function over the shaded rectangle.

23. http://www-wds.worldbank.org/external/default/WDSContentServer/WDSP/IB /2016/02/03/090224b08413deeb/1_0/Rendered/PDF/Within0our0gra0orgetown0 University.pdf.

24. The Lorenz curve is a graphic device, showing cumulatively for each percentage of the population their cumulative share of total income.

25. Much has been written on multidimensional inequality and poverty, and no attempt is made here to summarize the literature. For excellent references, see Chakravarty 2009, chapters 5 and 6; Aaberge and Brandolini 2015; and Alkire et al. 2015.

26. In 2014 and 2015, the *Human Development Report* contained both the OPHI MPIs, based on the 2010 specification, and MPIs calculated by the Human Development Report Office (UNDP 2015, table 6).

27. OPHI has been much engaged in the construction of national MPIs, and coordinates the Multidimensional Poverty Peer Network: http://www.mppn.org /participants/.

28. I am most grateful to Sabina Alkire for providing the information summarized in this table.

29. See the valuable discussion of this issue, and the next, by Alkire and Santos 2014 and by Alkire et al. 2015, 220–26.

30. The issues that arise when indicators are applied globally are considered in Marlier and Atkinson 2010 and Atkinson and Marlier 2010 and 2011.

31. For further discussion of the EU Social Indicators, see, among others, Guio, Gordon, and Marlier 2012 and 2016, Frazer et al. 2014, Guio and Marlier 2016, and Atkinson, Guio, and Marlier 2016.

32. On the theory of multidimensional poverty indexes, see, among others, Tsui 2002; Bourguignon and Chakravarty 2003; Atkinson 2003; Duclos, Sahn, and Younger 2006; Maasoumi and Lugo 2008; Kakwani and Silber 2008; Rippin 2010; Lustig 2011; Aaberge and Brandolini 2015; and Alkire et al. 2015.

33. Recent research has made use of copula functions to study the multivariate association among different components of well-being across two or more joint distributions (Atkinson and Marlier 2011). What is the copula function? Suppose that there are two dimensions, measured by variables denoted by x and y, with marginal distributions $F(x)$ and $G(y)$. The first two dials on the dashboard tell us how

many people are separately deprived on the dimensions x and y. Then, from a remarkable mathematical theorem (Sklar's Theorem), there is a copula function C{F,G} that binds the two marginal distributions to yield the joint distribution of x and y (Nelsen 1999, 20). It is the additional information contained in this copula function (over and above that contained in the marginal distributions) that summarizes the interdependence at the level of the household or individual. However, it does not reduce the joint distribution to a single number, and the procedure, while a valuable analytical tool, is not readily explained to a wide audience.

34. Information supplied by Sabina Alkire at the Launch of the Report on July 13, 2016.

35. Reference may also be made to the Key Indicators Survey, which has been the subject of pilot work: http://dhsprogram.com/What-We-Do/Survey-Types/KIS.cfm.

References

Aaberge, R., and A. Brandolini. 2015. "Multidimensional Poverty and Inequality." In *Handbook of Income Distribution*, Vol. 2A, edited by A. B. Atkinson and F. Bourguignon. Amsterdam: Elsevier.

Alkire, S. 2014. "Towards Frequent and Accurate Poverty Data." OPHI Research in Progress Series 43b, University of Oxford, Oxford, U.K.

Alkire, S., and J. Foster. 2011a. "Counting and Multidimensional Poverty Measurement." *Journal of Public Economics* 95: 476–87.

Alkire, S., J. Foster, S. Seth, M. S. Santos, J. M. Roche, and P. Ballon. 2015. *Multidimensional Poverty Measurement and Analysis*. Oxford, U.K.: Oxford University Press.

Alkire, S., and M. E. Santos. 2014. "Measuring Acute Poverty in the Developing World: Robustness and Scope of the Multidimensional Poverty Index." *World Development* 59: 251–74.

Allen, R. C. 2013. "Poverty Lines in History, Theory, and Current International Practice." Department of Economics Discussion Paper 685, University of Oxford, Oxford, U.K.

———. 2016. "Absolute Poverty: When Necessity Displaces Desire." Economics and Social History Working Paper 141, College, University of Oxford, Oxford, U.K.

Appleton, S. 1999. "Changes in Poverty in Uganda, 1992–1997." Centre for the Study of African Economies Discussion Paper 99.22, University of Oxford, University of Oxford, Oxford, U.K.

Atkinson, A. B. 1969. *Poverty in Britain and the Reform of Social Security*. Cambridge, U.K.: Cambridge University Press.

———. 1987. "On the Measurement of Poverty." *Econometrica* 55: 749–64.

———. 1995. "Capabilities, Exclusion, and the Supply of Goods." In *Choice, Welfare, and Development*, edited by K. Basu, P. Pattanaik, and K. Suzumura. Oxford, U.K.: Clarendon Press, 17–31.

———. 2003. "Multidimensional Deprivation: Contrasting Social Welfare and Counting Approaches." *Journal of Economic Inequality* 1: 51–65.

————. 2015. *Inequality: What Can Be Done?* Cambridge, MA: Harvard University Press.

Atkinson, A. B. and F. Bourguignon. 2000a. "Pauvreté et inclusion dans une perspective mondiale." *Revue d'économie du développement* 2000 8: 13–32.

————. 2000b. "Inclusion from a World Perspective." In *Governance, Equity and Global Markets*, edited by Jean Louis Beffa, et al., 179–92. Paris: La Documentation Française (English version).

Atkinson, A. B., and A. Brandolini. 2010. "On Analyzing the World Distribution of Income." *The World Bank Economic Review* 24: 1–37.

Atkinson, A. B., B. Cantillon, E. Marlier, and B. Nolan. 2002. *Social Indicators: The EU and Social Inclusion.* Oxford, U.K.: Oxford University Press.

Atkinson, A. B., A.-C. Guio, and E. Marlier, eds. 2016. *Monitoring Social Europe.* Luxembourg: Publications Office of the European Union.

Atkinson, A. B., and E. Marlier. 2010. *Analysing and Measuring Social Inclusion in a Global Context.* New York: United Nations Department of Economic and Social Affairs.

————. 2011. "Human Development and Indicators of Poverty and Social Exclusion as Part of the Policy Process." *Indian Journal of Human Development* 5: 293–320.

Basu, K. 1999. "Child Labor: Cause, Consequence, and Cure, with Remarks on International Labor Standards." *Journal of Economic Literature* 37: 1083–1119.

————. 2001. "On the Goals of Development." In *Frontiers of Development Economics*, edited by G. M. Meier and J. E. Stiglitz, 61–101. Oxford, U.K.: Oxford University Press.

————. 2013. "Shared Prosperity and the Mitigation of Poverty: In Practice and in Precept." Policy Research Working Paper 6700, World Bank, Washington, DC.

Basu, K., and L. F. López-Calva. 2011. "Functionings and Capabilities." In *Handbook of Social Choice and Welfare*, Vol. 2, edited by K. J. Arrow, A. Sen, and K, Suzumura, 53–187. Amsterdam: Elsevier.

Batane, Y., M. Bussolo, and J. Cockburn. 2013. "Global Extreme Poverty Rates for Children, Adults and the Elderly." *Economics Letters* 120: 405–07.

Becker, G. S. 1965. "A Theory of the Allocation of Time." *Economic Journal* 75: 493–517.

Bourguignon, F. 2015. *The Globalization of Inequality.* Princeton, NJ: Princeton University Press.

Bourguignon, F., A. Bénassy-Quéré, S. Dercon, A. Estache, J. W. Gunning, R. Kanbur, S. Klasen, S. Maxwell, J.-P. Platteau, and A. Spadaro. 2010. "The Millennium Development Goals: An Assessment." In *Equity and Growth in a Globalizing World*, edited by R. Kanbur and M. Spence, 17–40. Washington, DC: World Bank.

Bourguignon, F., and S. R. Chakravarty. 2003. "The Measurement of Multidimensional Poverty." *Journal of Economic Inequality* 1: 25–49.

Bourguignon, F., and H. Moreno. 2015. "On the Construction of Synthetic Panels." Working Paper, Paris School of Economics.

Bourguignon, F., and C. Morrisson. 2002. "Inequality among World Citizens, 1820–1992." *American Economic Review* 92: 727–44.

Bradshaw, J., and E. Mayhew. 2011. *The Measurement of Extreme Poverty in the European Union*. Brussels: European Commission, DG Employment, Social Affairs and Inclusion.

Calvo-Gonzãlez, O. 2016. "Why Are Indigenous Peoples More Likely to Be Poor?" World Bank Data Blog.

Case, A., and A. Deaton. 2002. "Consumption, Health, Gender and Poverty." Research Program in Development Studies, Princeton University, Princeton, NJ.

Castillo Añazco, R., and F. Jácome Pérez. 2016. *Medición de la Pobreza Multidimensional en Ecuador*. Guayaquil: Instituto Nacional de Estadística y Censos (INEC). http://www.ecuadorencifras.gob.ec/documentos/web-inec/Sitios/Pobreza_Multidimensional/.

Castleman, T., J. Foster, and S. C. Smith. 2015. "Person Equivalent Headcount Measures of Poverty." Institute for International Economic Policy Working Paper Series 2015-10, George Washington University, Washington, DC.

Chakravarty, S. R. 2009. *Inequality, Polarization, and Poverty*. New York: Springer.

Chakravarty, S. R., N. Chattopadhyay, J. Silber, and G. Wan. 2015. "Measuring the Impact of Vulnerability on the Number of Poor: A New Methodology and an Empirical Illustration Based on Asian Data." Mimeo.

Chen, S., and M. Ravallion. 2013. "More Relatively-Poor People in a Less Absolutely-Poor World." *Review of Income and Wealth* series 59: 1–28.

CONEVAL (Consejo Nacional para la Evaluacion de la Politica de Desarrolo Social). 2010. *Methodology for Multidimensional Poverty Measurement in Mexico*. Mexico City: CONEVAL.

CONPES (Consejo Nacional de Politica Economica y Social, Documento Conpes Social). 2012. *Official Methodology and Institutional Arrangements for the Measurement of Poverty in Colombia*. Bogota: CONPES (in Spanish). Available at: colaboracion.dnp.gov.co/CDT/Conpes/150.pdf.

Cruces, G., P. F. Lanjouw, L. Lucchetti, E. Perova, R. Vakis, and M. Viollaz. 2011. "Intra-Generational Mobility and Repeated Cross-Sections: A Three Country Validation Exercise." Policy Research Working Paper 5916, World Bank, Washington, DC.

Cruz, M., J. Foster, B. Quillin, and P. Schellekens. 2015. "Ending Extreme Poverty and Sharing Prosperity: Progress and Policies." Policy Research Note, World Bank, Washington, DC.

Dang, H.-A., and P. Lanjouw. 2013. "Measuring Poverty Dynamics with Synthetic Panels Based on Cross-Sections." Policy Research Working Paper 6504, World Bank, Washington, DC.

———. 2014. "Welfare Dynamics Measurement: Two Definitions of a Vulnerability Line and Their Empirical Application." Policy Research Working Paper 6944, World Bank, Washington, DC.

———. 2015. "Toward a New Definition of Shared Prosperity: A Dynamic Perspective from Three Countries." Policy Research Working Paper 7294, World Bank, Washington, DC.

Dang H.-A., P. Lanjouw, J. Luoto, and D. McKenzie. 2014. "Using Repeated Cross-Sections to Explore Movements In and Out of Poverty." *Journal of Development Economics* 107: 112–28.

Datt, G., K. Simler, S. Mukherjee, and G. Dava. 2000. "Determinants of Poverty in Mozambique, 1996–97." FCND Discussion Paper No 78, Food Consumption and Nutrition Division, International Food Policy Research Institute, Washington, DC.

Deaton, A. 1997. *The Analysis of Household Surveys: A Microeconometric Approach to Development Policy.* Baltimore, MD: Johns Hopkins University Press.

Deaton, A., and J. Drèze. 2009. "Food and Nutrition in India: Facts and Interpretations." *Economic and Political Weekly* 44 (7): 42–65.

Decancq, K., and M. A. Lugo. 2012. "Weights in Multidimensional Indices of Well-Being: An Overview." *Econometric Reviews* 32: 7–34.

Decerf, B. 2015. "A New Index Combining the Absolute and Relative Aspects of Income Poverty: Theory and Application." CORE Discussion Paper 2015/50, Center for Operations Research and Econometrics, Louvain-la-Neuve, Belgium.

Dell'Aglio, D., W. Cunningham, S. Koller, V. C. Borges, and J. S. Leon. 2007. "Youth Well-Being in Brazil: An Index for Cross-Regional Comparisons." Policy Research Working Paper 4189, World Bank, Washington, DC.

Dorfman, R., P. A. Samuelson, and R. M. Solow. 1958. *Linear Programming and Economic Analysis.* New York: McGraw-Hill.

Drèze, J., and A. Sen. 2013. *An Uncertain Glory: India and Its Contradictions.* London: Allen Lane.

Duclos, J.-Y., and A. Araar. 2006. *Poverty and Equity.* Ottawa: Springer.

Duclos, J.-Y., D. E. Sahn, and S. D. Younger. 2006. "Robust Multidimensional Poverty Comparisons." *Economic Journal* 116: 943–68.

Erikson, R. 1993. "Descriptions of Inequality: The Swedish Approach to Welfare Research." In *The Quality of Life,* edited M. Nussbaum and A. Sen, 67–87. Oxford, U.K.: Clarendon Press.

European Commission. 2016. *The Dutch Food Basket.* Brussels: European Commission.

FAO (Food and Agriculture Organization). 2001. *Human Energy Requirements.* Food and Nutrition Technical Report 1. Rome: FAO.

———. 2008. *FAO Methodology for the Measurement of Food Deprivation: Updating the Minimum Dietary Energy Requirements.* Available at: http://www.fao.org /fileadmin/templates/ess/documents/food_security_statistics/metadata /undernourishment_methodology.pdf.

Ferreira, F. H. G., and M. A. Lugo. 2013. "Multidimensional Poverty Analysis: Looking for a Middle Ground." *World Bank Research Observer* 2: 220–35.

Foster, J., J. Greer, and E. Thorbecke. 1984. "A Class of Decomposable Poverty Measures." *Econometrica* 52: 761–76.

Frazer, H., A.-C. Guio, E. Marlier, B. Vanhercke, and T. Ward. 2014. "Putting the Fight against Poverty and Social Exclusion at the Heart of the EU Agenda: A Contribution to the Mid-Term Review of the Europe 2020 Strategy." OSE Paper Series, Research Paper 15, OSE, Brussels.

Gibson, J. 2005. "Statistical Tools and Estimation Methods for Poverty Measures Based on Cross-Sectional Household Surveys." Chapter 5 in *Handbook on Poverty Statistics: Concepts, Methods and Policy Use.* New York: United Nations Statistics Division.

Global Coalition of Partners to End Child Poverty. 2015. Submission to the Global Poverty Commission.

Goedemé, T., B. Storms, T. Penne, and K. Van den Bosch, eds. 2015. *The Development of a Methodology for Comparable Reference Budgets in Europe—Final Report of the Pilot Project.* Luxembourg: Publications Office of the European Union.

Government of Chile. 2015. *Nueva Metodología de Medición de Pobreza por Ingresos y Multidimensional.* Documentos Metodológicos 28. Santiago: Gobierno de Chile Ministerio de Desarrollo Social.

Government of Costa Rica. 2015. *Methodology of the Costa Rican Multidimensional Poverty Index (MPI).* San José: El Instituto Nacional de Estadística y Censos (INEC).

Government of El Salvador. 2015. *Multidimensional Measurement of Poverty: El Salvador.* Secretaría Técnica y de Planificación de la Presidencia y Ministerio de Economía, a través de la Dirección General de Estadística y Censos (STPP and MINEC-DIGESTYC), El Salvador. (In Spanish). Full text available at: http://www .secretariatecnica.gob.sv/medicion-multidimensional-de-la-pobreza-el-salvador/.

Greenberg, J. 2014. "Meet the 'Zombie Stat' that Just Won't Die." PunditFact, July 3, http://www.politifact.com/punditfact/article/2014/jul/03/meet-zombie-stat -just-wont-die/.

Grosh, M., and P. Glewwe. 1995. "A Guide to Living Standards Measurement Surveys." LSMS Working Paper 120, World Bank, Washington, DC.

Guio, A.-C., D. Gordon, and E. Marlier. 2012. "Measuring Material Deprivation in the EU: Indicators for the Whole Population and Child-Specific Indicators." Eurostat Methodologies and Working Papers, Office for Official Publications of the European Communities (OPOCE), Luxembourg.

———. 2016. "Measuring Child Material Deprivation in the EU." In *Monitoring Social Europe,* edited by A. B. Atkinson, A.-C. Guio, and E. Marlier. Luxembourg: Publications Office of the European Union.

Guio, A.-C., and E. Marlier. 2016. "Amending the EU Material Deprivation Indicator: Impact on the Size and Composition of the Deprived Population." In *Monitoring Social Europe,* edited by A. B. Atkinson, A.-C. Guio, and E. Marlier. Luxembourg: Publications Office of the European Union.

Handoussa, H. 2010. "Egypt Human Development Report 2010," executed by the Institute of National Planning, Egypt, under the project document

EGY/01/006 of technical cooperation with the United Nations Development Programme (UNDP).

ILO (International Labour Organization). 2013. *Marking Progress against Child Labour—Global Estimates and Trends 2000–2012.* Geneva: ILO International Programme on the Elimination of Child Labour (IPEC).

———. 2015. *World Report on Child Labour 2015: Paving the Way to Decent Work for Young People.* Geneva: International Labour Office.

International Movement ATD Fourth World. 2015. Submission to the Global Poverty Commission.

Jencks, C. 2016. "Why the Very Poor Have Become Poorer." *New York Review of Books,* June 9.

Jolly, R. 2012. "Foreword: UNICEF, Children and Child Poverty." In *Global Child Poverty and Well-Being: Measurement, Concepts and Action,* edited by A. Minujin and S. Nandy, xxix–xxxii. Bristol, U.K.: Policy Press.

Kakwani, N., and J. Silber. 2008. "Introduction: Multidimensional Poverty Analysis: Conceptual Issues, Empirical Illustrations and Policy Implications." *World Development* 36: 987–91.

Kakwani, N., and H. Son. 2015. "Measuring Food Insecurity: Global Estimates." ECINEQ Working Paper Series 370, Society for the Study of Economic Inequality, Verona, Italy.

Kanbur, R. 1987. "Measurement and Alleviation of Poverty: With an Application to the Effects of Macroeconomic Adjustment." *IMF Staff Papers* 34: 60–85.

Lakner, C., and B. Milanovic. 2015. "Global Income Distribution: From the Fall of the Berlin Wall to the Great Recession." *World Bank Economic Review* 10.1093 /wber/lhv039.

Lustig, N. 2011. "Multidimensional Indices of Achievements and Poverty: What Do We Gain and What Do We Lose? An Introduction to JOEI Forum on Multidimensional Poverty." *Journal of Economic Inequality* 9 (2): 227–34.

Maasoumi, E., and M. A. Lugo. 2008. "The Information Basis of Multivariate Poverty Assessments." In *Quantitative Approaches to Multidimensional Poverty Measurement,* edited by N. Kakwani and J. Silber, 1–29. Basingstoke, U.K.: Palgrave Macmillan.

Mack, J., and S. Lansley. 1985. *Poor Britain.* London: Allen and Unwin.

Malaysia Department of Statistics. n. d. "Poverty Line Income: Malaysia's Experiences." Azahari Mohd Raslan, Prices, Income and Expenditure Statistics Division, Kuala Lumpur.

Marcoux, A. 1998. "The Feminization of Poverty: Claims, Facts, and Data Needs." *Population and Development Review* 24: 131–39.

Marlier, E., and A. B. Atkinson. 2010. "Indicators of Poverty and Social Exclusion in a Global Context." *Journal of Policy Analysis and Management* 29: 285–304.

Marlier, E., A. B. Atkinson, B. Cantillon, and B. Nolan. 2007. *The EU and Social Inclusion: Facing the Challenges.* Bristol, U.K.: Policy Press.

Martinez, A., M. Western, M. Haynes, and W. Tomaszewski. 2013. "Measuring Income Mobility Using Pseudo-panel Data." *Philippine Statistician* 62 (2): 71–99.

Moatsos, M. 2015. "Global Absolute Poverty: Behind the Veil of Dollars." CGEH Working Paper 77, Centre for Global Economic History, Utrecht University, Utrecht.

Morciano, M., R. Hancock, and S. Pudney. 2012. "*Disability Costs and Equivalence Scales in the Older Population.*" ISER Working Paper Series 2012-09, Institute for Social and Economic Research, University of Essex, U.K.

Morelli, S., T. M. Smeeding, and J. P. Thompson. 2015. "Post-1970 Trends in Within-Country Inequality and Poverty: Rich and Middle Income Countries." In *Handbook of Income Distribution*, Vol. 2A, edited by A. B. Atkinson and F. Bourguignon, 697–805. Elsevier-North Holland.

Nandy, S., and D. Gordon. 2015. "Policy Relevant Measurement of Poverty in Low, Middle and High Income Countries." In *Poverty and Inequality in Middle Income Countries: Policy Achievements, Political Obstacles*, edited by E. Braathen, J. May, and G. Wright 16–43. CROP, London: Zed Books.

Narayan, D., R. Chambers, M. K. Shah, and P. Petesch. 2000. *Voices of the Poor: Crying Out for Change.* New York: Oxford University Press.

Narayan, D., R. Patel, K. Schafft, A. Rademacher, and S. Koch-Schulte. 2000a. *Voices of the Poor: Can Anyone Hear Us?* New York: Oxford University Press.

Narayan, D., and P. Petesch, eds. 2002. *Voices of the Poor: From Many Lands.* New York: Oxford University Press.

Narsey, W. 2008. *The Quantitative Analysis of Poverty in Fiji.* Fiji Islands Bureau of Statistics and the School of Economics, University of the South Pacific.

Nelsen, R. B. 1999. *An Introduction to Copulas.* New York: Springer.

Nickel, J. W. 2014. "What Future for Human Rights?" *Ethics and International Affairs* 28: 213–23.

Nussbaum, M. 1988. "Nature, Function, and Capability: Aristotle on Political Distribution." *Oxford Studies in Ancient Philosophy* Supplement: 145–84.

———. 2000. *Women and Human Development: The Capabilities Approach.* New York: Cambridge University Press.

———. 2000a. *Sex and Social Justice.* Oxford, U.K.: Oxford University Press.

———. 2003. "Capabilities as Fundamental Entitlements: Sen and Social Justice." *Feminist Economics* 9: 33–59.

Nussbaum, M., and J. Glover, eds. 1995. *Women, Culture, and Development: A Study of Human Capabilities.* Oxford, U.K.: Clarendon Press.

Office of the Federal Register. 2015. *Federal Register* 80 (14 Thursday, January 22). Washington, DC: Office of the Federal Register.

Orshansky, M. 1965. "Counting the Poor: Another Look at the Poverty Profile." *Social Security Bulletin* 28: 3–29.

Pakistan Ministry of Finance. 2013. *Pakistan Economic Survey 2013–14.* Government of Pakistan.

Pemberton, S., D. Gordon, S. Nandy, C. Pantazis, and P. Townsend. 2007. "Child Rights and Child Poverty: Can the International Framework of Children's Rights Be Used to Improve Child Survival Rates?" *PLoS Medicine* 4: e307.

Planning Institute of Jamaica. 2007. "The Poverty-Environment Nexus: Establishing an Approach for Determining Special Development Areas in Jamaica." Planning Institute of Jamaica, Sustainable Development and Regional Planning Division.

Ravallion, M. 1998. "Poverty Lines in Theory and Practice." LSMS Working Paper 133, World Bank, Washington, DC.

———. 2011. "On Multidimensional Indices of Poverty." *Journal of Economic Inequality* 9: 235–48.

———. 2016. "Toward Better Global Poverty Measures." *Journal of Economic Inequality* 14: 227–48.

———. 2016a. *The Economics of Poverty: History, Measurement, and Policy.* New York: Oxford University Press.

Ravallion, M., and S. Chen. 2011. "Weakly Relative Poverty." *Review of Economics and Statistics* 93: 1251–61.

———. 2013. "A Proposal for Truly Global Poverty Measures." *Global Policy* 4: 258–65.

Ravallion, M., G. Datt, and D. van de Walle. 1991. "Quantifying Absolute Poverty in the Developing World." *Review of Income and Wealth* series 37: 345–61.

Ravallion, M., K. Himelein, and K. Beegle. 2016. "Can Subjective Questions on Economic Welfare Be Trusted?" Policy Research Working Paper 6726, World Bank, Washington, DC.

Reddy, S. G., and T. W. Pogge. 2010. "How *Not* to Count the Poor." In *Debates on the Measurement of Global Poverty,* edited by S. Anand, P. Segal, and J. E. Stiglitz, 42–85. Oxford, U.K.: Oxford University Press.

Rippin, N. 2010. "Poverty Severity in a Multidimensional Framework: The Issue of Inequality between Dimensions." Poverty, Equity and Growth Discussion Paper 47, Courant Research Centre, University of Göttingen, Göttingen, Germany.

Robertson, D. H. 1954. "Utility and All What?" *Economic Journal* 64: 665–78.

Robeyns, I. 2003. "Sen's Capability Approach and Gender Inequality: Selecting Relevant Capabilities." *Feminist Economics* 9(2/3): 61–92.

———. 2011. "The Capability Approach." In *The Stanford Encyclopedia of Philosophy, Summer 2011 Edition,* edited by N. Z. Edward. Available at: http://plato.stanford.edu/archives/sum2011/entries/capability-approach/.

Robinson, M. 2002. Statement at the World Summit on Sustainable Development, Johannesburg, August 29. Available at: http://www.un.org/events/wssd/statements/unhchrE.htm.

Roemer, J. 1998. *Equality of Opportunity.* Cambridge, MA: Harvard University Press.

Rowntree, B. S. 1901. *Poverty: A Study of Town Life.* London: Longmans, Green and Co.

Sala-i-Martin, X., and M. Pinkovskiy. 2010. "African Poverty is Falling . . . Much Faster Than You Think!" NBER Working Paper 15775, National Bureau of Economic Research, Cambridge, MA.

Saunders, P. 2015. Submission to the Global Poverty Commission.

Saunders, P., Y. Naidoo, and M. Griffiths. 2008. "Towards New Indicators of Disadvantage: Deprivation and Social Exclusion in Australia." *Australian Journal of Social Issues* 43 (2): 175–94.

Saunders, P., and M. Wong. 2012. "Promoting Inclusion and Combating Deprivation: Recent Changes in Social Disadvantage in Australia." Social Policy Research Centre, University of New South Wales, Sydney.

Sen, A. K. 1976. "Poverty: An Ordinal Approach to Measurement." *Econometrica* 44: 219–31.

———. 1982. "Introduction." In *Choice, Welfare and Measurement*, 1–39. Oxford, U.K.: Basil Blackwell.

———. 1983. "Poor Relatively Speaking." *Oxford Economic Papers* 35: 153–69.

———. 1985. *Commodities and Capabilities.* Amsterdam: North-Holland.

———. 1992. *Markets and Governments.* Institute for Economic Development, Boston University.

———. 1999. *Development as Freedom.* Oxford, U.K.: Oxford University Press.

———. 2009. *The Idea of Justice.* London: Allen Lane.

Sen, A. K., and J. E. Foster. 1997. *On Economic Inequality.* Expanded edition. Oxford, U.K.: Clarendon Press.

Shorrocks, A. F. 1995. "Revisiting the Sen Poverty Index." *Econometrica* 63: 1225–30.

Shue, H. 1996. *Basic Rights.* Second edition. Princeton, NJ: Princeton University Press.

Social Protection Committee Indicators Sub-Group. 2015. *Portfolio of EU Social Indicators for the Monitoring of Progress towards the EU Objectives for Social Protection and Social Inclusion (2015 Update).* Brussels: European Commission.

Sri Lanka Department of Census and Statistics. 2004. *Official Poverty Line for Sri Lanka.* Colombo.

Statistics Ghana. 2014. *Ghana Living Standards Survey Round 6 (GLSS 6): Poverty Profile in Ghana (2005–2013).* Accra: Statistics Ghana.

Statistics South Africa. 2008. *Measuring Poverty in South Africa: Methodological Report on the Development of the Poverty Lines for Statistical Reporting.* Technical Report D0300. Pretoria: Statistics South Africa.

Stigler, G. J. 1945. "The Cost of Subsistence." *Journal of Farm Economics* 27: 303–14.

Storms, B., T. Goedemé, K. Van den Bosch, and K. Devuyst. 2013. "Towards a Common Framework for Developing Cross-Nationally Comparable Reference Budgets in Europe." ImPRovE Methodological Paper 13/02, Antwerp.

Subramanian, S. 2009. "'How Many Poor in the World?': A Critique of Ravallion's Reply." *Economic and Political Weekly* 44 (5): 67–71.

———. 2011. "'Inclusive Development' and the Quintile Income Statistics." *Economic and Political Weekly* 46 (4): 69–72.

————. 2011a. "Money-metric Poverty Identification: A Cautionary Note." *Journal of Economic Analysis* 2: 46–55.

Sukhatme, P. V. 1961. "The World's Hunger and Future Needs in Food Supplies." *Journal of the Royal Statistical Society, Series A* 124: 463–525.

Sutherland, H., and D. Piachaud. 2001. "Reducing Child Poverty in Britain: An Assessment of Government Policy, 1997–2001." *Economic Journal* 111: F85–F101.

Tanzania National Bureau of Statistics. 2014. *Household Budget Survey Main Report 2011/12*. Dar es Salaam: Ministry of Finance.

Tobin, J. 1970. "On Limiting the Domain of Inequality." *Journal of Law and Economics* 13: 263–77.

Townsend, P. 1979. *Poverty in the United Kingdom: A Survey of Household Resources and Standards of Living*. Harmondsworth, U.K.: Allen Lane.

Townsend, P., and D. Gordon. 2002. *World Poverty: New Policies to Defeat an Old Enemy*. Bristol, U.K.: Policy Press.

Trinidad and Tobago Ministry of Social Development. 2007. *Analysis of the Trinidad and Tobago Survey of Living Conditions 2005*. Port of Spain: Ministry of Social Development.

Tsui, K. Y. 2002. "Multidimensional Poverty Indices." *Social Choice and Welfare* 19: 69–93.

UNDESA (United Nations Department of Economic and Social Affairs). 2016. *Provisional Proposed Tiers for Global SDG Indicators*. New York: United Nations.

UNDP (United Nations Development Programme). 2010. *Human Development Report 2010*. New York: United Nations.

————. 2015. *Human Development Report 2015*. New York: United Nations.

UNDP (United Nations Development Programme) and Institute of National Planning, Egypt. 2010. *Youth in Egypt: Building Our Future, Egypt Human Development Report 2010*. Cairo: UNDP and Institute of National Planning.

United Nations. 1948. *Universal Declaration of Human Rights*. New York: United Nations.

————. 1954. *International Definition and Measurement of Standards and Levels of Living*. New York: United Nations Publications.

————. 2015. "Draft Outcome Document of the United Nations Summit for the Adoption of the Post-2015 Development Agenda." Draft resolution submitted by the President of the General Assembly, United Nations, New York.

————. 2015a. *The Millennium Development Goals Report 2015*. New York: United Nations.

UNPFII (United Nations Permanent Forum on Indigenous Issues). 2016. "Indigenous Peoples: Conflict, Peace and Resolution." Fifteenth Session of the UNPFII, May 9–20, New York.

USAID (U.S. Agency for International Development). 2015. *Vision for Ending Extreme Poverty*. Washington, DC: USAID.

Walzer, M. 1983. *Spheres of Justice: A Defense of Pluralism and Equality.* New York: Basic Books.

World Bank. 1990. *World Development Report 1990: Poverty.* New York: Oxford University Press.

———. 2001. *World Development Report 2000/2001: Attacking Poverty.* New York: Oxford University Press.

———. 2015. *A Measured Approach to Ending Poverty and Boosting Shared Prosperity: Concepts, Data, and the Twin Goals.* Policy Research Report. Washington, DC: World Bank.

———. 2015a. *World Bank Group Gender Strategy (FY16-23): Gender Equality, Poverty Reduction and Inclusive Growth.* Washington, DC: World Bank.

———. 2016. *Indigenous Latin America in the Twenty-First Century: The First Decade.* Washington, DC: World Bank.

———. 2016a. "Individual Poverty Measurement: Submission to the Commission on Global Poverty." World Bank, Washington, DC.

World Bank Group. 2016. *Global Monitoring Report 2015/2016: Development Goals in an Era of Demographic Change.* Washington, DC: World Bank.

Zheng, B. 1997. "Aggregate Poverty Measures." *Journal of Economic Surveys* 2: 123–62.

———. 2000. "Poverty Orderings." *Journal of Economic Surveys* 14: 427–66.

Making It Happen

In order for the extreme poverty goal to be effectively monitored, and in order for a set of Complementary Indicators to be properly developed, there are a number of prerequisites. This final part of the Report highlights two aspects that seem essential—investment in statistics and an appropriate external governance structure—and asks how a coalition of support can be created for the work of the World Bank in this field. As already signaled at the outset, the Report does not consider the internal governance of the World Bank or the responsibilities of different parts of the World Bank.[1]

Investing in statistics

There is wide agreement among international organizations that there needs to be a significant additional investment in statistics if there is to be effective monitoring of the Sustainable Development Goals (SDGs). In the Draft resolution submitted by the President of the United Nations (UN) General Assembly in September 2015, the section on "Follow-up and review" stated clearly that "quality, accessible, timely and reliable disaggregated data will be needed to help with the measurement of progress and to ensure that no one is left behind.

Such data is key to decision-making" (United Nations 2015, para 48). The *Millennium Development Goals Report 2015* talked of the need for a "data revolution":

> As the post-2015 development agenda is being established, strengthening data production and the use of better data in policymaking and monitoring are becoming increasingly recognized as fundamental means for development. The MDG monitoring experience has clearly demonstrated that effective use of data can help to galvanize development efforts . . . sustainable development demands a data revolution to improve the availability, quality, timeliness and disaggregation of data to support the implementation of the new development agenda at all levels. (United Nations 2015a, 9)

In August 2014, the UN Secretary-General asked an Independent Expert Advisory Group to make concrete recommendations on how to bring about such a data revolution. In the case of the World Bank, the recent Review of DEC (the Development Economics Group) concluded that "to monitor the SDGs in an authoritative way for the global policy community . . . will require a major investment in the World Bank's capacity in data and statistics" (World Bank 2015, 8). In October 2015, the World Bank President Jim Yong Kim said,

> we will not be able to reach our goal unless we have data to show whether or not people are actually lifting themselves out of poverty. Collecting good data is one of the most powerful tools to end extreme poverty. We pledge, working alongside our partners in countries and international organizations, to do something that makes common sense and is long overdue: to conduct surveys in all countries that will assess whether people's lives are improving.[2]

The call for a substantial increase in the investment in data is reiterated here. Indeed, to echo the President, without such an investment by the World Bank, there must be significant doubt whether it can satisfactorily continue to fulfill the function of supplying the global poverty numbers, let alone to develop a response to the criticisms that have been made. There has to be a step upward in the resources available for the monitoring of global poverty:

> Recommendation 20: There should be a major investment in statistical sources and analysis, with these activities being accorded a high priority in the work of the World Bank.

Availability of data depends, first, on there being relevant surveys, and, second, on there being access for the World Bank to make use of the surveys. There can be little doubt that access is a major issue. For a variety of reasons, it is not possible for the World Bank to make full use of all data relevant to its remit of measuring global poverty. In the case of Africa, the World Bank study, *Poverty in a Rising Africa* (Beegle et al. 2016) identified 180 surveys over the period 1990–2012, but about a fifth were not available in the microdata library. Overcoming this second hurdle depends crucially on collaboration with national statistical offices. The achievement of better data on extreme poverty rests on the resources available to these institutions and on their own organization and priorities. It depends on the engagement of the national offices. Lack of data availability in the past may be due to other statistical operations taking precedence. There may, as in many countries, be insufficient coordination between the national accounts and household statistics. Recipients of development assistance may have been subject to conflicting donor preferences. Translating the increased investment by the World Bank into improved data at the country level requires therefore careful negotiation, taking account of each country's specific circumstances. Progress will not be achieved overnight. (After all, it should not be forgotten that official measures of poverty are a relatively recent phenomenon in many high-income countries—dating in the United States from the 1960s War on Poverty.)

The aim of Recommendation 20 is, therefore, not only to increase resources but also to signal the need for higher priority to be given to poverty statistics—by both the World Bank and by national statistical offices. In seeking to bring this about, the World Bank may be able to benefit from enhanced collaboration with other international bodies and related institutions. There is already considerable collaboration of this kind, but, as the Report has stressed from the outset, there is scope for this to be increased to make more effective use of the world's statistical resources and to avoid duplication. There are lessons that can be learned in this regard from regional collaboration, such as those involving the Development Banks. In the case of the European Union, Eurostat brings together the National Statistical Institutes of the Member States in joint activities to develop new statistics: for example, the development of the common statistical framework, EU–SILC (EU Statistics on Income and Living Conditions) (see Atkinson and Marlier 2010). In the global context, the Report has referred specifically to the World Bank's making greater use of Joint Statistical Working Parties, which can engage national and regional official statisticians and academic researchers funded by foundations and other nongovernmental sources.[3] Establishment of a more formal structure for this kind of collaboration would allow the World Bank to carry out a number of the investments urged in this Report via more effective employment of the sum of resources available in this field.

Data Priorities

On the assumption that the World Bank is willing to make the serious additional investment in statistics that is required, working in conjunction with national statistical agencies, what would this investment involve? Here attention is focused on the requirements for the measurement of global poverty along the lines recommended in this report.

In the course of the Report, a long "shopping list" for investments in improving the statistical base has been compiled. These include:

- Extending the country coverage of household surveys, including access to existing surveys
- Increasing the frequency of the basic household surveys
- Improving the reliability of national consumer price indexes (CPIs)
- Development of nonmonetary poverty indicators, allowing for multidimensional measures
- Engagement in participatory studies designed to obtain information about alternative poverty lines and the composition of the portfolio of Complementary Indicators
- Reconciliation of national accounts and household survey measures of consumption (and income)
- Improving population figures, and the post-census extrapolation
- Improving the quality of the measures of consumption within household surveys
- Research on those "missing" from the survey populations
- Investigating CPIs for the poor
- Work program on basic needs indicator
- Conducting rapid response and/or limited consumption surveys

The above list is arranged in a broad order of descending priority, but this is only a first attempt at a ranking. Any final decision must depend on information about feasibility and cost that cannot be assessed here.

There are, however, some general points to be highlighted. The first point concerns the choice of countries on which to focus. There is the perennial tension between allocating data resources to countries where the poverty rate is likely to be proportionately more affected by improvements and countries where there is a large number of poor. The appropriate allocation will depend on the subject under investigation: for example, in the case of country coverage, the Middle East and North Africa (MENA) region appears a priority and it may be a location suitable for experimentation with rapid response surveys; but it would not be the most obvious place to conduct pilot studies of price indexes for the poor. In the case of the population figures, there may be a case for concentrating initially on the largest countries. Some 60 percent of the population of Sub-Saharan Africa live in just six countries (the Democratic Republic of Congo, Ethiopia, Kenya, Nigeria, South Africa, and Tanzania). In reaching these judgments, an important role could be played by the National Poverty Statistics Reports, which could identify priorities for additional resources.

The second aspect concerns the availability and documentation of data. The World Bank is rightly commended for its efforts to make data available, and PovcalNet is much valued for its accessibility.[4] A remarkable number of those making submissions to the Commission on Global Poverty had employed PovcalNet data in studies of global poverty. At the same time, a constant refrain when discussing the statistics produced by the World Bank is the need for better documentation. The same concerns regarding documentation and access apply to survey data collected at the national level. Here the World Bank has no direct responsibility, but it could use its influence to secure easier access to data for outside researchers.

Building Statistical Capacity at the National Level

In the UN declaration concerning the SDGs, it was stated by heads of government that "We will support developing countries, particularly African countries, least developed countries, small island developing States and landlocked developing countries, in strengthening the capacity of national statistical offices and data systems to ensure access to high-quality, timely, reliable and disaggregated data" (United Nations 2015, para 48). It is indeed evident that the successful measurement of global poverty depends crucially on the statistical capacity of national (and lower-level) governments.

The need for such investment has long been recognized by the World Bank (see, for example, World Bank 2002). The World Bank was a founding member in 1999 of PARIS21 (Partnership in Statistics for Development in the 21st Century) along with the United Nations, the European Commission, the Organisation for Economic Co-operation and Development (OECD), and the International Monetary Fund (IMF). PARIS21 is a global forum and network to promote, influence, and facilitate statistical capacity development and the better use of statistics. In contemporary terms, the Review of DEC (World Bank 2015, 33) notes that significant resources are being devoted to supporting the building of statistical capacity. The work in this area includes the development of funding streams for country capacity development, the coordination of standard development and technical assistance with the UN and other multilateral bodies, the development of a global partnership on data for sustainable development, working with partners to "cost" the data required for monitoring SDGs, and so on. The importance of these activities does not need underlining. Without investment in capacity building, many of the recommendations in the Report will be ineffectual.

Governance Structure and External Accountability

The high political profile of the statistics considered in this Report means that issues of governance necessarily arise. They arise in two key respects. First, the World Bank is the leading global agency for collecting and analyzing data on the progress toward achieving Goal 1.1 and other important Goals. As such, its activities are of wide interest: "given the profile of global goals for poverty reduction and the Bank's leadership position among international development partners, the Bank's poverty agenda is of great interest to internal and external stakeholders" (World Bank 2013, 9). Second, the World Bank is providing the data to monitor its own performance according to the Twin Goals of ending extreme poverty and promoting shared prosperity. While the World Bank's activity is only one of many contributors to the world's success in achieving these goals, the Bank has established these criteria as defining its raison d'être. One has therefore to ask about the adequacy of the existing monitoring structure to ensure that there is appropriate external validation.

Governance in General

These issues of governance should be seen in their wider context. For all statistical bodies, the proper institutional structure is essential to ensure that they can carry out their functions and to guarantee the legitimacy of their findings. Historically, the production of statistical evidence has frequently played a key political role, not least in the field of poverty; and its imprint can be found in the development of welfare states, in the impact of colonial regimes, in the growth of independence movements, and in controversies about liberalization (Kanbur 2014). In such delicate areas, it is vital that there be a proper balance between independence of the producers of statistics and external audit of their operations.

The growth of official statistics has accompanied the spread of democracy, and the latter is seen as requiring the independence of the former. According to the Director General of Statistics Finland, "in a democratic society the independence of official statistics has the same status as the freedom of speech for the citizens" (Jeskanen-Sundström 2007, 1). In recent years, there have been moves in a number of countries to insulate statistical services from political interference and increase their degree of independence. For example, in April 2015, the European Parliament adopted new regulations governing the professional independence and integrity of statistical authorities. At the same time, the existence of regulations underlines that independence is a matter of degree and is not unconditional. The Finnish Director General went on to say that, "in order for official statistics to fulfil their important social task, they must be based on clear, publicly stated operating principles. Only thus is it possible to guarantee the quality of statistics and the trust among the users and providers of data towards compilers of statistics" (Jeskanen-Sundström 2007, 1). External scrutiny of these principles, and of the extent to which they are followed, is essential.

It is within this wider context that the governance issues are considered here. As has been argued in several submissions to the Commission, there is need for greater transparency and for an outside audit of the statistics used to assess the World Bank's performance.

External Accountability

The success of the World Bank in creating viable estimates of the extent of global poverty, and in facilitating the creation of the SDGs regarding poverty, means the assembly of the key statistics can no longer be regarded as a purely "in-house" activity; there has to be a degree of external accountability. As it has been put to the Commission,

> the absence of institutionalized protections for the transparency and credibility of the process has become a concern. In a similar vein, the Bank's adoption of an explicit target for the headcount ratio introduces a conflict of interest that must be contained in some transparent way if the determination of the line—as distinct from monitoring against that line—is to remain within the Bank. (USAID 2015, 1)

The case for introducing a degree of external accountability is convincing. How can this best be achieved? The first possibility is that this function could be performed by the Independent Evaluation Group (IEG), which is an independent unit within the World Bank charged with objectively evaluating the World Bank Group's activities. The head of IEG, the Director-General, Evaluation, reports directly to the World Bank Group's Board of Executive Directors and not to World Bank Group management. The reports of the IEG are peer-reviewed, and external experts could be involved at all stages. It is, however, open to question whether critics of the Global Poverty measures would regard this mechanism as sufficiently external to the World Bank. If the Bank wishes to ensure the maximum degree of credibility, then it is recommended that

> Recommendation 21: The International Poverty Line estimates and the proposed Complementary Indicators should be audited on a regular basis by a body fully external to the World Bank, and this body should be consulted about major changes in methodology.

The external review body should be established by the World Bank on a permanent basis, making regular published reports. (An example of such a body in a European Union context is the European Statistical Governance Advisory Board.) Membership should be drawn from academic and other experts, as well as statisticians from national and regional bodies. While the creation of such a review body has evident internal implications for the World Bank, it is the assurance of the external reputation that should be the primary guide.

Building a Coalition of Support

The Report is directed at providing recommendations that will aid the Chief Economist and other senior members of the World Bank in carrying out their responsibilities for monitoring the SDG goals and the Bank's twin objectives. At the same time, the drawing up of the Report has been greatly helped by the outside views that have been expressed. The Advisory Board has been especially helpful in this regard, as have the 122 submissions received in the consultation carried out by the Commission, which have come from individuals and organizations concerned with this field. These have contained a number of criticisms of the World Bank's monitoring of the poverty goals to which the Report has sought to respond. The recommendations in chapter 1 for monitoring Goal 1.1 up to 2030 reflect this, as do those for a set of Complimentary Indicators in chapter 2. In quite a number of cases, the proposals are a natural continuation of developments already in train within the Bank. If the recommendations are in general followed, at least in spirit if not in detail, then the World Bank should be able to build a coalition of external support. The recommendations with regard to external audit and the establishment of an external body should be seen as a step in this direction.

The estimation of the extent of global poverty is an exercise in description, and the field of this Report has been limited in this way. The Report has not sought to take the further steps of prescription or prediction. It has not gone beyond description to prescription of policies to achieve the SDG Goal 1.1; it has not sought to predict the future evolution of global poverty. As Commission member Amartya Sen (1980, 353) has written, "description as an intellectual activity is typically not regarded as very challenging." However, as he goes on to say, "description isn't just observing and reporting; it involves the exercise—possibly difficult—of selection . . . description can be characterized as choosing from the set of possibly true statements a subset on grounds of their relevance" (Sen 1980, 353–54). It is the choices to be made regarding the description of the extent of global poverty that this Report has tried to illuminate. Understanding the choices underlying the monitoring indicators, and their full implications, is indeed challenging. There will doubtless be differences of view regarding the selection embodied in the recommendations of the Report, but it is hoped that the ensuing debate will bring together all those concerned and provide a basis for action to tackle one of the gravest problems facing the world today.

Notes

1. The implications for data handling have been briefly described in "Assessment: Monitoring over Time" in chapter 1 of this Report.
2. For the full press release, see http://www.worldbank.org/en/news/press-release /2015/10/15/world-bank-new-end-poverty-tool-surveys-in-poorest-countries.
3. Just one example is the framework for poverty analysis provided by the Progress out of Poverty Index (Grameen Foundation 2014).
4. See PovcalNet (database), World Bank, Washington, DC, http://iresearch .worldbank.org/PovcalNet/index.htm?1,0.

References

Atkinson, A. B., and E. Marlier, editors. 2010. *Income and Living Conditions in Europe.* Luxembourg: Eurostat.

Beegle, K., L. Christiaensen, A. Dabalen, and I. Gaddis. 2016. *Poverty in a Rising Africa*, volumes 1 and 2. Washington, DC: World Bank.

Grameen Foundation. 2014. *Progress Out of Poverty Index.* Washington, DC: Grameen Foundation.

Jeskanen-Sundström, H. 2007. "Independence of Official Statistics—A Finnish Experience." Seminar on "Evolution of National Statistical Systems," United Nations, February 23.

Kanbur, R. 2014. "Statistics for Colonial Rule, for the Independence Struggle, and for Inclusive Governance: The Indian Experience." Presentation at Conference on 100th Anniversary of Egyptian Official Statistics, CAPMAS, Cairo, December 8.

Sen, A. K. 1980. "Description as Choice." *Oxford Economic Papers* 32: 353–69.

United Nations. 2015. "Draft Outcome Document of the United Nations Summit for the Adoption of the Post-2015 Development Agenda." Draft resolution submitted by the President of the General Assembly, United Nations, New York.

———. 2015a. *The Millennium Development Goals Report 2015.* New York: United Nations.

USAID (U.S. Agency for International Development). 2015. Submission to Global Poverty Commission.

World Bank. 2002. *Building Statistical Capacity to Monitor Development Progress.* Washington, DC: World Bank.

———. 2013. "Getting to Poverty: Lessons from the World Bank's Record on Supporting Poverty Reduction in Country Programs." Approach paper by Independent Evaluation Group, World Bank, Washington, DC.

———. 2015. *Evaluation Panel Review of DEC.* Washington, DC: World Bank.

Index

Boxes, figures, notes, and tables are indicated by *b, f, n,* and *t* following the page number.

www.ingramcontent.com/pod-product-compliance
Lightning Source LLC
Chambersburg PA
CBHW071851270326
41929CB00013B/2189